Women and Inequality in a Changing World

Women and Inequality in a Changing World explores the obstacles women continue to face to their equal participation in all areas of daily life—political, social, and economic—which persist despite the growth in the education of girls, large-scale social movements, and political waves.

The volume widens and deepens understanding of women in relation to the inequalities they face, based not only on gender, but also on race, class, religion, and more. It also highlights the progress that women have made, and how this progress contributes to the creation of more peaceful and prosperous societies. This interdisciplinary book brings together leading scholars and practitioners from across the globe to provide a wide range of perspectives and experiences, examine crucial questions, and offer new ideas and innovative solutions to increasing the role of women moving forward.

This book will be of great interest to students and scholars of gender studies, women's studies, and political science, as well as practitioners working at the intersection of women and global issues.

The Open Access version of this book, available at http://www.taylorfrancis.com, has been made available under a Creative Commons Attribution-Non Commercial-No Derivatives (CC-BY-NC-ND) 4.0 license.

Hoda Mahmoudi is Research Professor and has held the Bahá'í Chair for World Peace at the University of Maryland, College Park, USA, since 2012. As director of this endowed academic program, she collaborates with a wide range of scholars, researchers, and practitioners to advance interdisciplinary analysis and open discourse on global peace.

Jane L. Parpart is Emeritus Professor and former Lester Pearson Chair in International Development at Dalhousie University, Canada; and Adjunct Research Professor in the Sociology and Anthropology Department at Carleton University, Canada, the Institute of Feminist and Gender Studies Department at the University of Ottawa, Canada, and in the School of International Development and Global Studies at the University of Massachusetts Boston, USA. She specializes in gender analysis, class implications, and the importance of thinking about both gender and class with a global perspective.

Kate Seaman is Assistant Director of the Bahá'í Chair for World Peace at the University of Maryland, USA. Her research interests include the concept of state responsibility, United Nations peacekeeping operations, global security governance, the ethics of international interventions, and the development of the responsibility to protect.

Gender in a Global/Local World

Series Editors: **Jane Parpart**, *University of Massachusetts Boston, USA*, **Marianne H. Marchand**, *Universidad de las Américas Puebla, Mexico, and* **Rirhandu Mageza-Barthel**, *University of South Africa (UNISA)*.

Gender in a Global/Local World critically explores the uneven and often contradictory ways in which global processes and local identities come together. Much has been and is being written about globalization and responses to it but rarely from a critical, historical, gendered perspective. Yet, these processes are profoundly gendered albeit in different ways in particular contexts and times. The changes in social, cultural, economic and political institutions and practices alter the conditions under which women and men make and remake their lives. New spaces have been created - economic, political, social - and previously silent voices are being heard. North-South dichotomies are being undermined as increasing numbers of people and communities are exposed to international processes through migration, travel, and communication, even as marginalization and poverty intensify for many in all parts of the world. The series features monographs and collections which explore the tensions in a 'global/local world', and includes contributions from all disciplines in recognition that no single approach can capture these complex processes.

Recent titles in the series include:

The Politics of Trauma and Integrity
Stories of Japanese "Comfort Women"
Sachiyo Tsukamoto

Women, Migration, and Aging in the Americas
Analyzing Dependence and Autonomy in Old Age
Edited by Marie-Pierre Arrizabalaga

Women and Inequality in a Changing World
Exploring New Paradigms for Peace
Edited by Hoda Mahmoudi, Jane L. Parpart and Kate Seaman

The Politics of Silence, Voice and the In-Between
Exploring Gender, Race and Insecurity from the Margins
Edited by Aliya Khalid, Georgina Holmes and Jane L. Parpart

For more information about this series, please visit: https://www.routledge.com/Gender-in-a-GlobalLocal-World/book-series/GENDERLOCAL

Women and Inequality in a Changing World
Exploring New Paradigms for Peace

Edited by
Hoda Mahmoudi, Jane L. Parpart
and Kate Seaman

LONDON AND NEW YORK

First published 2024
by Routledge
4 Park Square, Milton Park, Abingdon, Oxon OX14 4RN

and by Routledge
605 Third Avenue, New York, NY 10158

Routledge is an imprint of the Taylor & Francis Group, an informa business

© 2024 selection and editorial matter, Hoda Mahmoudi, Jane L. Parpart and Kate Seaman; individual chapters, the contributors

The right of Hoda Mahmoudi, Jane L. Parpart and Kate Seaman to be identified as the authors of the editorial material, and of the authors for their individual chapters, has been asserted in accordance with sections 77 and 78 of the Copyright, Designs and Patents Act 1988.

Trademark notice: Product or corporate names may be trademarks or registered trademarks, and are used only for identification and explanation without intent to infringe.

The Open Access version of this book, available at www.taylorfrancis.com, has been made available under a Creative Commons Attribution-Non Commercial-No Derivatives 4.0 license. Please note that Chapter 6 is excluded from this Creative Commons license. Pieces of this chapter were previously published in: Golan, G., 'Autobiographical Note' in Galia Golan: An Academic Pioneer on the Soviet Union, Peace and Conflict Studies, and a Peace and Feminist Activist (PAHSEP, Vol. 22), published 2018, Springer International Publishing, reproduced with permission of SNCSC. The author is grateful to the publisher for permission to reuse the material, which is still copyright protected and owned by the publisher.

An electronic version of this book is freely available, thanks to the support of libraries working with Knowledge Unlatched (KU). KU is a collaborative initiative designed to make high quality books Open Access for the public good. The Open Access ISBN for this book is 978-1-003-28138-2. More information about the initiative and links to the Open Access version can be found at www.knowledgeunlatched.org.

British Library Cataloguing-in-Publication Data
A catalogue record for this book is available from the British Library

Library of Congress Cataloging-in-Publication Data
Names: Mahmoudi, Hoda, editor. | Parpart, Jane L., editor. | Seaman, Kate, editor.
Title: Women and inequality in a changing world : exploring new paradigms for peace / edited by Hoda Mahmoudi, Jane L. Parpart and Kate Seaman.
Description: Abingdon, Oxon ; New York, NY : Routledge, 2024. |
Series: Gender in a global/local world | Includes bibliographical references and index.
Identifiers: LCCN 2023028902 (print) | LCCN 2023028903 (ebook) |
ISBN 9781032250649 (hardback) | ISBN 9781032250687 (paperback) |
ISBN 9781003281382 (ebook)
Subjects: LCSH: Sex discrimination against women. | Equality. | Women and peace.
Classification: LCC HQ1237 .W65 2024 (print) | LCC HQ1237 (ebook) |
DDC 327.1/72082--dc23/eng/20230814
LC record available at https://lccn.loc.gov/2023028902
LC ebook record available at https://lccn.loc.gov/2023028903

ISBN: 978-1-032-25064-9 (hbk)
ISBN: 978-1-032-25068-7 (pbk)
ISBN: 978-1-003-28138-2 (ebk)

DOI: 10.4324/9781003281382

Typeset in Times New Roman
by Taylor & Francis Books

Contents

List of illustrations vii
List of contributors viii
Foreword xii

Introduction: Women and Inequality in a Changing World: Exploring New Paradigms for Peace 1
HODA MAHMOUDI

PART I
Transformation, Intervention, and Disruption, Before and Now 13

1 Historical Antecedents: African American Women's Enduring Commitment to an Intersectional Peace 15
BRANDY THOMAS WELLS

2 Chicanas and Latinas in the Academic Borderlands: Resistance, Empowerment, and Agency 35
DENISE SEGURA

3 Interrogating the Image of the '21st Century Woman' 51
LAURA SJOBERG

PART II
Activating Rights and Securing Institutional Equality 69

4 Does Corporate Social Responsibility Matter to Gender Inequality During Times of Crisis? 71
JINYOUNG LEE, C.K. LEE AND JANE L. PARPART

5 The Untapped Potential of the Human Security Paradigm for
Indian Women Construction Workers: The Gender, Agency,
Human Security Nexus 95
CHANTAL A. KRCMAR

6 What Blocks Equality for Women?: Recollections from a
Feminist Life 114
GALIA GOLAN

PART III
**Challenging Boundaries, Subverting Expectations, and
Emphasizing Potential** 129

7 Shifting Perceptions of Women in the World: The Implications of
Place, Space, and Time 131
KATE SEAMAN AND HODA MAHMOUDI

8 Exploring the Power of Silence, Voice and the In-between in a
Troubled World 148
JANE L. PARPART

9 Paradise Lost, Paradigm Found?: Revisiting Assumptions for a
New Paradigm for Women in the World 159
TIFFANI BETTS RAZAVI

Conclusion: Women and the Potential for New Paradigms for
Peace 178
KATE SEAMAN, HODA MAHMOUDI AND JANE L. PARPART

Index 185

Illustrations

Figure

9.1 Features of a new paradigm — 172

Tables

4.1 Characteristics of the Selected Companies — 92
4.2 Modes of Reporting — 92
4.3 Mode of Guidelines and Third-Party Assurance — 92
4.4 The Total Pages of CSR Reports — 93
4.5 WEP 1 – Leadership Promotes Gender Equality — 93
4.6 WEP 2 – Equal Opportunity, Inclusion and Nondiscrimination — 94
4.7 WEP 3 – Health, Safety and Freedom from Violence — 94
4.8 WEP 4 – Education and Training — 94

Contributors

Tiffani Betts Razavi is Visiting Research Professor at the Bahá'í Chair for World Peace at the University of Maryland, College Park, USA. Based at the Bahá'í World Centre in Haifa, Israel since 2003, she coordinates curriculum development for a worldwide program of education based on spiritual values. Through ongoing action research, she spearheads the writing of materials, conducts teacher seminars, and manages the participation of volunteer teachers working with children's groups in villages and neighborhoods in Africa, Asia, Australia, Europe, and the Pacific Islands. She is a member of the Board of Directors of a non-profit organization dedicated to the improvement of international education through research-driven practical training, a newspaper and interactive website, and a growing number of special projects for children with compromised access to education. As a senior staff writer for *The International Educator*, her regular series of articles curates and communicates research findings and global trends relevant to educators, recently exploring the changing nature of work and education, highlighting findings and implications for women.

Galia Golan is Darwin Professor Emerita, formerly Chair of the Political Science Department, founder of the Lafer Center for Women's Studies, and of Israel's first women's studies program in 1981, all at the Hebrew University, Israel. She is a member of the Board of the Tami Steinmetz Center for Peace Studies, a member of the national executive of Meretz, associate editor of the *International Feminist Journal of Politics*, and a member of the editorial board of the *Palestine-Israel Journal*. She was a founding leader of Peace Now; today she is a leading member of Combatants for Peace. She was also a founding member of the Jerusalem Link: A Joint Israeli-Palestinian Women's Venture for Peace. She received the International Studies Association 2019 Distinguished Scholar/Activist Award and 2016 Distinguished Scholar Award in Peace Studies; the 2007 Israel Political Science Association Award for lifetime achievement; the 1999 Gleitsman Foundation International Activist Award; and the 1995 New Israel Fund Award for Women in Leadership.

Valerie M. Hudson is University Distinguished Professor and George H.W. Bush Chair at the Bush School of Government at Texas A&M University,

USA. She directs the Bush School's Program on Women, Peace, and Security. She is an expert on international security and foreign policy analysis as well as gender and security. In 2009, *Foreign Policy* named her one of the top 100 Most Influential Global Thinkers, and she was also recently named a Distinguished Scholar of Foreign Policy Analysis by the International Studies Association. She has also received national book awards. She has developed a nation-by-nation database on women, the WomanStats Database (www.womanstats.org/), that has triggered both academic and policy interest. Using this data, she and her co-principal investigators from the WomanStats Project have published a wide variety of empirical work linking the security of women to the security of states, with research appearing in *International Security, American Political Science Review, Journal of Peace Research, Political Psychology*, and *Politics and Gender*.

Chantal A. Krcmar earned her PhD in Global Governance and Human Security from the University of Massachusetts Boston, USA. Her focus areas are Human Security, the informal economy, Indian labor issues, qualitative research methods, and feminism and postcolonialism. She has been published in the *New Security Beat* and by Tradeswomen Building Bridges. Additionally, she served as Research Assistant for the Tradeswomen Building Bridges Delegation to Kerala, India (2019), as well as for Susan Moir, founder of Tradeswomen Building Bridges and Fulbright Scholar, at the "Making Non-traditional Livelihoods Work for the Marginalized" conference in Delhi (2019). She also conducted research for SEWA Bank in Ahmedabad, India. She has taught at a number of institutions of higher education, including UMASS Boston, Three Rivers Community College, and Simmons University, all in the USA.

C.K. Lee is Assistant Professor at James Madison University, USA. He received a PhD in Entrepreneurship at Syracuse University, USA. His research interests are entrepreneurial failure, entrepreneurial entry decisions, social entrepreneurship, and corporate social responsibility.

Jinyoung Lee is Assistant Professor at Sellinger Business School at Loyola University, Maryland, USA. She received a PhD in Global Governance and Human Security at University of Massachusetts-Boston, USA. Her research interests are corporate social responsibility, gender and workplace, and social entrepreneurship.

Hoda Mahmoudi is Research Professor and has held The Bahá'í Chair for World Peace at the University of Maryland, College Park, USA, since 2012. As director of this endowed academic program, she collaborates with a wide range of scholars, researchers, and practitioners to advance interdisciplinary analysis and open discourse on global peace. Before joining the University of Maryland faculty, she served as the coordinator of the Research Department at the Bahá'í World Centre in Haifa, Israel. Prior to that, she was Dean of the College of Arts and Sciences at Northeastern

Illinois University, USA, where she was also a faculty member in the Department of Sociology.

Jane L. Parpart is Emeritus Professor and former Lester Pearson Chair in International Development at Dalhousie University, Canada; and Adjunct Research Professor in the Sociology and Anthropology Department at Carleton University, Canada, the Institute of Feminist and Gender Studies Department at the University of Ottawa, Canada, and in the School of International Development and Global Studies at the University of Massachusetts Boston, USA. She had been associated with the University of Massachusetts Boston's very exciting program on Conflict Resolution, Global Governance and Human Security. She has a long history of teaching, researching, and writing about gender and development issues. She has done her research in many parts of the world, particularly Africa. She specializes in gender analysis, class implications, and the importance of thinking about both gender and class with a global perspective.

Kate Seaman is Assistant Director of the Bahá'í Chair for World Peace at the University of Maryland, USA. She previously held positions at the University of Baltimore, USA, the University of Bath, UK, and was Postdoctoral Fellow at the University of East Anglia, UK. She received her Ph.D. from Lancaster University, UK. She has written and edited several books and her research has also been published in the journals *Global Governance* and *Politics and Governance*. Her research interests include the concept of state responsibility, United Nations peacekeeping operations, global security governance, the ethics of international interventions, and the development of the responsibility to protect.

Denise Segura is Professor of Sociology and Affiliated Professor in the respective departments of Chicana/o Studies and Feminist Studies at the University of California, Santa Barbara, USA. Her research and teaching center on Chicana/x feminisms, Chicana/Mexicana employment, and Latina/o education. She has received a number of awards for her research, teaching, and mentorship, including the 2019 Founders Award from the Section on Latina/o/x Sociology from the American Sociological Association, the 2015 Feminist Mentor Award from Sociologists for Women in Society, the Outstanding Latino/a Faculty in Higher Education (Research Institutions) Award in 2009 by the American Association of Hispanics in Higher Education, and the award for Lifetime Distinguished Contributions to Research, Teaching, and Service from the American Sociological Association, Latina/o Sociology Section in 2007. She is currently engaged in research on the perceptions of the origins and significance of Chicana/o/x and Latina/o/x sociology to diverse generations of scholar-activists.

Laura Sjoberg is British Academy Global Professor of Politics and International Relations at Royal Holloway University of London, UK. She specializes in gender, international relations, and international security, with work on war theory and women's political violence. Her work has been published in more than four dozen journals of politics, international relations, gender studies, geography, and law. She is author or editor of 15 books.

Brandy Thomas Wells is Assistant Professor of History at Oklahoma State University, USA. Her research interests focus on transnational activism, citizenship diplomacy, and gender, religion, and empire. Her work has appeared in the *Journal of African American History*, the *Journal of Civil and Human Rights, Women and Social Movements in Modern Empire*, and edited books. Her current work examines how activists in the National Council of Negro Women and the National Association of Colored Women envisaged and pursued peace, freedom, and civil and human rights in the 20th century.

Foreword

"Woman, Life, Freedom!" As this volume goes to press, this is the rallying cry in Iran. The uprising in that country was catalyzed by the death of a young woman, Mahsa Amini, at the hands of the Iranian state's morality police who did not believe she was wearing her hijab correctly. Women have spearheaded the uprising, cutting their hair and removing their headscarves. Women in Afghanistan then also took up the cry "Woman, Life, Freedom" as they braved the whips of the Taliban for protesting their banishment from education and employment.

It is no coincidence that these three words have become entwined, for there is a deep connection between them. The first political order in any society is the sexual political order—the order established between the two halves of humanity who only together can create a future for their kind. A grave choice thus lies before us in every generation, for that sexual order could be based on equity, equal standing, equal participation in decisionmaking, equal access to that which is deemed of value in the society. But in the case of men and women throughout human history, it is far too often based on inequity, unequal standing, unequal participation in decisionmaking, and unequal access to valuable resources. Indeed, it is far too often based on ubiquitous male-on-female violence.

This matters, for that first, sexual political order colors all else in the society. If men treat their partners in humanity's future—women—with violence and disregard, they themselves will find a similar destiny. The outcomes for the group will be tragic—instability, violence, terror, corruption, autocracy—because the group's foundation is built upon the same characteristics at the level of the first, sexual political order: domestic violence, domestic terror, domestic corruption, domestic autocracy. Furthermore, such a society will also experience additional related consequences at the nation-state level: poor health, food insecurity, low economic performance, rentierism, demographic woes, lack of attention to environmental security.

It's almost as if there is an iron law of social science: what you do to your women, you do to your nation-state. If you deny freedom to women, you deny it for all. If you curse your women, you curse your nation-state.

This excellent volume is thus a welcome one. There is no greater undertaking than "Woman, Life, Freedom!" and the chapters herein challenge us to realize the enormity of the effort involved. I strongly resonated with Galia Golan's realization that "we have to change society, because society was not built for us ... I came to realize that joining the existing institutions would not change basic power relations. Society's institutions and norms had to be overhauled. This is a revolutionary task, a radical task, but necessary."

Amen, amen, amen. I am reminded of that beautiful Baha'i saying:

> The world of humanity is possessed of two wings: the male and the female. So long as these two wings are not equivalent in strength, the bird will not fly. Until womankind reaches the same degree as man, until she enjoys the same arena of activity, extraordinary attainment for humanity will not be realized; humanity cannot wing its way to heights of real attainment. When the two wings ... become equivalent in strength, enjoying the same prerogatives, the flight of man will be exceedingly lofty and extraordinary.

May this volume bring that day closer ...

Valerie M. Hudson
December 2022

Introduction

Women and Inequality in a Changing World: Exploring New Paradigms for Peace

Hoda Mahmoudi

Undefinable Losses

The global crisis of gender inequality poses a great challenge to the progress and development of all people and their societies. Women's inequality in educational attainment, work, economic empowerment, legal status, their contributions to the arts and sciences or in any other sphere of activity and expression, not only violates their agency and human rights, it also blocks the potential for the constructive advancement of women and men within the global community. The lack of women's full participation in all branches of human society blocks the progress and development of all societies.

Women all over the world know that in order to survive, much less thrive, they must navigate the systemic impediments placed before them. As pointed out by Helen Lewis, "[f]eminism will always be difficult. It tries to represent half of humanity ... drawn from every race, class, country and religion" (2020: 307). The sagging costs of this reality presses its weight on the moral, ethical, spiritual, and material possibilities of women everywhere; it also constrains women in a vice of limited possibility. The absence of women – and its costs to the world – handicaps human potential, freezes innovation, and clouds the future of our world.

This book, in large measure, outlines the performance and *presence* of women in difficult, extraordinary circumstances. It also offers a harsh cartography of the debilitating systems which constrain women. But before one can examine women's presence, one must examine women's *absence*, and the loss that occurs in a world without women.

These are the losses of the never happened. Tragedies of new possibilities never formed, new knowledge and scientific discoveries never enacted, and a world without access to the creativity that grows out of a fuller diversity and participation. And even on a more basic level the intimacy of friendships never experienced, wise words of counsel never heard, and unique understandings and perspectives never shared. Our world bears all the hallmarks of the absence of women. There is a poignant elegy that looms over our global community – a story of missed opportunities, unused potential, and of human capacities never reached.

It is as if billions of people were silenced in an instant. But it is also much worse than that. It is the reality of continuing systems that were created and sustain such conditions, systems which condemn us to repeat the same abject failures, ad infinitum.

The 'voids of the never-happened' is impossible to trace empirically. It is a vast, deflated moral space that echoes with a kind of muted anti-energy.

Its absence also vitiates against all of us. All bear the loss – the loss of possibility, the lack of consolation. While the statistics tell of material failure, a robust moral imagination is needed to comprehend the spiritual loss of so much life consigned to the wayside. This *void* of women creates a moral exemplar of loss. It is a predicate world – a world in a kind of ongoing Peter Pan youth that never matures to its full seriousness.

Today, women all over the world are confronted with many serious issues and setbacks in relation to their basic human rights, security, and well-being. Many of the obstacles are outlined in the United Nations' *Progress on the Sustainable Development Goals: The Gender Snapshot 2022*. For example, the document reported that women are more likely than men to suffer from food insecurity. During the COVID-19 pandemic, food insecurity among women rose from 27.5 percent in 2019 to 31.9 percent in 2021. According to the same UN report, one in three women experienced moderate to severe food insecurity. The triple impact of conflict, climate change, and COVID-19 posed a significant threat to women's food insecurity. Likewise, COVID-19 increased extreme poverty levels for both women and girls, and it is projected that the trend will continue to worsen. Decline in healthcare systems, and the backlash against women's sexual and reproductive health and rights have left poorer women without care, leading to a decline in their physical and mental health (United Nations, 2022b). Globally, one in every ten women and girls aged 15–49 were subjected to sexual and/or physical violence by intimate partners (United Nations, 2022b).

Other examples of the human rights violations faced by women are highlighted by the Missing and Murdered Indigenous Women and Girls (MMIWG) movement in the United States and Canada, which advocates for the end of violence against Native women and to raise awareness about the high rates of disappearances and murders of women and girls. The brute facts about MMIWG show Native women facing murder rates ten times that of the national average, and three times more than that of white women. About four out of five Native women have experienced violence and are twice as likely as white women to experience violence (WERNATIVE, 2023).

For African American women, the intersectionality of race, gender, and socioeconomic status negatively impacts their health and well-being, especially as evidenced during the COVID-19 pandemic. Black women were disproportionately impacted by COVID-19, leading to higher morbidity and mortality rates compared to other racial and ethnic groups (Chandler et al., 2021). Black women have a higher prevalence of heart disease, stroke, cancers, diabetes, maternal morbidities, obesity, and stress (Chinn et al., 2021). As explained by

Chinn et al., "[s]ubstantial evidence exists that racial differences in socioeconomic (e.g., education and employment) and housing outcomes among women are the result of segregation, discrimination, and historical laws purposed to oppress Blacks and women in the United States" (2021). Finally, the gender wage gap for Black women shows that despite having the highest labor force participation rates, Black women in 2020 earned 64 cents for every $1.00 earned by white, non-Hispanic men (Center for American Progress, 2021).

In Afghanistan, women are restricted from public office and from working in the judiciary. They have been removed from many governmental jobs. Women and girls are subjected to strict dress code and travel restrictions. Choice is not an option for these women and girls. Only girls under the age of 12 are allowed to go to school. In public, women must be completely covered by a burkha or face severe beatings (United Nations, 2023a; UNESCO, 2023; Afary and Anderson, 2022).

In Iran, under the current laws enforced by the Islamic Republic of Iran, women are not only marginalized but controlled by laws that enforce an Islamic dress code in schools, public events, and national media. Women are under surveillance by the morality police charged with cracking down on hijab violators. Other laws passed by the Islamic Republic of Iran also serve to control women's agency. The legal marriageable age for women is 13. A woman who wishes to marry must obtain permission from her father, paternal grandfather, or a civil court. Legally, there is no such thing as rape between spouses. Divorce laws are no longer under the authority of secular family courts where wives and husbands had a comparable right to divorce. Now only husbands have a unilateral right to divorce. A woman's custody rights are limited, and a husband has absolute rights over his wife. Women are not free to travel or obtain passports without a male guardian's written permission. Similar to the women in Afghanistan, Iranian women cannot ride bicycles in public and are obligated to wear some form of hijab (headscarf) and a long coat or some type of clothing that covers their bodies down to the ankles. The recent Iranian women's movement, 'Woman, Life, Freedom,' has shown the extent to which Iranian women are willing to risk their lives by removing their hijab in public in order to bring an end to gender apartheid (Mahmoudi, 2019).

The war in Ukraine has made women increasingly vulnerable to sexual violence and domestic abuse. Rape as a weapon of war against Ukrainian women and girls has been reported since the start of the war. Women in Ukraine face significant emotional, physical, and economic challenges with the disappearance of their social support systems. Ukrainian women are also shouldering responsibility for the care of their children and older parents or relatives who, because of the war, are no longer receiving assistance from the state (Amnesty International, 2023; United Nations, 2023b). These are but a few of the examples of gender inequality and its implications for women.

There are countless more examples. Examples in every culture, in every region of the world (World Bank, 2022). Together they form a kind of human catalog of lost possibilities. Yet this book seeks to not simply map what has been lost, but to reveal what still can be gained by drawing attention to possibilities yet extant. *Women and Inequality in a Changing World: Exploring New Paradigms for Peace* grapples with the immensity of our shared challenge. It examines the conditions needed to not only imagine a new world, but to honestly survey the failures of the old world. If the ontology of absence defines the historical experience of women in the world, the epistemologies of possibility must define their future. But before we examine new opportunities, we must sift through the ruins of the old system's failure, if only to convince ourselves that what is broken cannot be mended. For small patches to the fabric of old conventions will not change our world – an entirely new *paradigm* is needed.

Toward a New Paradigm

A paradigm may be defined as a new way of thinking or a new system to replace an old and outdated one. Paradigms are based on a set of assumptions, concepts, values, and practices that constitute a way of viewing reality; this way of viewing reality may change, but such changes usually occur slowly. Indeed, paradigm shifts are often turbulent, and can be met with great resistance. A particular paradigm will generally be accepted until irregularities arise that question its basic concepts or assumptions. Yet even with emerging anomalies that challenge the legitimacy of an existing paradigm, deeply entrenched opinions and attitudes generate major obstacles. Indeed, for a new paradigm to take hold, the deep roots of the old paradigm must be pulled out. The shift to a new paradigm demands a radical change within social systems – change at the individual, institutional, and societal level.

To achieve a future which fully includes women, the existing paradigm – the paradigm that excludes women – must change. The previous paradigm and its inheritors gave birth to – through ignorance, indifference, pointed violence, and simple dismissal – a vast and empty spiritual quarter. Such a paradigm could be called many things, and it contains many features, but the most oft-repeated referent is that of *patriarchy*. Patriarchy refers to a system of societal organization where men are the predominant decision-makers and power holders. In feminist theory, patriarchy refers to the social structures used to enforce or institutionalize male-dominated systems. Like all systems of social organization, patriarchal systems come with a full moral, ethical, and metaphysical ecology of practices, symbols, values, and approaches to life.

In exploring a new paradigm for global peace, an understanding of the old paradigm – patriarchy – is essential. But that understanding cannot be strictly material; it must display the trenchant spiritual harm that has occurred for centuries. For there are times when, before we usher in a new paradigm, we must catalogue the harms of the old system so that we might have a kind of truth and reconciliation moment, identifying the wrongs of the past in order to prepare for a better future.

Cataloguing the Old Paradigm

The old paradigm of patriarchy has preserved the unequal status of women throughout the world. Though less acknowledged by some, systemic patriarchy restrains women in their fight for gender rights and equality. Hudson et al. (2012: 94) note that gendered hierarchies are linked with the "violence associated with nationalism." Hierarchical differences between women and men are at the root of systemic inequality and violence against women (see also Garcia, 2021: 17–19). Marie E. Berry in her book, *War, Women, and Power*, speaks of the re-emergence of patriarchal norms as "reflecting men's 'perennial sense of entitlement to women's bodies'" (Cockburn, 2013: 3 as cited in Berry, 2018). Berry (2018: 201) writes that "[p]atriachial norms underscore women's day-to-day life around the globe, typically through disproportionate time use, as well as subtle forms of intimidation and violence that ensures women's subordinate status to men."

This system of patriarchy or gender hierarchies, which continues today, hampers women's lives, opportunities, security, and well-being. In *Are Women Human?*, Catharine MacKinnon (2006: 41–42), offers a dark and poignant account of what women face:

> If women were human, would we be a cash crop shipped from Thailand in containers into New York's brothels? Would we be sexual and reproductive slaves? Would we be bred, worked without pay our whole lives, burned when our dowry money wasn't enough or when men tired of us … sold for sex because we are not valued for anything else? … Would we, when allowed to work for pay, be made to work at the most menial jobs and exploited at barely starvation level? … Would we be trafficked as things for sexual use and entertainment worldwide in whatever form current technology makes possible? Would we be kept from learning to read and write? … Would we have little voice in public deliberations and in government in the countries where we live? … Would we be raped in genocide to terrorize and eject and destroy our ethnic communities, and raped again in that undeclared war that goes on every day in every country in the world in what is called peacetime? … And, if we were human, when these things happened, would virtually nothing be done about it?

In her 1938 classic novel, *Three Guineas*, Virginia Woolf responds to a letter received from an unnamed correspondent who asks for her help with his efforts to "prevent war." Woolf replies, "[t]hough we see the same world, we see it through different eyes." She responds by asking how women can prevent war when they are denied education, professional advancement, and opportunities to enter the public sphere. Woolf goes on to criticize patriarchy, militarism, and totalitarianism. She suggests that women should focus their energies and creativity on forming their own institutions. Essentially, she is saying that war is impossible to prevent when patriarchal systems exist.

Historian Judith Bennett gives a sense of patriarchy's long age when she describes women's wage inequality in the United Kingdom from the early fourteenth century to present. According to Bennett (2006: 102–103):

> [E]ver since a wage-earning sector emerged in the Middle Ages, the wage gap has fluctuated within a fairly stable range, with women paid about one-half to three-quarters the wages of men: this was true of female laborers in the early fourteenth century; of female harvesters in the early fifteenth century; of female agricultural workers in the nineteenth century; and of women working the modern wage market. There is very little that the economy of a fourteenth-century Westminster manor shares with a Westminster business today, but in both, Women's wages fell significantly short of the wages earned by men.[1]

Women continue to be overrepresented in low-paying jobs and underrepresented in senior positions (Ortiz-Ospina and Roser, 2018). Also, women's work at home is unpaid and undervalued.

But it is violence toward women which most drastically shows the need for a new paradigm. When it comes to acts of violence against women, the World Health Organization estimates that "globally about 1 in 3 (30%) women worldwide have been subjected to either physical and/or sexual intimate partner violence or non-partner sexual violence in their lifetimes" (World Health Organization, 2021). In a recent study from the UK, 97 percent of women between the ages of 18 and 24 reported being sexually harassed at some point (United Nations Women UK, 2021). In the United States, 20 percent of women have reported being the victims of an attempted sexual assault. Statistics are harder to come by outside the world's 'advanced' countries, but it is not mere projection to assume some of these statistics are even worse in poorer countries. Too often, physical violence against women occurs at alarming rates throughout the world with little legal or other institutional intervention. Violence against women is perpetuated by rape, forced prostitution, sexual abuse (including children), and sexual harassment. Other forms of violence against women and girls include trafficking, cyber-harassment, female genital mutilation, sexual harassment at work, and violence against women in politics (United Nations Women, 2022). Legal and moral measures, where in place, fall short of addressing the root causes of violence against women. Simply put, the most damning aspect of the evil of the old paradigm is that it has failed to protect and preserve women's lives. Without exception, where women find themselves without power, women find themselves at the mercy of those in power.

And even when women's lives are not threatened, their possibilities are limited through unequal treatment. Markers of women's inequality include the significant biases that are prevalent in public spaces, health care, and product design. In *Invisible Women* (2021), Caroline Criado Perez notes that "[w]hen planners fail to account for gender, public spaces become male spaces by default" (p.66) Perez's research shows how the world is built by and for men. Examples include how the lack of streetlights contributes to women's lack of safety; cell phones that are too big for women's hands; doctors' misdiagnosis of women's health issues; and prescribing drugs that are wrong for women's bodies. Other examples include the lack of workplace childcare facilities and unpaid household and care work. Perez explains that until 2011, US carmakers used male dummies in all crash tests despite the fact that on average, women weigh less and are shorter than men. As a result, women are 47 percent more likely to be seriously injured than men and 17 percent more likely to die in automobile accidents.

> [M]ale universality is also a cause of the gender data gap: because women aren't seen and aren't remembered, because male data makes up the majority of what we know, what is male comes to be seen as universal. It leads to the positioning of women, half the global population, as a minority. With a niche identity and subjective point of view. In such a framing, women are set up to be forgettable. Ignorable. Dispensable – from culture, from history, and from data. And so, women become invisible.
> (Criado Perez, 2021: 25)

Another serious bias against women is in medical research (Temkin et al., 2022). Until the 1990s, medical research concerning women in the United States "focused primarily on diseases affecting fertility and reproduction, and women were excluded from most clinical trials" (see Regensteiner and Reusch, 2022). A summary report from the Office of Research on Women's Health of the National Institute of Health reported that "[f]undamental basic and translational knowledge gaps in many female-specific conditions and diseases with sex-specific presentations, symptoms, or responses to treatments have hampered the generation of robust scientific data needed to provide high-quality, evidence-based care to women" (Temkin et al., 2022).

Women's lack of inclusion and equal participation in society remains a major barrier to the progress of peoples and societies everywhere; women do not enjoy equal rights in social institutions – family, legal systems, work, educational systems, government, or religious organizations. Women's inequality impedes the possibility for the international community to achieve its highest moral, social, economic, and political aspirations. Despite countless efforts on the part of many well-intentioned and powerful organizations throughout the world to empower women as equal decision-makers, women continue to face significant barriers. Seventy years after the UN adopted the Universal Declaration of Human Rights – which states "All human beings are born free and equal in dignity and rights. They are endowed with reason and conscience and should act towards one another in a spirit of brotherhood" – the international community is nowhere near reaching the goal. Indeed, the statement itself leaves out the notion of *sisterhood*, and we see that, unfortunately, not "[e]veryone is entitled to all the rights and freedoms set forth in this declaration."

Building a New Paradigm

Yet imagining a new paradigm cannot simply be a rehashing of the failures of the past paradigm, necessary as that must be. It also cannot simply be a counter-argument, a switching out of genders to the same platforms of power that infused the older system. Women – and men – need fresh imaginations, fresh analysis, and fresh opportunity to consider how to achieve what has never been achieved. For women, the attainment of social justice means that they, like all other members of society, should enjoy equal treatment and rights in all the various branches of society. It also means that women should be equal and full participants in shaping a different paradigm, which over time becomes instrumental in the advancement of a social order toward peace.

The scholars in this edited volume examine both the missed opportunities of the past and the potential for better futures to come. Some track women's efforts to overcome mistreatment; others propose principles that should underlie new paradigms. These scholars remind us that to argue for new possibilities is in and of itself an act of faith in a better, more hopeful future. Considering new possibilities is tangible evidence of humankind's ability to commit to new ways, new undertakings, new futures to come.

Women and Inequality in a Changing World: Exploring New Paradigms for Peace takes an interdisciplinary approach, gathering numerous scholars who all wrestle with the thorny problem of converting an old paradigm to a new one. Considering how new paradigms are built, identifying the precise steps to take, determining how the old system has failed, and outlining how the new system should be constructed are all valid undertakings. An artful mix of honest empiricism and considered possibilities reminds us that the future has not been promised, that the past has not been frozen in time. Though all of the authors, through quite different means, arrive at essentially the same conclusion – namely that the defunct patriarchal paradigm has failed to deliver a viable framework for peace – they are not wallowing in the mire of frozen possibilities. For though utopias emerge through rich imagination, practicable paradigms are built with full attention to social, political, and societal realities (though they must not be fully constrained by those). New worlds are built at the influx of possibility and actuality, and our human race is capable of great things. We can find a way; we must find a way, to normalize, value, and celebrate the contributions of women in our world.

Structure of the Book

The nine chapters in this volume explore the existing paradigm by which women's full equality remains unrealized; these chapters also describe scholarly and practical approaches towards deconstructing an old paradigm and developing a new one. The book is organized into three sections: (I) Transformation, Intervention, and Disruption, Before and Now; (II) Activating Rights and Securing Institutional Equality; and (III) Challenging Boundaries,

Subverting Expectations, and Emphasizing Potential. The sections are organized in order to place chapters in conversation with each other based on their overlapping or connected themes.

Part I, 'Transformation, Intervention, and Disruption, Before and Now,' brings together three chapters that examine the intersecting challenges that women face on a daily basis, which vary depending on their positionality and identity. The chapters in this section also highlight how the lived identities of women can provide a means of solidarity and a foundation for challenging the status quo.

Brandy Thomas Wells' 'Historical Antecedents: African American Women's Enduring Commitment to an Intersectional Peace' begins Part I and examines the often-overlooked contribution of African American women to the fight for world peace. Wells shows in particular the difficulties these peace-leaders encountered – at the intersections of race, sex, and class – and how particular individuals and groups navigated these fraught paths. The chapter sheds light on how the fight for world peace – or any broad-based undertaking – must take into account the complexities of lived identity if such an undertaking is going to be successful.

'Chicanas and Latinas in the Academic Borderlands: Resistance, Empowerment, and Agency' by Denise Segura, tracks the dismal rates of Chicana/o/x and Latina/o/x individuals within university faculties and further contextualizes the data by describing the author's own experiences within the academic world. Segura describes in detail the commitment of a relatively small group of scholars who supported one another's work and helped to create traditions and standards of excellence. Utilizing the theme of the *Borderlands*, she describes how Chicana/o/x and Latina/o/x scholars challenge prevailing academic research narratives, by, for example, remaining deeply committed to the communities they come from.

Laura Sjoberg examines how the image of the '21st Century Woman' both limits and caricatures women's agency and ability. Her chapter, 'Interrogating the Image of the "21st Century Woman",' describes the uneven progress and barriers to equality that women continue to face. Sjoberg focuses on three key realities: the disturbing remnant of gender subordination that is further distributed within categories such as class, ethnicity, and gender identity; the flat essentialism that tends to describe policy, advocacy, and academic approaches to gender equality; and the noxious mixture of representation and expectation that prods women to do more than men while simultaneously limiting the scope of their goals.

Part II, 'Activating Rights and Securing Institutional Equality,' delves deeper into the experiences of women in the workplace, and connects these experiences to wider questions of equality. Jinyoung Lee, C.K. Lee, and Jane L. Parpart begin Part II with their chapter, 'Does Corporate Social Responsibility Matter to Gender Inequality During Times of Crisis?' The authors describe how the changes brought about by the COVID-19 emergency gave people the opportunity to rethink the concept of corporate social responsibility. The authors remind us that institutional change must be both broad and deep if we are to have a lasting impact on the fight for women's equality.

In 'The Untapped Potential of the Human Security Paradigm for Indian Women Construction Workers: The Gender, Agency, Human Security Nexus', Chantal A. Krcmar shows us how institutional possibilities for change remain a ripe arena for women's empowerment. Krcmar's scholarship demonstrate that patterns of change and possibilities are often pre-existing in current institutions, if we would but listen to the different and dynamic ways women are engaging in the fight for equality. By examining what "'local-local' understandings" of security looks like, this chapter explores issues of agency in key regions of the Global South and describes how women are already doing the critical work of building new, more equal frameworks for equality.

Chapter 6 features Galia Golan and her many decades of experience in the fight for women's equality. 'What Blocks Equality for Women? Recollections from a Feminist Life' examines all that has changed – and all that has not changed – at the intersection between academic undertakings of peace and equality, governmental and legal projects, and civil society efforts. Golan describes not only the changing *activities* of peace and equality but the surrounding *ideas* which gave rise to – and did not give rise to – major shifts in the world's paradigms surrounding women's equality.

Part III, 'Challenging Boundaries, Subverting Expectations, and Emphasizing Potential,' takes a broader view of the ongoing challenges to gender equality, and each chapter utilizes a different conceptual approach to identify the limitations of the current paradigm, and the critical need for new approaches.

Kate Seaman and Hoda Mahmoudi begin the final section with their chapter, 'Shifting Perceptions of Women in the World: The Implications of Place, Space, and Time,' which examines the ways in which women are continually pushing for change, breaking down barriers, and shattering glass ceilings. By examining the intersections of gendered power relations within different spaces, places, and times, the authors explain how, why, and where the barriers to women's agency still exist, and what more needs to be done to push for real change in the future.

Chapter 8 explores how demonstrative and affirmative assertions of equality are often counterbalanced with more muted approaches. Jane L. Parpart's 'Exploring the Power of Silence, Voice and the In-between in a Troubled World' is particularly concerned with the importance of integrating the full range of possible approaches in the fight for equality. Parpart argues that the intersections of activity and rest illuminate methods and perspectives that shed light on our ability to rethink and redesign a more humane existence.

Tiffani Betts Razavi's 'Paradise Lost, Paradigm Found? Revisiting Assumptions for a New Paradigm for Women in the World' takes a sweeping, mile-high view of the complex challenges to women's full equality. In this concluding chapter of Part III, Razavi clearly shows that the prevailing paradigm has not been up to the task; a new framework must be developed. Razavi discusses multi-disciplinary data and research – in social, economic, political, and legal realms – in order to both identify the assumptions that underlie the current paradigm and prescribe alternative approaches to usher in a new framework. She argues for a new paradigm based on spiritual values and collective concern for the well-being of humanity – a paradigm defined by shared identity and common purpose.

The volume closes with 'Conclusion: Women and the Potential for New Paradigms for Peace,' a final chapter from the editors, Kate Seaman, Hoda Mahmoudi, and Jane L. Parpart. Uniting the contributions in this volume are the different perspectives on the radical changes necessary within our social systems, at the individual, institutional, and societal levels. The conclusion provides an overview of these changes, that are designed to end the current patriarchal paradigm, and to open up the possibility for us to imagine a new paradigm or paradigms, an imagining of a better world.

Note

1 www.pay-equity.org/info-time.html

References

Afary, Janet and Kevin B. Anderson (2022) "Woman, Life, Freedom: The Origins of the Uprising in Iran," *Dissent*, December 2. www.dissentmagazine.org/online_articles/women-life-freedom-iran-uprising-origins. Accessed May 30, 2023.

Amnesty International (2023) "Ukraine: Women Face Grave Risks as Russia's Full-Scale Invasion Enters its Second Year," March 8. www.amnesty.org/en/latest/news/2023/03/ukraine-women-face-grave-risks-as-russias-full-scale-invasion-enters-its-second-year/. Accessed May 30, 2023.

Bennett, Judith M. (2006) *History Matters: Patriarchy and the Challenges of Feminism*. Philadelphia: University of Pennsylvania Press.

Berry, Marie E. (2018) *War, Women, and Power: From Violence to Mobilization in Rwanda and Bosnia-Herzegovina*. Cambridge: Cambridge University Press.

Center for American Progress (2021) "Women of Color and the Wage Gap," www.americanprogress.org/article/women-of-color-and-the-wage-gap/. Accessed May 9, 2023.

Chandler, R., D. Guillaume, A.G. Parker, A. Mack, J. Hamilton, J. Dorsey, and N.D. Hernandez (2021) "The Impact of Covid-19 among Black Women: Evaluating Perspectives and Sources of Information," *Ethnicity & Health*, 26(1): 80–93.

Chinn, J.J., I.K. Martin and N. Redmond (2021) "Health Equity Among Black Women in the United States," *Journal of Women's Health*, 30(2): 212–219.

Cockburn, C. (2013) "Sexual Violence in Bosnia: How War Lives on in Everyday Life," https://www.opendemocracy.net/en/5050/sexual-violence-in-bosnia-how-war-lives-on-in-everyday-life/. Accessed May 9, 2023.

Criado Perez, Caroline (2021) *Invisible Women: Exposing Data Bias in a World Designed for Men*. New York: Abrams Books.

Garcia, Manon (2021) *We are Not Born Submissive: How Patriarchy Shapes Women's Lives*. Princeton: Princeton University Press.

Hudson, V.M., M. Caprioli, D.L. Bowden, and R. McDermott (2012) *Sex and World Peace*. New York: Columbia University Press.

Lewis, Helen (2020) *Difficult Women: A History of Feminism in 11 Fights.* London: Penguin Random House.

MacKinnon, Catharine A. (2006) *Are Women Human? And Other International Dialogues.* Cambridge, MA: The Belknap Press of Harvard University Press.

Mahmoudi, Hoda (2019) "Freedom and the Iranian Women's Movement," *Context*, 18(3): 14–19. Ortiz-Ospina, Esteban and Max Roser (2018) "Economic Inequality by Gender," *OurWorldInData.org*, https://ourworldindata.org/economic-inequality-by-genderRegensteiner, Judith G. and Jane E.B.Reusch (2022) "Sex Differences in Cardiovascular Consequences of Hypertension, Obesity, and Diabetes: JACC Focus Seminar 4/7," *Journal of American Cardiology*, 79(15): 1492–1505.

Temkin, Sarah M., Samia Noursi, Judith G. Regensteiner, Pamela Stratton, and Janine A. Clayton (2022) "Perspectives from Advancing National Institutes of Health Research to Inform and Improve the Health of Women," *Obstetrics & Gynecology*, 140(1): 10–19.

UNESCO (2023) "Let Girls and Women in Afghanistan Learn!" www.unesco.org/en/articles/let-girls-and-women-afghanistan-learn. Accessed May 30, 2023.

United Nations (2022a) "Facts and Figures: Women's Leadership and Political Participation," www.unwomen.org/en/what-we-do/leadership-and-political-participation/facts-and-figures. Accessed August 2, 2022.

United Nations (2022b) "Progress on the Sustainable Development Goals: The Gender Snapshot 2022," www.unwomen.org/en/digital-library/publications/2022/09/progress-on-the-sustainable-development-goals-the-gender-snapshot-2022?gclid=Cj0KCQjwu-KiBhCsARIsAPztUF0QvpdnVM164vnpzEkTtqJLlmAtN72XMr9JcY8d2TtHA0gJXOPeMGEaAkpuEALw_wcB. Accessed May 8, 2023.

United Nations (2023a) "Afghanistan: UN Experts Say 20 Years of Progress for Women and Girls' Rights Erased Since Taliban Takeover," www.ohchr.org/en/press-releases/2023/03/afghanistan-un-experts-say-20-years-progress-women-and-girls-rights-erased. Accessed May 30, 2023.

United Nations (2023b) "War Crimes, Indiscriminate Attacks on Infrastructure, Systematic and Widespread Torture Show Disregard for Civilians, Says UN Commission of Inquiry on Ukraine," www.ohchr.org/en/press-releases/2023/03/war-crimes-indiscriminate-attacks-infrastructure-systematic-and-widespread. Accessed May 30, 2023. United Nations Women (2022) "Facts and Figures: Ending Violence Against Women," www.unwomen.org/en/what-we-do/ending-violence-against-women/facts-and-figures. Accessed June 7, 2022.

United Nations Women UK (2021) "Public Spaces Need to be Safe and Inclusive for All. Now," www.unwomenuk.org/safe-spaces-now. Accessed October 16, 2022.

WERNATIVE (2023) "What is the MMIW Movement?" www.wernative.org/articles/what-is-the-mmiw-movement. Accessed May 9, 2023.

Woolf, Virginia (1966 [1938]) *Three Guineas.* Houghton Mifflin Harcourt.

World Bank (2022) "Female Labor Force Participation," https://genderdata.worldbank.org/data-stories/flfp-data-story/. Accessed June 4, 2022.

World Health Organization (2021) "Violence Against Women," www.who.int/news-room/fact-sheets/detail/violence-against-women

Part I
Transformation, Intervention, and Disruption, Before and Now

Part 1

1 Historical Antecedents

African American Women's Enduring Commitment to an Intersectional Peace

Brandy Thomas Wells

On June 3, 2020, Jessica Murrey, a Black peace activist, and communications expert, took to the internet to grieve the murder of George Floyd, a 40-year-old Black man who died while in the public custody of a Minneapolis police officer. The officer had pressed his knee on Floyd's neck for nearly ten minutes. Murrey was devastated. She had dedicated her life to stopping human suffering by training young peace activists and peacebuilders on nearly every continent under the aegis of Search for Common Ground, a Nobel Peace Prize-nominated organization and one of the largest peace bodies in the world. As Murrey reflected on Floyd's murder, she sought to reconcile the "despair and rage [that] threaten to swallow me whole" with the fact that "I am also a peacebuilder." Looking to map a way forward for herself, peace activists, and people everywhere, Murrey called for a rethinking of peace and justice and a realization that "there is no true peace without justice" (Murrey, 2020).

Long before Murrey, African American female peace activists had made similar arguments and appeals. Even before Johan Galtung defined "positive peace" in 1969 and Kimberlé Crenshaw coined the phrase "intersectionality" in 1989, Black women demanded a peace that eradicated structural violence and that limited the lives and potential of marginalized populations. They articulated the links between international cooperation, disarmament, non-proliferation, economic progress, and racial equality, and explicated the relationship between the local and global. In one space after another, Black women peace activists articulated a paradigm for peace that challenged the damaging effects of patriarchy and how it works in tandem with other systems of oppression.[1]

Despite their long commitment, Black women's peace activism and ideologies largely remained on the margins of the Women's Peace and Security (WPS) agenda and understandings of women's peace activism. Many scholarly works identify Black women activists as civil rights activists rather than peace activists, regardless of their lifelong commitment to the latter. This gap is hardly surprising since too few works present the Black freedom struggle and peace movements as related struggles.[2] While feminist studies have enriched our understanding of peace, consideration of race and racism remains dubious (Berlowitz, 2002). However, as M. Azarmandi (2018: 69–77) clarifies,

DOI: 10.4324/9781003281382-3

"It is crucial to include race as an analytic within the field of Peace Studies as has been done with gender because racism continues to be a defining feature on which Western societies are built, structured, and economically reliant on." Even at the United Nations, where Resolution 1325 (UNSCR1325) reaffirms the significance of women in maintaining negotiations, peace, and security, the emphasis is narrowly on women's needs and opportunities, their leadership, or victimhood. Where intersectionality appears, it focuses mainly on women in conflict and post-conflict societies and is divorced from Black women's theories and methods. As Laura Shepherd and others have argued, the contemporary WPS agenda and the National Action Plans (NAPs) it has spurred privilege gender more than race, class, or sexuality (Shepherd, 2016, 2011).

Through a historical examination of the activities, goals, and motivations of Black women peace activists, this chapter posits a rethinking of the WPS agenda that is fuller in its treatment of women and its understanding of the violence, vulnerabilities, and inequalities they face. It uncovers the tenacity of African American female peace activists as they worked for intersectional peace for more than a century, from the earliest women's peace organizations, including the Women's Peace Party (WPP), and to interstate bodies like the United Nations, to contemporary bodies, including the Women of Color Advancing Peace, Security & Conflict Transformation (WCAPS). Even when disappointments over segregation, racism, and narrowly conceived agendas frustrated their work, Black women remained steadfast in their commitment to ensuring peace and security. Even when repression in the interwar and Cold War eras restricted more radical forms of activism, Black female activists, particularly those on the left, risked their livelihood and freedom to bring about a peaceful world built on parity. The issues that Black female peace activists raised in times past continue to reverberate today including in contemporary bodies, like the WCAPS. This enduring agenda across time and space may prove critical to reimagining a WPS agenda that leads to agency, inclusion, and justice.

Since the beginning of the feminist peace movement in the United States, Black women have insisted on the centrality of justice, freedom, and equality in pursuing peace. They sought to make this part of the goals of the WPP, formally established in January 1915 as the country's first women's peace organization (Alonso, 1993; Ramdani, 2015). Working alongside the body's founder and president, Jane Addams, Mary Church Terrell, Mary Burnett Talbert, Charlotte Atwood, Mary Fitzbutler Waring, and Addie Waites Hunton helped the predominately White, middle-class organization to stimulate public interest and civic commitment to peace (Rief, 2004). The WPP sought to convince Americans that the world needed to rid itself of the scourge and horrors of war and that women, especially as wives and mothers, were vital contributors to enduring peace. As such, the WPP connected world peace with women's suffrage (Alonso, 1993).

While sharing similar beliefs with their White colleagues, Black women peace activists also revealed that they defined peace and peace activism differently. Nearly all of the Black women who labored beside Addams were founding members of the National Association of Colored Women (NACW), the first national body of Black women's civic clubs. Through collective action, the women worked to improve Black Americans' economic, political, and social conditions. Given this experience and their broader experiences as racialized women in the United States, Black WPP members held that despite being a double minority and a small segment of an already small movement, they had much to share with and teach their colleagues. They contended that it was precisely because of their status that they could understand and advocate for fuller peace.

One of the principles that Black WPP members promoted was that peace was not simply the absence of direct violence but the presence of justice. They advocated for what we term positive peace today, which means eradicating wars and conflicts and abolishing structural harms that prevent human beings from living full lives. As social reformers on the local and national levels, Black WPP members knew that the harms Black Americans faced were many—from discrimination in jobs and housing to unequal access to education to the loss of life and loved ones in the form of lynching.[3] Thus, these activists contended that the work for peace and harmony must not only focus on faraway places but instead begin at home.

Black WPP members also called for an intersectional approach in the women's peace agenda, which required all activists to understand that groups of women experienced life differently as they contended with discrimination not simply on the account of sex, but also because of race, class, nationality, and other intersecting social and political identities. In 1915, an exacerbated Talbert, a WPP member in Buffalo, New York, asserted in *Crisis*, a national Black magazine, that: "It should not be necessary to struggle forever against popular prejudice, and with us as colored women. This struggle becomes two-fold, first, because we are women and second because we are colored women" (Talbert, 1915: 184). As they worked for peace, Black female activists invited their White colleagues to root peace work in the issues of racialized peoples and women.

The early history of Black women's peace activism reveals that these activists frequently understood war through complicated lenses. Where many protested wars, they mainly did so because American intervention often distracted from critical civil rights matters at home, because Black troops endured military racism despite their invaluable contributions, and because American military engagement, such as in the Pacific, led to U.S. imperialism. In these instances, Black peace activists, joined by their more radical White colleagues, called out the links between war, militarism, racism, and imperialism (Alonso, 1993). In other cases, many Black women peace activists clarified that they believed war could be justified. Even when they held the WPP viewpoint that militaries were a microcosm of exaggerated power, abuse, and exploitation, and that wars created widows and orphans, many happily remembered Black military service in the U.S. Civil War that led to Black emancipation. Reveling in Haiti's example of Black self-determination, they also celebrated the Haitian Revolution that led the country to become the second free republic and first free Black nation in the Western hemisphere (Parker, 2021: 47). Seeing war as a potential battleground to settle matters of equality and citizenship, extend freedom, and dismantle American racism and global White supremacy, many Black WPP members soon departed from their White colleagues concerning the First World War (Ramdani, 2015).

At the outbreak of fighting in Europe in 1914, NACW resolutions show that Black female activists rejected the "horrible slaughter and frightful suffering to thousands of hopeless human beings" (NACWC, 1993). Still, while professing Black Americans' "consistent adherence to the teachings of the Prince of Peace," they also argued that peace "must be accompanied by righteous and indignant protest against injustice."[4] The proliferation of injustices at home included President Woodrow Wilson's screening of the racist film *Birth of a Nation* at the White House. When and where Black women female peace activists shifted their stance on the war, it was less because they believed in Wilson's call for the extension of democracy to the world and instead because they hoped to make this rhetoric a reality for Black Americans through wartime sacrifices and patriotic participation. Many, including Ida Gibbs Hunt, a British Columbian and Black clubwoman who made her home in France, extended this hope to foreign populations. As early as 1915, she argued that the "war must change things for the darker races"—not simply those who lived under German imperialism.[5] Seeking this change, WPP members like Talbert and Hunton led Black women in war relief work and overcame a myriad of denials to serve as nurses to Black troops in the war theater and make justice a plank in postwar discussions.

In their European work, Black female activists sought to create an intersectional peace that freed colonized populations, drew attention to countries' localized conditions that flew in the face of international promises about harmony and democracy, and made room for the voices of women and people of color. Their ability to bring this agenda to fruition was severely limited. As women and non-statesmen, they were not invited to formally participate in the Versailles Peace Conference, which brought together state leaders from Allied Nations together in a conference to establish the League of Nations. When women's peace and rights advocates were briefly permitted to appear before the conference to present their ideas, finances and continued passport denials for Black travelers prevented Black women's participation. Instead, their commitment to seeking a peace that "blott[ed] out hate and its train of social and civil injustices" appeared in spaces beyond the corridors of the state meeting hall (Wells, 2015).

In February 1919, Hunton attended W.E.B. DuBois's Pan-African Congress that called attention to the needs of Black populations that were being ignored at the Peace Conference. Many historians have noted that the meeting worked "in contrast to peace organizations dominated by Euro-Americans" by "consistently interjecting an anti-colonial/anti-imperialist emphasis in international struggles for peace" (Berlowitz, 2002: 61–65). As one of the few female speakers at the conference, Hunton highlighted Black women's significant role in "the world's reconstruction and regeneration of today" (Chandler, 2005: 278–280; Geiss, 1974: 239–240). Though funding difficulties prevented Talbert from joining Hunton as she had hoped, she still worked to give American and global racism an international hearing. Delivering lectures before large crowds of socialites and distinguished families throughout France she argued that the arrival of peace had to be met by the arrival of equality and freedom for Black Americans (Wells, 2015).

Terrell made similar points about the intersection of peace and racial justice in her participation in the international women's congress in Zurich in May 1919. At the meeting, women from the U.S., Britain, France, Germany, and neutral and Central Powers nations gathered to argue for a women's charter with the League of Nations and advocate for broader peace terms. Terrell delivered two speeches: one for women's inclusion in the League of Nations and one for racial equality in the peace movement. Anticipating that many Zurich delegates might respond that their countries did not need to deal with issues of race since they came from majority White lands, Terrell reminded them that European empires were composed of people of color that matched or outnumbered White citizens at the metropole. Thus, she implored the gathering to recognize that there was no way around race and that "Lasting peace is impossible as long as the colored races are subject to injustice" (Parker, 2021: 356–376).

Afterward, Terrell submitted a resolution imploring the body to grant its full attention, power, and efforts to ending racial discrimination. While the passing of the resolution indicated a broader acceptance of Terrell's efforts within the growing international women's peace movement, Terrell's autobiography reveals that her White American colleagues had worked to soften its language before its adoption (Church Terrell, 2005). Additionally, Emily Green Balch, who would become the leader of the American section in 1935, recorded in her diary her quiet seething over Terrell's approach. She believed that it contained "too much militarism" (Siegel, 2021: 81). These ideological differences would come to a head a short while later; in the meantime, Terrell celebrated that she had won a significant victory for Black women's peace activism.

In the decade following the war, Black women primarily pursued their search for a positive, intersectional peace through women's organizations. They joined their colleagues in arguing against federal funds earmarked for a peacetime army rather than funds directed at promoting world peace and dealing with social ills. In the NACW, Addie Hunton created the organization's first-ever Peace Department, which soon changed its name to Peace and Foreign Relations to reflect Black women's interests in international relations, especially connections to Africa. During the early 1920s, African missionaries steadily appeared at the NACW's biennial conventions, where they found financial and social support for their endeavors (Wells, 2015). Black female peace activists also joined interracial feminist peace bodies like the National Committee on the Cause and Cure of War (NCCCW). Funded in 1924 by Carrie Chapman, the NCCCW was the last major and most progressive women's peace organization before the Second World War. Though serving as a clearinghouse for women's efforts and bringing together 11 national women's groups that allowed the body to claim by 1930 that it represented one of every five American women, no Black women's organization was invited to join (Plastas, 2011: 6). Organizational minutes and write-ups in Black newspapers reveal that Black women got around their exclusion by participating as members of the Young Women's Christian Association or church groups. At NCCCW meetings, they contributed to the body's understanding of war, including its public position that psychological, economic, racial, and political factors were often the basis of conflicts.[6]

Black women peace activists also pushed for broader peace discussions in the WPP, now rechristened as the American section of the Women's International League of Peace and Freedom (WILPF), to reflect the organization's new goals following the war and transnational configuration. The organization's ever-growing identification of the relationship between peace and racial injustice, in part helped by Terrell's efforts, strongly convinced Black women activists to become league members (Blackwell, 2004: 62). Through the WILPF, these activists, including many of the original WPP members, found success in gaining federal attention for their interests, including their concerns about how the U.S. occupation of Haiti adversely shaped the conditions of this population, especially women and children. In 1920, the WILPF appointed a commission to study the matter. In 1926, it conducted a Haitian study with the Fellowship of Reconciliation and the American Friends Service Committee. By publishing its findings in the report, *Occupied Haiti*, the WILPF successfully pushed for a formal federal investigation which led to a new treaty arrangement and the withdrawal of Marines (Plastas, 2011: 116).

These and other successes did not automatically mean that Black female peace activists had created a fuller and fairer understanding of peace in peace work. Historians Melinda Plastas, Joyce Blackwell, and others reveal that the relationship between Black and White peace activists remained fraught. One telling example is the WILPF's response to 1921 allegations that Black American troops stationed in occupied German territory after the war frequently assaulted German women. Though an anti-war organization, the WILPF did not call for the removal of all soldiers but instead just Black ones. In response, Terrell, who was then a member of the organization's executive board, argued that the resolution was "a direct appeal to race prejudice," refused to sign, and offered her resignation should it prove necessary. At Addams's intervention, Terrell remained on the board, and the organization elected not to pursue action (Plastas, 2011; Blackwell, 2004). Undoubtedly, because of the harm that she endured in this incident and others, Terrell distanced herself from her colleagues. In 1923, her colleagues did not re-elect her to the board, citing her supposed lack of commitment. For her part, Terrell surmised that her termination came because her colleagues lacked the "grit" to do the work needed for true peace (Church Terrell, 2005: 426–427; Mjagkij, 2001: 702; Schott, 1997: 138). The Terrell incident and growing postwar conservativism that likened peace activists to un-American spies and radicals, kept many Black women away from the WILPF in the 1920s.

In the face of these troubles, Black women peace activists often turned to separate organizing that allowed them to explore peace, women's rights, and racial equality from their perspectives in the 1920s. In 1922, Terrell, Hunton, Talbert, and others became founding members of the International Council of Women of the Darker Races (ICWDR). This small organization emphasized world unity and peace with a mission to educate people of color worldwide. The group sought to proclaim the accomplishments of women of color and encourage them to join together in common need and interest (Rief, 2004: 214–215). In 1926, Hunton created the Circle for Peace and Foreign Relations to bring together a group of women believing in the "universality of the race problem" (Geiss, 1974: 248–251; Aptheker, 1993 [1973]: 548). Believing that the Pan-African Congress remained one of the most promising bodies for positive, intersectional peace, the New York-based organization fundraised for the body, which had not been able to meet for years because of poor finances.[7]

Another ICWDR member, Mary McLeod Bethune, worked to increase Black women's international activism under the NACW umbrella. In her 1926 presidential address, she called for Black women to fulfill their global responsibilities for peace and reform. She argued that this work meant study and work within national borders and foreign travel that permitted "actual observation and touch" (McCluskey and Smith, 1999: 163–164). When financial limitations limited the NACW's follow through on an international excursion, Bethune joined a small band of physicians touring Europe in the summer of 1927. Bethune worked hard to make the sight-seeing trip a "tour of investigation and good-will." At her departure, she lectured 200 women aboard the ship on the problem of race in the United States.[8] When she arrived in Scotland, she met with Edith McLeod of the National Women's Council and talked with her about the activism and needs of African American women.[9] Bethune's actions reveal that despite continued setbacks and limitations, Black women took every opportunity to enrich and improve women's activism in ways that served all women.

In the 1930s, Black women's peace activists remained steadfast even as the economic effects of the Great Depression wreaked havoc in their personal lives and organizational endeavors. In the NACW, even when the Peace and Foreign Relations Department was demoted from a department to a committee to cut organizational costs, a fate that nearly every department faced, the body remained committed to peace and freedom. Now led in this effort by Alice Dunbar Nelson, the NACW cooperated with the work of the Quaker-run American Friends Service Committee (ASCF). As a leader of the ASCF's American Interracial Peace Committee, Nelson used her work detailing world affairs to create a yearly program for the Association's local and regional clubs to ensure they considered peace activism as integral to the race's survival as they did working to improve the community's economic condition.[10] Reflecting its organizational relationship to the ASCF, the NACW change the name of its committee from Peace and Foreign Relations to Peace, Disarmament, and Concord to mirror the former's emerging concerns in the early 1930s. While Nelson brought this focus into the NACW, she also successfully expanded the ASCF's peace consciousness by demanding that the organization pay as much attention to the local racial issues in the U.S. as it did foreign relations (Plastas, 2011: 165).[11]

Disturbed by the worsening conditions of Black Americans during the economic downturn, many Black peace activists increased their calls for attention to local injustices in the pursuit of peace and harmony. They called out the paradoxes they saw in peace activism. In her 1935 presidential address for the NACW, Mary Fitzbutler Waring, one of the first Black WPP members and a dedicated member of the WILPF, dedicated a portion of her speech to the explication of peace and justice. She wondered aloud if "Pacificists, Philanthropists, and other groups" considered how Black Americans felt to "live in a country where they could neither travel, eat or even purchase the necessities of life without being reminded that they are different, inferior, or undesirable." Questioning these individuals, who clamored for money and attention for peace work in foreign lands, she reminded them to look more closely at home and to realize that "there can be no peace while such practices continue."[12] Though Waring did not directly speak about ongoing issues in the WILPF, it is likely that her statements reflected ongoing troubles in the body. Though the League's Black membership had grown in its first decade of existence, Black members were subjected to segregation within the body, often invited to serve only on interracial committees, and excluded from events and meetings because of local prejudices. In 1935, as a result of continued Jim Crowism in women's peace activism, Hunton resigned from the Interracial Committee, and African American leaguers in Philadelphia, one of the most active branches among Black Leaguers, staged a walkout, never to return (Blackwell, 2004: 73–74).

Moderate female peace activists did not have to wait long to find another organization to situate their global interests. In December 1935, Bethune proposed an umbrella organization that strengthened the voices and power of Black women by bringing national bodies together on a unified agenda (McCluskey and Smith, 1999: 172). Under the auspices of the National Council of Negro Women's (NCNW), Black women made clear their beliefs that domestic and international peace relations were intertwined and that everyone, including people of color, who were often excluded and overlooked, needed to be included at peace- and policy-making tables. Four years after its birth, the Council hosted its first international night program, which revealed this belief. In the auditorium of the Labor Department, meeting under the theme of "Human Relations in Transition to Peace," Black women dialogued with representatives from foreign embassies, including the Philippines,

Liberia, Costa Rica, and China about the state of world affairs (McCluskey and Smith, 1999: 172). The NCNW hoped to make clear to government leaders, peace organizations, and the public that "peoples of all countries must work together if world freedom is to exist, and we are to gain universal peace."[13]

Reflecting its belief that peace was inseparable from freedom and justice, the NCNW also lobbied U.S. Congress to repeal the Neutrality Act that same year. Concerned about the plight of European Jews, particularly the development of the Nuremberg Laws, which stripped German Jews of their most elementary civil rights, the NCNW, like Black female peace activists in former years, argued that war could be justified. At its 1938 convention, the body succinctly made their position clear: "As members of an oppressed group in the United States of America, we sympathize with the Jewish minority group in Germany as can no others" (Kiesel, 2019: 155).

In December 1941, spurred by the Japanese attack on Pearl Harbor, the United States entered the Second World War. The Council threw itself into the cause, hoping to create a postwar peace that better addressed the needs of the world's oppressed populations. Like many Black Americans, members of the NACW and NCNW also redirected their efforts, seeking what the Black newspaper, the *Pittsburgh Courier*, called a "Double Victory": Victory against fascism abroad and victory for equality at home. Thus, Black women committed themselves to work that tackled racial and gender inclusion and equality in the military and war industries, child welfare, educational equality, housing, voting, and anti-lynching efforts (Tuuri, 2018: 18–20). Though the war shattered peace activism and delegitimized peace activists who voiced opposition, Black women peace activists eagerly looked forward to a postwar world where future wars would not be necessary (Danielson, 2015: 2–3).

As the Second World War drew to a close, Black women peace activists vowed to ensure that the intertwinement of peace, freedom, and equality was understood by world leaders. The NCNW's commitment to this agenda signaled its desire to participate in and support the United Nations, which would serve as the successor to the League of Nations. Akin to earlier claims made by Black WPP activists, Black peace activists of the 1940s asserted that Black women were the vanguard of change. Like their WPP predecessors, they argued that their long experience with multiple forms of oppression and their dedication to speaking for the masses of oppressed people, especially the colonized populations of Africa, made them indispensable at the peace table. Once again, the women would find their perspectives sidelined.

Even after the United States reversed its earlier decision to allow non-governmental participants to consult with the nation's delegation at the founding of the United Nations, it contended that Black women's voices were not needed. Instead, it suggested that Black women's issues could be separated and represented by the five predominately White women's organizations and the only organization for people of color invited to attend.[14] Like they had at the Versailles Peace Conference, Black female activists worked to circumvent their exclusion and to bring forward a more universal vision of peace. The NCNW formed an unofficial delegation that supported Bethune (who received a last-minute appointment to the NAACP delegation) and connected with African and Indian nationalists, including Vijaya Lakshmi Pandit of India, to strike up a global alliance of women of color (Wells, 2023).

In its commitment to global peace, many Black women peace activists continued to support the United Nations after its birth, including efforts to overcome the organization's shortcomings, especially those concerning colonial territories and the domestic jurisdiction clause, that shielded nations from investigation and intervention on domestic matters (which could, ironically, be determined by the very nation). Members of the NACW and NCNW also supported the peace activism of the International Council of Women (locally, the U.S. National Council of Women) and the Women's Action Committee for Victory and Lasting Peace, in many ways, the NCCCW's successor (Litoff and Smith, 2000: 5). In 1946, the NACW as a body and several members of the NCNW as individuals supported the founding of the Congress of American Women, the American branch of the Women's International Democratic Federation.[15] The latter organization reflected the growing dynamism of women's peace activism, as women from the political left, right, and center came together to form a progressive feminist agenda that argued that equality, freedom, and justice for women and marginalized racial groups were necessary to preventing another war.

Unsurprisingly, when the long, uneasy wartime alliance between the U.S. and Soviet Russia turned cold, left-liberal unified activism and peace work came under attack from anti-communists. Some argued that the U.S. was not as tough on the Soviets at it needed to be. As a political tool, even more argued that this approach had corrupted labor, feminist, and civil rights activism, as well as New Deal programming, and all needed to be stopped. In this new environment, many moderate Black women peace activists shifted their approach to avoid organizational repression and personal ruin. Rather than continue publicly calling out the nation's complicity in violence, especially considering its foreign policy—by far one of the most significant focuses of the postwar American peace movement—these activists backed away from the Congress of American Women, the Women's International Democratic Federation, and other progressive sites of activism. Indeed, akin to other mainstream women's organizations, safely within their bodies and with work alongside the state the moderate activists of the NACW and NCNW hoped to *inspire* peace by strategically utilizing American rhetoric about the nation's mission to lead the world (Danielson, 2015: 4–5; Tuuri, 2018: 181–187; Wells, 2023).

Some Black women freedom and peace activists refused to bow to Cold War pressures even as the dangers threatening their livelihood and freedom increased in the 1950s Holding firm to the leftist position that many developed during the Great Depression and the Second World War, they continued to call out the connections between disarmament, nonproliferation, and racial equality. They also held that the competition between the U.S. and Russia disproportionally impacted non-White and poor populations by dragging newly decolonized countries into the conflict (McDuffie, 2011). While many moderate Black women peace activists could agree on these matters, they parted ways on the outright rejection of capitalism and contention that the Soviet Union was the rightful leader of the postwar world. As many contemporary historians have rightly revealed, continued rejection of this viewpoints by scholars, as well as the illumination of the hypocrisies of the Soviet Union's claims, has led to what historian Robbie Lieberman calls "the missing peace" of the Black Left. Attention to this population's efforts reveals that even in the tempestuous, restrictive nature of the Cold War, some Black women publicly maintained their commitment to a positive, intersectional peace (Lieberman, 2015: 83–87).

Two of these women, Charlotta Bass and Claudia Jones, working from opposite coasts in the U.S., advocated for a peace focus that brought the issues of Black women to the front. At work in Los Angeles, Bass called attention to the ways that the commitment to anti-communism was being used to quiet calls for freedom at home and potentially squash emerging movements for independence in Africa, Asia, and the Middle East. Because of her concerns, she supported Henry Wallace, former Secretary of Commerce, who was fired in 1946 because of his criticism of American foreign policy, in his bid for president. Bass was attracted to Wallace's platform that called for the U.S. to shed its overseas bases, abandon the draft and nuclear stockpile, and terminate anti-communist policies like the Marshall Plan and Truman Doctrine. Undeterred by a devastating defeat in the 1948 national election, Bass sought to work out her peace approach through international conferences, including the Defenders of Peace conference in Prague in 1949. When she returned home, she used her *California Eagle* newspaper to circulate news of a Stockholm Appeal that called for an absolute ban on nuclear weapons (Lynn, 2022). In 1952, Bass became the first Black woman in the U.S. to run for vice president. She ran as a progressive candidate that called for a peace that "will bring an end to the war in Korea. Peace which will bring an end to the war on the negro people here at home" (Lieberman, 2015: 93).

From Harlem, Jones offered similar arguments about American postwar policy. She also authored treatises that outlined Black women's necessity to the peace movement.

One of her most famous pieces emanated from a 1950 speech that she gave on the significance of International Women's Day. In it, she argued that Black women could not be overlooked in commitments to peace precisely because

> imperialism was played out through the bodies of their husbands and sons – their men were subjected to violence in the armed forces that matched the lynch mob violence against Black civilians and veterans alike, and war threatened to permanently militarize and conscript their youth.
>
> (Lieberman, 2015: 93)

Jones did not stop there. Studies by Carole Boyce Davies, Charisse Burden-Stelly, Denise Lynn, Zifeng Liu, and Derefe Chavennes reveal that Jones had long held that Black women's freedom stood at the center of an intersectional movement that brought together broader Black liberation, peace activism, women's rights, and working-class struggles. Her argument that peace work and "women's lives" were essential to "building a proletarian internationalism" influenced other activists including W.E.B. DuBois (Burden-Stelly, 2019; Lynn, 2019).

In 1951, Jones and Bass joined the new organization, Sojourners for Truth and Justice (SJT), a short-lived organization that linked peace and freedom. The body was born both out of protest to the war in Korea and the lack of justice evident in cases like Rosa Lee Ingram and her sons, Black Georgians who were sentenced to death in 1948 for shooting the White man who attempted to assault her sexually (Lieberman, 2015: 93). While Black women continued to push for their issues to be included on the agendas of broader progressive and leftist organizations, they developed the SJT as a site to solidify their political vision. Together, sojourners sought to "rally Black women to defend their men" and to organize wives and mothers "of the legally lynched ... of those imprisoned and threatened with prison ... widowed by police brutality ... [and] who mourn [their] sons dead in foreign wars" (Lieberman, 2015: 93).

Cold War repression subjected Jones and Bass to endure FBI monitoring and harassment, though, in Jones's case, it also led to her imprisonment and, ultimately, her deportation. Even when virulent anti-communism could not quell radical Black women's activism, it virtually destroyed the American peace movement (McDuffie, 2011; Gore, 2011). One historian declares the period to be a "midcentury nadir" as protests against war and American foreign policy became limited to a few pacifists, communists, and die-hard isolationists. It was not until the 1960s that moderate Black women peace activists en masse returned to the peace movement, helping to draw connections between this agenda and the rapidly growing civil rights movement (Lieberman, 2015: 93; Adams, 1985: 12). Their peace activism showed all over.

Many of these peace activists worked in enduring bodies. A second generation of Black women peace activists joined the WILPF between 1946 and 1975, linking anti-racism and peace with increased fervor. The membership included people like Angela Davis, Shirley Chisolm, Eartha Kitt, Inez Jackson, Shirley Chisholm, Angela Davis, Coretta Scott King, and Fannie Lou Hamer (Blackwell, 2004: 170). While King's anti-war arguments were premised mainly on arguments of political femininity, Hamer's calls for peace primarily called out the racist undertones of war and its relationship to local problems. For her part, Davis brought to bear the political consciousness generated by her work with the Black Panther Party and the Communist Party. This small but influential group of politically diverse women transformed the WILPF's critiques of war and foreign policy and its pursuit of human rights and justice (Blain, 2022: 97–107).

Peace activism led some Black women activists to become members in new bodies like Women Strike for Peace (WSP), which grew out of an anti-nuclear-testing protest in 1961. Using maternalist arguments, the women argued for an end to the Vietnam War and against nuclear weapons. Where the women disagreed was whether non-proliferation and disarmament were related to racism. The tension showed in the organization's first national conference in 1962 when four Black women from Detroit called on the organization to "ban the bomb and end segregation." Reminiscent of earlier arguments from the 1920s through the 1940s, many White WSP members, even those sympathetic to racial issues, questioned the wisdom of what they believed was a co-mingling of issues. In the end, the WSP strategically sidestepped the issue by refusing to bring the matter to a vote or issue official policy statements. Continued efforts by members, including Coretta Scott King, who made clear that "Peace among nations and peace in Birmingham, Alabama cannot be separated," led the WSP to participate in broader civil rights and social welfare activism after 1968 (Swerdlow, 1993: 90–93).

Many Black female peace activists created bodies that allowed them to forge an international fight against the oppressions that restricted their lives. Founded in 1967 in Washington, D.C., the National Welfare Rights Organization (NWRO) drew together dozens of local welfare activist groups with a central focus on poor women's problems. As Frankie Chappell has shown, these women

> drew on their material reality as Black, poor mothers to examine the economic and social ways in which the government's war impacted on them, by requiring them to produce labor and fighting power for the country through raising children but refusing to reimburse them accordingly.
> (Chappell, 2021)

In 1969, Black Puerto Rican, Chicana, Asian, and Indigenous women united to create the Third World Women's Alliance (TWWA). Like the NWRO, the TWWA depicted the U.S. military budget and the draft as tools that destroyed families and subjected children in foreign countries to violence and death—all while ignoring the needs of American children who faced hunger, homelessness, and despair (Chappell, 2021). Like their predecessors, Black peace activists in the TWWA did not equate peace and anti-war to pacificism. They fully supported the efforts of oppressed people to liberate themselves (Farmer, 2017: 168–192).

In 1974, a small band of New York City women began the Women for Racial and Economic Equality (WREE), in some ways the successor to the Congress of American Women. The interracial body responded to the vacuum they witnessed in the women's rights movement and the peace movement, namely issues surrounding the needs of women of color and poor people. (Alonso, 1993: 234) Under the umbrella of peace activism, members confronted fundamental issues, such as racism, sexism, welfare reform, reproductive rights, childcare, housing, health care, food, and employment (Alonso, 1993: 235). Like the WSP and WILPF, WREE used traditional demonstrations, lobbying, and petitioning methods to conduct its work. Differently, though, this organization re-connected itself to a global militant movement that sought participation among younger, poorer women of color (Alonso, 1993: 237). By the 1990s, backlash and repression in the conservative landscape led the group to disband.

Despite the difficulties of the period, Black peace activists remained committed to broadening conversations about national and global peace. In 1995, a group formed a caucus to attend the Fourth World Conference on Women in Beijing. The conference was called "to build on consensus and progress made at previous UN conferences and summits ... [and] to [a]chieve the full and effective implementation of the Nairobi Forward-looking Strategies for the Advancement of Women." As such, it would offer a Platform for Action in which participating nations would agree to continue to work to eliminate discrimination against women (Levitt, 2017: 156). Calling upon Kimberlé Crenshaw's work on "intersectionality," published in 1989, the women gathered in Washington, D.C., in mid-June 1995 to craft their arguments for intersectionality in human rights law.

When they arrived in China in September, they merged with an NCNW delegation to bring together nearly 100 Black women to enrich the discussion of women, peace, and security (Levitt, 2017: 155). Working with other women of color, including Native American/Indigenous women, Asian Americans, and Latinas, the group developed three position papers that emphasized broadened conversations about gender inequity in the peace agenda to include racism, poverty, unequal access to health care, and environmental justice issues.[16] The final Beijing Declaration and Platform for Action reflected their efforts. It made use of an intersectionality framework, which included an explicit recognition that some subgroups of women face barriers to full equality and advancement because of factors such as race, age, language, ethnicity, culture, religion, or disability. The document also acknowledged that some groups of women and children are more vulnerable to violence, especially those of refugee, rural and impoverished, and minoritized populations. These acts of violence include those within the home and the community and those perpetuated and condoned by the state. These harms instilled fear and insecurity in women's lives and are obstacles to achieving equality and to development and peace (UN Women, 1995: 17, 49).

Reflecting on this success and the more extensive history on which it stood, Black female peace activists likely expected more from the WPS agenda when it was formalized in October 2000. Spurred by the long and rich activism of women's rights and peace movement as extensive lobbying by non-governmental organizations, United Nations Resolution 1325 (UNSCR1325) reaffirms the significance of women in maintaining negotiations, peace, and security, as well as humanitarian missions and postwar and post-conflict reconstruction. The landmark resolution also directs state attention to gender-based violence, especially crimes of sexual assault during armed conflict. Making clear its commitment to implement UNSCR1325, national actors created NAPs to lay out their comprehensive plan of governmental actions and chart their progress.

While notable in these goals, a more than 20-year history reveals that the WSP and the NAPs it inspired remain relatively flat and limited. Activists and scholars alike have noted that the framework is "racialised, patriarchal, classist, heteronormative and Western-centric at its core" (Martin de Almagro, 2017: 18). Goals concerning women are narrowly and superficially focused on women's inclusion as leaders or fixated on their experiences in conflict-related sexual violence. This limited focus means that where "women" are made visible, they do so as essentialized beings who are devoid of race, class, sexual orientation, and other realities of experiences (Shepherd, 2011, 2016). Rather than develop policies that recognize that these reciprocally constructed phenomena shape women's experiences as a whole and cannot be examined independently, current NAPs make these categories subsidiaries of gender. Even more, where the term "intersectionality" emerges, it primarily does so as a "heuristic device" that captures the experiences of women affected in conflict and post-conflict settings. As Susan Smith, Elena B. Stavrevska, and others point out, this emphasis, while an important one, does not go as far as intersectionality requires (Smith and Stavreska, 2022: 66). Given these limitations, it is little wonder that Black women activists have created organizations and alternative spaces to address their intersectional needs and perspectives.

In 2017, the WCAPS was created to diversify peace and security and conflict transformation by providing a sustained voice from LGBTQIA+ women and gender-diverse persons of color. The organization works to cultivate and advance leadership and development skills (WCAPS, n.d.). The number of bodies committed to tackling the structural violence that Black Americans faced has also accelerated. In 2013, three Black female organizers, Alicia Garza, Patrisse Cullors, and Opal Tometi, created the Black Lives Matter Movement to draw attention to Black Americans' continued experiences with police brutality (Black Lives Matter, n.d.). Since the movement mostly focuses on the violence against Black men, the African American Policy Forum (AAPF) and Center for Intersectionality and Social Policy Studies (CISPS) created the #SayHerName campaign to bring awareness to Black women and girls victimized by police violence (Jacobs, 2017: 42).

Other peace activists pursue their work through bodies like the Black Alliance for Peace and Search for Common Ground. Born in April 2017, the Black Alliance for Peace continues the traditional of radical peace activism by resisting racism in its many forms and militarization ranging from state warmongering to the militarization of police (Burden-Stelly, 2019). Emerging in the Cold War, Search for Common Ground continues to creatively bring peaceful solutions through actions ranging from "traditional diplomacy and mediation to video games and virtual exchange" (Search for Common Ground, n.d.a). In 2014, the organization joined with others to compel the

United Nations to adopt Resolution 2250 to bring young people like Murrey into solutions of peace (Search for Common Ground, n.d.b).

After Floyd's murder in 2021, Murrey, who had run Search for Common Ground's communication department for six years, used her experiences and methods to inspire Americans and peace activists worldwide to develop a deeper understanding of the myriad of problems that plague Black Americans' peace. In pieces like "I'm Black. I'm a Peacebuilder. I Want Your Help" and "America's Identity Crisis: Race and Reconciliation from a Black Peacebuilder," she compelled readers to come to terms with the fact that "Justice is not only the acknowledgment of unfairness or the punishment that follows." Instead, "Justice is the replacement of systems that have caused disparities with systems that uphold human dignity for everyone." Though Murrey did not cite the long history of Black women making similar claims, her calls are nearly identical to those made by Black female peace activists of yesteryear.

A more than 100-year review of Black women's peace activism should reveal two key takeaways. First, this population has long remained committed to peace activism. Since the early 20th century, Black female activists have worked to bring about a positive, intersectional peace in civic organizations, interstate bodies, and the political process. Whether working on the right, left, or in the center, these activists contended that the arrival of peace was not the absence of direct violence but rather the presence of justice. They explicated the local and global relationship, calling on fellow citizens and activists to recognize that the hurdles to peace, harmony, and equality exist not only in foreign countries but also closer to home. They also clarified that a successful peace agenda required paying attention to the multiple and interlocking oppressions and examining the interplay between patriarchy, antiblackness, ethnocentricity, and heteronormativity.

The second takeaway is that the necessary shifts needed in the WPS agenda must involve the voices and perspectives of Black women and other women of color. Today, there is still no significant or sustained voice from LGBTQIA+ women and gender-diverse persons of color in discussions of international peace, security, and conflict transformation. The WPS agenda also has not gone far enough in recognizing that gender cannot be divorced from race, class, or sexuality and that women need and deserve more than a narrow focus that vacillates between leadership opportunities and victimhood. If the experiences of Black women peace activists and the history of the last several decades are to be believed, lasting peace is impossible until injustices are met head-on and soundly defeated (Murrey, 2020).

Notes

1 In this chapter, I use "African American" and "Black" to refer to people born in the United States with African ancestry. While "Black" also refers to dark-skinned people of African descent, no matter their nationality, many African Americans

consider this identifier as an interchangeable one or have no terminological preference. I capitalize "Black" in this chapter, not because it refers to a natural category but a social one that describes a collective and shared identity. I capitalize "White" to recognize the dialectical relationship between "Black" and "White" racialization and acknowledge the historical development of Whiteness, and because it is important not to see "White" as a fixed, self-evident, or unmarked category. For an introduction to these developments and approaches, see Morgan (2007), Martin (1991), and Sigelman et al. (2005).
2 For work on Black women and peace activism, see Blackwell (2004), Plastas (2011), Chandler (2005), and Ramdani (2015). Stephanie Y. Evans also considers how Black women chronicled experiences of personal peace and quests for peace, and social justice in their autobiographies (2014: 96).
3 For a history of Black women's club activism, see Gray White (2000).
4 Hunton and Johnson (1920; emphasis added).
5 Ida Gibbs Hunt to Mary Church Terrell, April 20, 1915, William Henry Hunt Papers, Moorland Spingarn Research Center, Howard University (Washington, D.C.).
6 "Women Discuss Causes of War in Conference," *New Journal and Guide* (Norfolk, Virginia), February 7, 1925: 8; "At Conventions," *Afro-American*, January 31, 1925.
7 Addie Hunton to Du Bois, November 17, 1926, Du Bois Credo Papers.
8 "Mrs. Bethune Writes from Abroad," *Pittsburgh Courier*, 6 August 1927; and "Mrs. Bethune Honor Guest at Banquet," *Chicago Defender*, August 20, 1927.
9 "The Onward March of the 'Jolly 14'," Box 1, Folder 26, Mary McLeod Bethune Papers, 1923–1942, Amistad Research Center at Tulane University, New Orleans, Louisiana. Also, see "Off to Europe? Who's Off?" [1927] in this same folder.
10 Barnes (2016: 108–109) and Williams and Boehm (1994: 42 and 48).
11 Barnes (2016: 90–91).
12 "Address of Mary F. Waring," 1935 NACW Minutes, NACW Microfilm, Reel 1.
13 *AfraAmerican* (October 1950): 3–4, Box 1, Folder 15, Series 13, NCNW Papers.
14 The five women's organizations were the General Federation of Women's Clubs, the National League of Women Voters, the American Association of University of Women, the U.S. section of the International Council of Women, and the Women's Action for Victory and Lasting Peace. The sole organization to represent racialized minorities was the National Association for the Advancement of Colored People. See Gallagher (2011: 96n10).
15 Mable Alston, "The Committee, in Accord with NACW, Stand," *Afro-American*, April 12, 1947.
16 Indigenous women also formed a caucus and held a related view about the heterogeneity of women's experience, explicitly adopting a framework of intersectionality as well. See Levitt (2017: Chapter 8).

References

Alonso, H. 1993. *Peace as a Woman's Issue: A History of the U.S. Movement for World Peace and Women's Rights.* Syracuse, NY: Syracuse University Press.
Aptheker, H. 1993 [1973]. "The Fourth Pan African Congress," in *A Documentary History of the Negro People in the United States, 1910–1932*, comp vol. 3. New York: Citadel Press.
Azarmandi, M. 2018. "The Racial Silence within Peace Studies," *Peace Review* 30, No. 1: 69–77.
Barnes, G.A. 2016. *A Centennial History of the American Friends Service Committee.* FriendsPress.

Berlowitz, M.J. 2002. "Eurocentric Contradictions in Peace Studies," *Peace Review* 14, No. 1.
Black Lives Matter. n.d. "Herstory." https://blacklivesmatter.com/herstory/. Accessed November 14, 2022.
Blackwell, J. 2004. *No Peace Without Freedom: Race and the Women's International League for Peace and Freedom 1915–1975*. Carbondale, IL: Southern Illinois University Press.
Blain, K.N. 2022. *Until I Am Free: Fannie Lou Hamer's Enduring Message to America*. S.l.: Beacon Press.
Burden-Stelly, Charisse. 2019. "Introduction to Claudia Jones: Foremother of World Revolution," *Journal of Intersectionality* 3, No. 1. Chandler, S. 2005. "Addie Hunton and the Construction of an African American Female Peace Perspective," *Affilia* 20, No. 3: 270–283.
Chappell, F. 2021. "'There Has Always Been A Black Women's Peace Movement': Women of Colour and Anti-War Activism in the U.S., 1968–1972," *Women's History Network*, October 4. https://womenshistorynetwork.org/there-has-always-been-a-black-womens-peace-movement-by-frankie-chappell/
Church Terrell, M. 2005 [1940]. *A Colored Woman in a White World*. Lanham, MD: Rowman & Littlefield.
Crenshaw, Kimberle. 1989. "Demarginalizing the Intersection of Race and Sex: A Black Feminist Critique of Antidiscrimination Doctrine, Feminist Theory and Antiracist Politics," *University of Chicago Legal Forum* 1: Article 8. http://chicagounbound.uchicago.edu/uclf/vol1989/iss1/8
Danielson, L. 2015. "The Peace Movement since 1945," in *Oxford Research Encyclopedia of American History*. Oxford: Oxford University Press.
Evans, S.Y. 2014. "Inner Lions: Definitions of Peace in Black Women's Memoirs. A Strength-based Model for Mental Health," *Peace Studies Journal* 7, No. 2.
Farmer, Ashley D. 2017. *Remaking Black Power: How Black Women Transformed an Era*. Charlotte, NC: University of North Carolina Press.
Gallagher, J.A. 2011. "The National Council of Negro Women, Human Rights, and the Cold War," in *Breaking the Wave: Women, Their Organizations, and Feminism, 1945–1985*, ed. Kathleen A. Laughlin and Jacqueline L. Castledine. New York: Routledge.
Galtung, J. 1969. "Violence, Peace, and Peace Research," *Journal of Peace Research* 6, No. 3: 167–191. www.jstor.org/stable/422690
Geiss, I. 1974. *The Pan-African Movement: A History of Pan Africanism in America, Europe and Africa*. New York: Africana Publishing Company.
Gore, D.F. 2011. *Radicalism At The Crossroads: African American Women Activists in the Cold War*. New York: NYU Press.
Gray White, D. 2000. *Too Heavy a Load: Black Women in Defense of Themselves, 1894–1994*. New York: W.W. Norton.
Hunton, A.W. and K.M. Johnson. 1920. *Two Colored Women with the American Expeditionary Forces* (No. 7460). Brooklyn: Eagle Press.
Jacobs, M.S. 2017. "The Violent State: Black Women's Invisible Struggle Against Police Violence," *William & Mary Journal of Women and the Law* 24, No. 1: 39–100.
Kiesel, D. 2019. *She Can Bring Us Home: Dr. Dorothy Boulding Ferebee, Civil Rights Pioneer*. Lincoln, NB: Potomac Books.
Levitt, J.I. 2017. *Black Women and International Law: Deliberate Interactions, Movements, and Actions*. Cambridge: Cambridge University Press.

Lieberman, R. 2015. "The Missing Peace: Charlotta Bass and the Visiton of the Balck Left in the Early Cold War Years," in *Lineages of the Literary Left: Essays in Honor of Alan M. Wald*, ed. Howard Brick, Robbie Lieberman, and Paula Rabinowitz. Ann Arbor: Michigan Publishing.

Litoff, J. and David C.Smith. 2000. *What Kind of World Do We Want? American Women Place for Peace.* Wilmington: SR Books.

Lynn, D. 2019. "Women Crusade for Peace: Claudia Jones and the Cold War Peace Movement," *Journal of Intersectionality* 3, No. 1.

Lynn, D. 2022. "Charlotta Bass and the Cold War Peace Movement," *Black Perspectives*, March 15. www.aaihs.org/charlotta-bass-and-the-cold-war-peace-movement/. Accessed July 18, 2022.

Martin, Ben L. 1991. "From Negro to Black to African American: The Power of Names and Naming," *Political Science Quarterly* 106, No. 1: 83–107.

Martin de Almagro, M. 2017. "Producing Participants: Gender, Race, Class, and Women, Peace and Security, Global Society," *Global Society*. DOI: doi:10.1080/13600826.2017.1380610

McCluskey, Audrey Thomas and Elaine M. Smith. 1999. "In Pursuit of Unalienable Rights: Mary McLeod Bethune in Historical Perspective (1875-1955)," in *Mary McLeod Bethune: Building a Better World*, ed. A.T. McCluskey and Elaine M. Smith. Bloomington: Indiana University Press.

McDuffie, E.S. 2011. *Sojourning For Freedom: Black Women, American Communism, and the Making of Black Left Feminism.* Durham, NC: Duke University Press.

Mjagkij, N. 2001. *Organizing Black America: An Encyclopedia of African American Associations.* New York: Garland.

Morgan, Sue (ed.). 2007. *The Feminist History Reader.* London: Routledge.

Murrey, J. 2020. "I'm Black. I'm a Peacebuilder. I Want Your Help," *Search for Common Ground*, June 3. https://sfcg.medium.com/im-black-i-m-a-peacebuilder-i-want-your-help-8ab32f84c572

NACWC. 1993 [1914]. *Convention Minutes, Wilberforce, Ohio, National Association of Colored Women's Clubs, 1895–1992, Part 1: Minutes of the National Conventions, Publications, and President's Office Correspondence.* Bethesda, MD: University Publications of America.

Parker, A.M. 2021. *Unceasing Militant: The Life of Mary Church Terrell.* Chapel Hill: The University of North Carolina Press.

Plastas, M.A. 2011. *'A Band of Noble Women': The WILPF and the Politics and Consciousness of Race in the Women's Peace Movement, 1915–1945.* Syracuse, NY: Syracuse University Press.

Ramdani, F. 2015. "Afro-American Women Activists as True Negotiators in the International Arena (1893–1945)," *European Journal of American Studies* 10, No. 1: 1–15.

Rief, M. 2004. "Thinking Locally, Acting Globally: The International Agenda of African American Clubwomen, 1880–1940," *Journal of African American History* 89, No. 3.

Schott, L.K. 1997. *Reconstructing Women's Thoughts: The Women's International League for Peace and Freedom Before World War II.* Stanford, CA: Stanford University Press.

Search for Common Ground. n.d.a. "About Us." www.sfcg.org/our-story/. Accessed November 14, 2022.

Search for Common Ground. n.d.b. "UNSCR 2250." www.sfcg.org/tag/unscr-2250/. Accessed November 14, 2022.

Shepherd, L. 2011. "Sex, Security, and Superhero(in)es: From 1325 to 1820 and Beyond," *International Feminist Journal of Politics* 13: 504–521.

Shepherd, L. 2016. "Victims of Violence or Agents of Change? Representations of Women in UN Peacebuilding Discourse," *Peacebuilding* 4.

Siegel, M. 2021. *Peace on Our Terms: The Global Battle for Women's Rights After the First World War*. Columbia, NY: Columbia University Press.

Sigelman, Lee, Steven A. Tuch, and Jack K. Martin. 2005. "What's in a Name? Preference for 'Black' versus 'African-American'," *Public Opinion Quarterly* 69, No. 3: 429–438.

Smith. S and E.B. Stavrevska. 2022. "A Different Women, Peace and Security is Possible? Intersectionality in Women, Peace and Security Resolutions and National Action Plans," *European Journal of Politics and Gender*, 5, No. 1.

Swerdlow, A. 1993. *Women Strike for Peace: Traditional Motherhood and Radical Politics in the 1960s*. Chicago: University of Chicago Press.

Talbert, M.B. 1915. "Women and Colored Women," *The Crisis*, August.

Tuuri, R. 2018. *Strategic Sisterhood: The National Council of Negro Women in the Black Freedom Struggle*. Chapel Hill, NC: University of North Carolina Press.

UN Women. 1995. *Report of the Fourth World Conference on Women Beijing*, September 4–15, pp. 17, 49. www.un.org/womenwatch/daw/beijing/pdf/Beijing%20full%20report%20E.pdf. Accessed November 14, 2022.

WCAPS. n.d. "Vision and Mission," *Women of Color Advancing Peace, Security & Conflict Transformation*. www.wcaps.org/mission. Accessed July 16, 2022.

Wells, Thomas B. 2015. "'She Pieced and Stitched and Quilted, Never Wavering nor Doubting': A Historical Tapestry of African American Women's Internationalism, 1890s–1960s," Ph.D. Dissertation, Ohio State University

Wells, Thomas B. 2023. "'And the Curtain Rises on the Drama': The National Council of Negro Women & the Tragedy of the United Nations," *Journal of Civil Rights and Human Rights* 8, No. 2: 34–66.

Williams, L.S. and R. Boehm. 1994. *Records of the National Association of Colored Women's Clubs*. Bethesda, MD: University Publications of America.

2 Chicanas and Latinas in the Academic Borderlands[1]

Resistance, Empowerment, and Agency

Denise Segura

> Activism is the courage to act consciously on our ideas, to exert power in resistance to ideological pressure—to risk leaving home. Empowerment comes from ideas—a revolution is fought with concepts, not guns, and it is fueled by vision. By focusing on what we want to happen, we change the present. The healing images and narratives we imagine will eventually materialize.
> (Gloria E. Anzaldúa [2002] cited in Lindsay Pérez Huber [2017])

Activism eloquently articulated by Gloria Anzaldúa in the epigraph that opens this chapter reminds us of the importance of individual and collective courage in the face of tremendous obstacles hurled dauntingly against many disenfranchised communities. Activism means actively reframing and contesting ideological and material forms of oppression to focus on social change that heals the mind, spirit, and the conditions under which we all live. In the United States today, children, cis-gender women and men, queer folks, transindividuals, migrants, Chicanas/os/x, people of Mexican descent, and Latinas/os/x[2] who trace their origins from Latin American countries are all under attack. Thousands of Latinx migrants have been imprisoned along the U.S.–Mexico border and children are being torn from the arms of their parents and loved ones to be locked up where they are not cared for, fed properly, and where even soap and diapers are not categorized as essential items (Jordan, 2018). It leads one to wonder: has social justice improved the quality of life for communities of color and levelled the chasm between opportunity and exclusion since the civil rights and feminist movements of the 1960s? Those social movements sought to heighten *concientización* – social justice consciousness and political activism within communities and universities – to ameliorate the gulf between historically disenfranchised communities of color and citizens privileged by color, class, gender, and sexuality (Luibheid and Cantú Jr., 2005; Suárez-Orozco et al., 2011).

Activism from those years resulted in a wide range of civil rights legislation designed to *prohibit* unequal access to voting rights, education, employment, fair housing, and health care. I italicize the term "prohibit" here to call attention to the fact that legislation and policy have rarely codified equality of outcomes but rather focused on neoliberal notions of promoting equal access.

The past several years have seen the rise of important social movements such as the Sanctuary Movement, the transnational Ni Una Más (Not One More – movement against feminicide), the Black Lives Matter movement, the MeToo movement, and many others. In solidarity with local communities, a number of scholar-activists are using their respective skill sets to affirm the voices of oppressed and politicized "others" by documenting what Latina critical race theorist Tara Yosso (2016; Yosso et al., 2009) has called "community cultural wealth." This approach seeks to challenge what is considered "legitimate" and "valuable" research, curriculum, or service in the academy, often through its focus on activism for social justice causes both in scholarship as well as in person advocacy. Scholar-activism is constantly developing with respect to Chicana/o/x and Latina/o/x; one example is the increasingly use of "Chicanx" and "Latinx" to signal inclusion and affirmation of gender-nonconforming subjects. Scholar-activism takes many forms and is not always well-recognized or considered legitimate by conventional academics as research by Dolores Delgado Bernal (1998), Ruth Zambrana (2013), and others has shown. Part of the challenge for legitimacy lies in scholars' activist origins and their advocacy of social justice.

This chapter discusses how scholar-activists, in particular Chicana/x and Latina/x, are navigating the academic world in order to participate in the empowerment of our communities. It combines an autoethnography methodology with a borderlands-intersectional framework that critiques canonical explanations for social inequality and taps into the insights of Chicana/x and Latina/x feminisms. My research examines the appearance of community cultural wealth in academic "borderlands" and seeks to determine alternative sites for empowerment that emphasize community assets. This chapter is also a first step toward a larger study that will examine what it means to be a Latina/x scholar-activist. I situate my discussion within the foundational concept of the *borderlands*, and how this idea has shaped a generation of scholars, including myself. I go on to show how in my own scholarship within the academy, the development and use of borderlands theory incorporates a durable metaphor and meaning-maker for intellectual engagement, cultural consolation, and rigorous, expansive scholarship challenging the status quo. The chapter concludes with some thoughts on the increasing significance of intersectional borderlands approaches and their ability to provide new insights into women's resistance, agency, and empowerment.

Borderlands

Borderlands is a concept whose multifaceted meanings and significance are beautifully theorized by Gloria Anzaldúa in the now-classic *Borderlands/La Frontera* (1987). Her work challenges the white, heteronormative research frame used to study communities of color, and instead emphasizes the importance of Chicanas' diverse identities and their creative "mestiza consciousness." Anzaldúa's writings offer a new language that liberates the "ser" from the "estar" – that "to be" is formed by the politics of place and space in the territorial and cultural space known as the borderlands. Liberated methodologically and linguistically, more and more Chicana/x activist scholars in sociology are moving beyond research *about* Chicanas/x to a *Chicana/x feminist sociology* dedicated to social change; her book has also inspired new intersectional approaches within queer theory.

Borderlands refer to spaces with spatial, social, and spiritual features. Anzaldúa states that:

> The U.S.-Mexico border *es una herida abierta* (an open wound) where the Third World grates against the first and bleeds. And before a scab forms it hemorrhages again, the lifeblood of two worlds merging to form a third country—a border culture. Borders are set up to define the places that are safe and unsafe, to distinguish us from them.
>
> (Anzaldúa, 1987: 5)

Within these spaces, marginalized "others" voice their identities and proclaim their resistance. All of these social, political, spiritual, and emotional transitions transcend geopolitical space. Anzaldúa's theoretical perspective joins research on intersectional connections that seeks to determine how power is wielded and contested by dominant and subordinate classes, races, sex/genders. A borderlands intersectionalities approach considers the structural, spiritual, and social-interaction forces that frame social life and pose potent barriers to social justice and well-being; this approach also researches power shifts where new hybridized identities emerge. Indeed, identities constantly shift and are negotiated in responses to forces from above and below – they are never fixed or bounded (Levitt, 2001: 237–238). Anzaldúa's borderlands thus inhabit physical and spiritual spaces that center on the movement of people, products, and ideas across the United States and Mexico. The borderlands are not confined to geographical spaces but refer to spaces where two or more cultures "edge" each other. These meetings are active and vibrant where social subjects negotiate for position, legitimacy, and place.

In the borderlands, empowerment is generated when individuals and communities who lack power in a particular context – schools, for instance – acquire knowledge and a language that assists them in unpacking institutional settings and power arrangements to change the conditions of their lives. The importance of energizing language to "deconstruct, construct" is an essential part of a borderlands feminist project (Anzaldúa, 1987: 104).

Anzaldúa's theoretical formulation of the borderlands disrupts Anglocentric nationalist histories, assimilationist paradigms, and Chicano nationalist agendas regarding the incorporation of Mexicans into the United States. Within the context of feminist ideology, women's narratives expand previous androcentric history texts and deconstruct the heteronormative patriarchal Chicano master narrative. Women-centered analyses expand previous versions of texts labeled politically "neutral" or "objective" by conventional social science that objectifies working-class, racial-ethnic, and queer communities.

One critical contribution of a Chicana/x *borderlands* perspective is its attention to the history of colonization and racialization of Mexicans which Chicanx theorist Emma Pérez refers to as a "decolonial imaginary" (1999). The confluence of Mexico and the United States creates specific social conditions for both Mexicanas/Mexicanos/Mexicanx and Chicanas/Chicanos/Chicanx. Race, gender, sexuality, and class are negotiated in the daily lives of Chicana/xs within the context of the borderlands and serve as a fertile ground from which individual and collective action arises. Borderlands theorists contextualize and substantiate myriad Mexicana/x and Chicana/x experiences as forms of adaptation and resistance to linguistic and cultural terrorism. In a transnational framework, borderlands scholars and activists emphasize coalitions with other *mujeres* (women) across the U.S.–Mexico geopolitical border. Hence, a borderlands feminist sociology interrogates and moves beyond a nation-bound discourse. Borderlands feminist research works to develop binational approaches that include structural forces and women's individual and collective agency, incorporating perspectives of women on both sides of the U.S.–Mexican border.

Anzaldúa has also used the term "spiritual activism" to describe the transformative potential of borderlands subjects. Drawing on Anzaldúa, Keating argues that spiritual activism "begins with the personal yet moves outward, acknowledging our radical interconnectedness. This is spirituality for social change, spirituality that recognizes the many differences among us yet insists on our commonalities and uses these commonalities as catalysts for transformation" (Keating and Anzaldúa, 2002: 18). Validating connections to our communities that center on women's voices and experiences is integral to spiritual activism, and to Chicana/x/Latina/x feminist sociology. In this vein, Chicana/x feminist sociology will explore how women express complex human agency within the transformations occurring in the borderlands between the United States and Mexico and beyond.

In the borderlands, "difference" becomes meaningful even as "sameness" is questioned. Marginality is revealed as a social reality marked by moments of transgression from the dominant culture as well as assertions of a unique and valuable "otherness" and "in-between" subject positions. Understanding otherness as a site of resistance and empowerment is a core concept within a Chicana/x feminist sociology situated in the borderlands. Segura and Zavella's (2007) review of key theoretical and methodological characterizations of borderlands in the social sciences finds a strong emphasis on transnational social formations, in particular economic, political, or sociocultural activities by individual and collective actors that transcend national borders, thereby "deterritorializing" politically drawn international boundaries. Increasingly, researchers who use this approach conduct field research in both "sending" and "receiving" communities, thereby revealing specifics of how deterritorialized processes unfold at micro and macro levels.

Segura and Zavella (2007: 176) argue further that a second approach to borderlands, centered in cultural studies, "emphasize[s] the ways in which identity formation is linked to multiple sites, both real and imagined, such that new hybridized and creolized identity forms emerge" but are rather fluid. One must be familiar with both approaches to get a sense of the multifaceted changes that women negotiate.

A borderlands feminist project focuses on women's construction of cultural identity and agency in the nebulous space of their lived realities, or what Segura and Zavella (2007) refer to as "subjective transnationalism." Women constantly negotiate economic and political space in geographic and psychic borderlands. Their activity disrupts traditional notions of gender within households, local communities, and the state. Rosa Linda Fregoso (2003) argues that violence against women in Ciudad Juárez, in the state of Chihuahua, and elsewhere illustrates the male-dominated state's efforts to reclaim women as subordinate objects. I argue that social movements against femicide exemplify subjective transnationalism where women's spiritual agency and borderless *concientización* seeks to reclaim their political and sexual subjectivities and reject all forms of domestic or state-sanctioned violence. Reclaiming women's voices and uncovering their paths to resist violence and assert their sexual subjectivity are feminist borderlands projects engaged in by such researchers as Patricia Zavella (2003, 2020), Gloria González-López (2006), Yvette Flores (2013) and Enriqueta Valdez Curiel (with Yvetta Flores, 2009), to name a few. These scholars are among a growing group of Chicana/x and Latina/x scholars making the case for a more inclusive, overlapping, intersectional approach to knowledge and understanding.

But it is Anzaldúa's (1987) conception of the *borderlands*, and its seductive hybrid of the material and immaterial, the imagined and the real, that opens space for us. Anzaldúa and Keating collaboratively argue "we are in symbiotic relationship to all that exists and co-creators of ideologies—attitudes, beliefs, and cultural values—motivates us to act collaboratively" (2002: 2). It is here that the broad, suggestive landscape of the *borderlands* ideal emerges, offering a vision of spiritual activism that bridges the community and the academy.

Scholarly Beginnings

Fifty years ago, community activists and scholar-activists including students, staff, and faculty gathered in Santa Barbara, California to craft *El Plan de Santa Barbara* (Chicano Coordinating Council on Higher Education, 1969). *El Plan* was a blueprint for institutional change that sought to diversify higher education and clarify the processes of educational exclusion toward people of color in the United States. It demanded programs to prepare and admit students from historically underrepresented groups and sought the hiring of staff and faculty from underrepresented groups to teach about the needs of Chicano and other oppressed communities. As scholar-activists, a term used then and now by many Chicana/o/x and Latina/o/x university faculty, staff, and students, they – we – committed ourselves to the hard work of bringing social justice to our communities including changing the range of "legitimate" knowledge claims within the university; holding the academy accountable to include historically disenfranchised subjects was, and is, paramount.

While the intent of *El Plan* was social justice, the voices of women were notably few, and the agenda was largely driven by patriarchal power dynamics. As Chicana feminist historian Cynthia Orozco ironically notes, "'El Plan' was a MAN-ifesto" (1984: 13). Moreover, creating Chicana Studies or Chicanx Studies was not part of the agenda during those turbulent times. In the face of considerable cultural policing that privileged race and class agendas in the Chicano Movement and the priority given to gender equality by second wave feminism, Chicana feminisms focused on challenging the "walls of silence" that shrouded Mexican-origin women's ability to (re)claim their unique funds of knowledge within existing organizational spaces and create alternative paths toward social and sexual agency.[3]

At the University of California, Santa Cruz, which I attended in 1972, there were no tenure-track Chicana faculty and only three Chicano male faculty members. My department, Sociology, had only two faculty members of color, both African American men. When I began my senior year, one of those faculty, Provost Herman Blake, called me to his office along with another Chicana undergraduate and convinced us to apply for graduate school for *la lucha* (or the struggle for self-determination and empowerment for our communities). Professor Blake had been involved in the Black Power movement and sponsored the political activist and Black Panther leader Huey Newton's attendance at UC Santa Cruz. He told us he believed my friend and I had what it took to enter PhD-granting institutions and secure faculty positions. Schooled within the Chicano Movement we questioned why he had singled us out, telling him that we had worked hard to earn teaching credentials while completing our respective majors so that we could serve our community.

Dr. Blake argued that the academy needed more scholar-activists of color and if we secured a PhD, we could serve our community in multiple ways including contributing new knowledge concerning our communities and by encouraging and supporting other students of color. We were both working-class, first-generation students of color and did not know what graduate school would involve, but we agreed to apply. I entered the Sociology PhD program at UC Berkeley and my friend entered a PhD program at Stanford. The challenges went beyond what we could have imagined but I was fortunate to have a strong Chicana/o support group and was able to work as a part-time teacher in a high school bilingual program which kept me connected to the community I loved and nurtured my commitment to scholar-activism.

The challenges I and other Chicanas faced in graduate school to both work within our communities and to do research on the under-studied area of Chicanas/Latinas required us (namely Beatriz Pesquera, Elisa Facio, Guadalupe Friaz, Teresa Córdova, Gloria Cuádraz, Deena González, and Patricia Zavella) to navigate what I call the academic borderlands.

These borderlands demanded that we navigate spaces where the graduate curriculum did not include the experiences of communities of color. We were often dismissed by faculty with the words, "I am not an expert in this but if *you* wish to do this kind of research you can." Fortunately, the Berkeley borderlands in sociology included feminist scholar Arlie Hochschild, African American scholar-activist Troy Duster, radical race theorist Robert Blauner, and Chicano historical sociologist Tomas Almaguer. I mention them not only because they were important role models to many graduate students of color, but because they always warned us that would have to "do more" as our research would be heavily scrutinized for political bias, our teaching would be evaluated for perceived inadequacies of breadth and rigor, and our efforts at community service would be disparaged if not altogether dismissed.

Several first- and second-generation scholar-activists of color within the academy – including Cherrie Moraga (1983), Patricia Arredondo (2019), and Yolanda Flores Niemann (1999) – have written autobiographical accounts about the complexity of navigating a system designed for white men. In their 1998 study of the academic environment for graduate students of color, Eric Margolis and Mary Romero (1998) wrote that "[t]he department is very male, very white, very old, and very conservative." In interviews with Chicana faculty I conducted with Beatriz Pesquera in 1998, we discussed the challenges scholar-activists experienced navigating the professoriate – from access to tenure-track positions to establishing the legitimacy of community-based research. Many faculty considered themselves scholar-activists, by which they meant doing research that would reflect the needs and agendas of communities of color as articulated by community members themselves. Across disciplinary boundaries, Chicana/x and Latina/x scholar activists developed new paradigms that critiqued tropes of cultural deficiency and created new knowledge claims that expanded the range of feminist and other theories.

In 1999, around the time I conducted these interviews with Beatriz Pesquera, less than 1 percent of all full-time faculty teaching in institutions of higher education in the United States were Latina. Of these, 0.4 percent were full professors, 0.7 percent associate professors, and 1.3 percent assistant professors (U.S. Department of Education, 1999). Given the paucity of Chicanas/Latinas in the academy it is not surprising that many of these women labored alone. However, others were able to develop strong collaborations with Latinas and others committed to social justice in the academy, the nation, and across the globe. Today, such collaborations are increasing as the number of Latina and Latinx faculty slowly rises. Still, less than 2 percent of full-time faculty members are Latinas (1.87 percent in 2016) (Kena et al., 2016). This is a woeful underrepresentation given that Latinx subjects are 17 percent of the nation's population and in California comprise over half of all public school students.

Despite the relatively low numbers of Latina and Latinx faculty, their intellectual, policy, and political impact cannot be underestimated. Among the theoretical innovations and foundational achievements of Chicanas and Latinas in the academy include Gloria Anzaldúa's theories of the borderlands mestiza consciousness, Emma Pérez's (1999) decolonial imaginary, Chela Sandoval's (1991, 2013) oppositional consciousness, Dolores Delgado Bernal's (2001) pedagogies of the home, and Tara Yosso et al.'s (2009) work on racial microaggressions and community cultural wealth. Their foundational work merges feminist theories with critical race theory while combining contexts from social movements and insights grounded in the realities of Chicana/o/x and Latina/o/x experiences and abilities. These scholars' insights inform further research by scholar-activists committed to exposing inequality in the world and in the halls of the academy – all with the goal of presenting alternative practices that increase the socioeconomic and spiritual life chances of Chicana/o/x and Latina/o/x people. Research by Dolores Delgado Bernal (2001) on "pedagogies of the home" and her theorizing with Octavio Villalpando (2002) on an "apartheid of knowledge" demonstrates the practices that marginalize and devalue the scholarship, epistemologies, and cultural resources of faculty of color within higher education. As they have written: "This apartheid of knowledge in the academy is sustained by the de facto racial segregation that exists in higher education institutions, across academic ranks, and within departments" (Bernal and Villalpando, 2002: 177). Their analysis, based on national data on faculty of color across different types of postsecondary institutions, academic ranks, and departments broadens our understanding of epistemological racism in education research. These scholars and others demonstrate how Eurocentric faculty rarely validate or legitimate research based on alternative systems of knowing – systems that focus on the assets of communities of color and disrupt Western colonial assumptions of merit and knowledge legitimacy (Bernal, 1998, 2002; Dillard, 1995, 2000; Elenes, 1997, 2011; Hurtado, 2003; Ladson-Billings, 1995, 2000; Tillman, 2006; Villenas, 1996, 2010). Such work illustrates a borderlands intersectionalities perspective which identifies the cartographies of oppression and the importance of spirituality and healing. This perspective also directs us to consider how oppressive spaces are navigated and contested. Such scholars have gone far in articulating a viable sociological and intellectual framework for scholarship. Chicana/x feminist sociology in the borderlands reveals the complex representations, experiences, and identities that Chicana/x and Mexicana/x construct in the contexts established by globalization, transnational migration, and social formations and imaginaries that span national borders. The challenge facing Chicana/x feminist researchers is to establish our own genealogy, that is, to understand and interrogate our own social locations within the borderlands with an eye to learning about women, families, and children presented as "others," with caring and respect that allows us to "risk being wounded" (Anzaldúa and Keating, 2002: 3).

In addition to operationalizing concepts such as "the borderlands," it is essential to interrogate the "new mestiza consciousness" within Chicana feminist sociology. Anzaldúa argues that the new mestiza consciousness validates Chicana selfhood by confronting traditions of male domination within our own communities, including men and male-identified women, and breaking down dualities of sexuality that promote heterosexism.

Recognizing the "indígena" in the new mestiza is essential in the development of a politicized, racialized, feminist Chicana. The new mestiza consciousness is a consciousness of the borderlands, which includes "mental nepantilism" (Anzaldúa, 1987: 100). "Nepantla" is a Náhuatl term meaning "in the middle," "tierra entre medio," or "in between," a state in which defining space(s) of mitigating and negotiating dualities takes place with the goal of healing and transformation.

But the work of social change does not exist solely within the academy. Agent-resistance and alternative visions of social justice can be found in every Chicana/o/x community. Much of this work reflects Chicana/x and Latina/x feminisms that validate connections to our communities and amplify women's voices and experiences. Chicana/x feminist sociology explores how women voice their complex human agency within economic, political, and cultural spheres along the borderlands between the U.S., Mexico, and beyond. Moreover, given the community praxis embodied within Chicana/x feminist sociology, developing research and policy initiatives and programs that address the economic struggles of women of all race-ethnicities and their families is essential.

SISTERS and ENLACE

Trained as a qualitative sociologist, I am well-versed in feminist methods that emphasize women's voices and experiences as critical analytical starting points for any program. I have sought to build, with Elisa Facio (Segura and Facio, 2008) and others, a borderlands community praxis that would draw on the theoretical nurturance Anzaldúa describes. Such activities blend key theoretical and applied developments in Chicana/x feminist sociology, with a focus on social justice.

Sisters of Color United for Education, or SISTERS, in Denver, Colorado; and ENLACE (Engaging Latino Communities for Education) at the University of California, Santa Barbara are two programs that sought to manifest what an effective borderlands approach could look like in the real world. SISTERS and ENLACE are two borderlands programs that embody three aspects of Anzaldúa's conceptualization of spiritual activism: transformative social change, community building, and a tolerance for ambiguity, that is, possessing mestiza consciousness. Anzaldúa's work on the contours of the mestiza consciousness also presented a new activist subject, the new mestiza. She goes on to present the work of Chicana sociologists as twofold: to continue to work in our communities by deploying a borderlands community praxis and to disrupt the master narrative of sociology by interpreting the lives of Chicanas through standpoints that bridge the academic with the indigenous, or as Sonia Saldívar-Hull (1991) states, a mestizaje consciousness. Ultimately, Anzaldúa reminds us that "[t]he struggle of the mestiza is above all a feminist one" (1987: 106).

SISTERS and ENLACE are programs built on Chicana/x and Latina/x community members' funds of existing knowledge and the principles of spiritual activism in these communities. These programs do not have Principal Investigators or faculty who define priorities or problems. Rather, these two programs seek to invert power relations while respecting local ways of knowing thereby bridging "the work of opening the gate to the stranger, within and without" (Anzaldúa and Keating, 2002). To eradicate hierarchies between the academy and local communities, bridges must be built across groups with different access to power and prestige. Anzaldúa and Keating argue that we must take responsibility for changing these social relations, and "we must risk being open to personal, political, and spiritual intimacy, to risk being wounded."

SISTERS is a nonprofit, community-based organization dedicated to improving comprehensive health and quality of life for women of color. Through indigenous community leadership, SISTERS develops and conducts culturally proficient models of prevention, empowerment, and information sharing. The fundamental values that guide SISTERS' community work are empowerment, individual growth, social justice, health care as a human right, respect for differences, and a belief that the indigenous community has the strength, wisdom, and ability to navigate in mainstream society. SISTERS has been heavily involved in a peer-led program to prevent HIV infection among Chicanas and Mexicanas in Denver.

Activist-scholar Elisa Facio (2014) argued that a Chicana feminist praxis shows how empowerment has a different meaning for Chicanas that participate in such intervention programs. Generally, empowerment entails accessing power structures rather than dismantling, eradicating, and/or changing structures that are oppressive to their communities. Women in intervention programs desire to institutionalize undertakings that support their communities' goals in creating healthy and productive environments. Consequently, terminology like "healing and transformation" has replaced the term "empowerment" in teaching materials and implementation strategies. The notions of healing and transformation are influenced by Anzaldúa's theory of a new mestiza consciousness, which illustrates how the new mestiza adopts new perspectives toward dark-skinned people, women, and queers. In other words, we need to understand and interpret our worlds from our own academic indigenous standpoints. Anzaldúa reminds us of the task we face when she states that "[w]ithin us and within *la cultura chicana*, commonly held beliefs of the white culture attack commonly held beliefs of the Mexican culture, and both attack commonly held beliefs of the indigenous culture" (1987: 78).

A program funded by the Kellogg Foundation, UC Santa Barbara, and three local community colleges, ENLACE utilized the perspective of pedagogies of the home and identified "best practices" in schools to improve the academic preparation of Latinas/os for higher education and enhance their retention in college.[4] This program, which I co-directed, sought to disrupt the hierarchical relations between educational professionals and parents (mainly mothers) and prioritize women's experiences and insights. ENLACE's goals included enhancing family involvement in schools, increasing the leadership capacity of students and parents, improving the community's knowledge of schools, developing effective family–school negotiation skills with parents, effecting school-centered systemic change (such as working with the schools to be more flexible in their curricular or "track" assignments), and helping sensitize schools to the needs of local families. The project assumed value and complexity within Chicanx and Latinx cultures – value that is all too often unrecognized. Parents guided a collaboration that resulted in programs that focused on the needs articulated by the community (for example, in Padres Adelante workshops). Concurrently, ENLACE trained undergraduates, 90 percent of whom were first-generation Chicanx and Latinx students, to work with families as mentors and advocates in schools. That the college students' backgrounds mirrored those of the high school students was particularly important for Latinas since sometimes their families are reluctant to let them stay after school for enrichment programs, but when Chicana or Latina mentors are assigned, the outcomes tend to be more positive. The success of the program was a strong symbol to the community that "*sí se puede*"! (or as Gloria Anzaldúa states: "I change myself, I change the world" [1987: 92]). ENLACE demonstrates that "community empowerment" is not just about giving information to Chicanx or Latinx families or other community-based organizations, it is a reciprocal, organic process that includes strengthening families' funds of knowledge of our own Latinx undergraduates and those of the faculty, the schools, and the university.

All 95 undergraduates who have worked in ENLACE graduated, and about two-thirds have gone on to master's degrees, credential programs, and other graduate programs. This project, which occurred between 1999 and 2005, was later institutionalized within UC Santa Barbara's academic preparation program and is currently strengthening partnerships with local schools, families, and community-based agencies. Due to programs like this and others, UC Santa Barbara is now considered a Hispanic Serving Institution.[5] The ENLACE y Avance experience demonstrates how a Chicana feminist praxis can facilitate empowerment of our local communities.

And though that word is bandied about quite a bit, it is important to remember what empowerment truly is. Empowerment is a process that changes the nature and distribution of power. SISTERS and ENLACE show how community empowerment in health care and education can deploy a Chicana feminist sociology anchored in an activist interpretation of Anzaldúa's borderlands, or what we refer to as a borderlands community praxis.

Looking Ahead

There are many places where the work of change continues. For instance, along the U.S.–Mexico border community and scholar-activism abounds. Latinx community activists, artevistas (artists visualizing social justice), journalists, and scholar-activists are documenting and disseminating images of the anguish faced by thousands of migrant children along the U.S.–Mexico border. Indeed, art can be a powerful vehicle for change (Cascone, 2019).

Artevistas and artist-activists that include members of local communities as well as members of the academy are devising alternative ways to protest injustice and try to heal the spirit through play.

One of these examples is the Pink See-Saw Project. As memorably described in the *New York Times* (Romero, 2019):

> For a brief moment — just a half-hour over the weekend — a simple piece of playground equipment served as a bridge between the United States and Mexico ... children smiled and giggled with glee as they bobbed up and down on three pink seesaws that had been inserted through the steel slats of a section of border wall in Sunland Park, New Mexico.

Ronald Rael, one the architects who designed the border seesaws, wrote in an Instagram post describing the unusual installation: "Actions that take place on one side have a direct consequence on the other side" (Rael, 2019).

This collaborative project brought together architects and scholars to highlight the plight of migrant children along the U.S.–Mexico border. It also reminded the public of the importance of the often-overlooked concept of "play" and its ability to help heal traumatized children.

The work of artevistas is also critical to social justice work and a feminist re-envisioning of society. Chicano history is replete with examples of how the power of art helped envision alternative futures. During the heyday of the Chicano Movement, a group of Chicana student activists developed a philosophy of sisterhood – *hermanidad* – and published a Chicana feminist newspaper, *Las Hijas de Cuauhtémoc*. *Las Hijas de Cuauhtemoc* reappropriated masculinist iconography such as the Aztec eagle, depicting the Aztec eagle overshadowing a woman trying to free herself from patriarchal oppression by cutting herself free with a machete.

Indeed, numerous Chicana and Chicanx artists express their feminisms by reinterpreting "appropriate" notions of gender depicted by key cultural icons such as Our Lady of Guadalupe. Artist Yolanda Lopez re-envisioned the traditional Virgen de Guadalupe figure by inserting an image of herself. Representing Chicana feminists asserting agency and power, Lopez depicts La Virgen as a marathon runner with muscular thighs and calves, holding a serpent in her hand like a staff of power. Crushed under her foot is an angel whose wings are red, white, and blue. She describes the angel as a middle-aged agent of patriarchy. Lopez explained in a talk delivered at the University of California, Irvine, that she depicted the Virgin of Guadalupe as "jumping off the crescent moon, jumping off the pedestal she's been given by Chicanos" (Gaspar de Alba, 1998). Chicana feminist critic Amalia Mesa-Baines argues that Lopez's series on Our Lady of Guadalupe (*The Guadalupe Triptych*) offers a "critique of traditional Mexican women's roles and religious oppression in a self-fashioning of new identities" (Griswold del Castillo et al., 1991: 137). After her painting was displayed, Lopez was harassed and physically threatened.

Borderlands intersectionalities guide many Chicanx and Latinx scholar-activists whose research examines processes where marginalized others assert their voices and claim their places. Chicana/x and Latina/x academic "others" develop new knowledge-claims steeped in the experiences of their beleaguered communities. Latinx scholar-activists document and disseminate the narratives of social inequality and new forms of border capital that are developed within local communities.

At their best, scholar-activists are humble listeners who provide advice when asked but focus on using their skill set to broaden the inclusionary mechanisms of an historically exclusionary academy. Broadening the legitimacy of community funds of knowledge and embracing counter-narratives of history and resistance is critical. Our challenge is to remain vigilant and ensure that these academic borderlands are nurtured and new plantings are sown across the academic terrain.

Notes

1 Pieces of this chapter were previously published in Facio, Elisa and Segura, Denise A. "23. Chicana Feminist Sociology in the Borderlands". *Bridging: How Gloria Anzaldúa's Life and Work Transformed Our Own*, edited by AnaLouise Keating and Gloria González-López, New York, USA: University of Texas Press, 2011, pp. 175–181. The author is grateful to the publisher for permission to reuse this material.
2 Chicanx and Latinx are gender-neutral terms that incorporate non-binary, gender-nonconforming and genderqueer individuals who claim Mexican American or Latin American heritage. In addition, using the "x" challenges conventional Spanish grammatical usage privileging the masculine "o" in Chicano or Latino, to refer to all members of these respective race-ethnic communities. This chapter uses each of these terms attentive to history and context; that is, when I refer to Chicano cultural nationalism that reflects the term used at the time. The current chapter focuses largely on women of Mexican and Latin American descent so uses either the terms "Chicana" and "Latina" when referring to cis-gender women or "Chicana/x" and "Latina/x" when I refer to the larger, more inclusive community of cis-gendered women, lesbian, transwomen, and genderqueer individuals.
3 For a different perspective on the importance of silence and voice in feminist movements, and both concepts connections with women's agency, see Jane Parpart's contribution to this volume, Chapter X.
4 ENLACE, "Engaging Latino Communities for Education," was funded by the W. K. Kellogg Foundation from 2000–2005 at the University of California, Santa Barbara under the direction of two Co-Principal Investigators, Denise A. Segura and Richard Durán.
5 Funds of knowledge refers to various forms of home literacy practices, home discourse styles, and familial/cultural resources (Moll et al., 2006).

References

Anzaldúa, G. 1987. *Borderlands—La Frontera: The New Mestiza*. San Francisco: Spinsters/Aunt Lute.

Anzaldúa, G. 2002. Preface: Unnatural bridges, (un)safe spaces. In G.E. Anzaldúa and A. Keating (eds.), *This Bridge We Call Home: Radical Visions for Transformation* (pp. 1–5). New York: Routledge.

Anzaldúa, G. and Keating, A. (eds.). 2002. *This Bridge We Call Home: Radical Visions for Transformation*. New York: Routledge.

Arredondo, P. 2019. Latina Administrators Practicing Resonant Leadership in the Borderlands. In P.A. Pérez (ed.), *The Tenure-Track Process for Chicana and Latina Faculty* (pp. 106–129). London: Routledge.

Bernal, D.D. 1998. Using a Chicana Feminist Epistemology in Educational Research. *Harvard Educational Review*, 68(4), pp. 555–583.

Bernal, D.D. 2001. Learning and Living Pedagogies of the Home: The Mestiza Consciousness of Chicana Students. *International Journal of Qualitative Studies in Education*, 14(5), pp. 623–639.

Bernal, D.D. 2002. Critical Race Theory, Latino Critical Theory, and Critical Raced-Gendered Epistemologies: Recognizing Students of Color as Holders and Creators of Knowledge. *Qualitative Inquiry*, 8(1), pp. 105–126.

Bernal, D.D. and Villalpando, O. (2002) An Apartheid of Knowledge in Academia: The Struggle Over the "Legitimate" Knowledge of Faculty of Color. *Equity & Excellence in Education*, 35(2), pp. 169–180.

Cascone, S. 2019. Artists Briefly Bridge the US-Mexico Border With a Heartwarming Seesaw Linking Kids in Both Countries. https://news.artnet.com/art-world/us-mexico-border-teeter-totter-wall-1612897

Chicano Coordinating Council on Higher Education. 1969. *El Plan de Santa Barbara*. Oakland: La Causa Publications. http://mechadeucdavis.weebly.com/uploads/9/7/0/4/9704129/el_plan_de_santa_barbara.pdf

Dillard, C.B. 1995. Leading with Her Life: An African American Feminist (Re) Interpretation of Leadership for an Urban High School Principal. *Educational Administration Quarterly*, 31(4), pp. 539–563.

Dillard, C.B. 2000. The Substance of Things Hoped For, the Evidence of Things Not Seen: Examining an Endarkened Feminist Epistemology in Educational Research and Leadership. *International Journal of Qualitative Studies in Education*, 13(6), pp. 661–681. Elenes, C.A. 1997. Reclaiming the Borderlands: Chicana/o Identity, Difference, and Critical Pedagogy. *Educational Theory*, 47(3), pp. 359–375.

Elenes, C.A. 2011. *Spiritual Mestizaje: Religion, Gender, Race, and Nation in Contemporary Chicana Narrative*. Durham, NC: Duke University Press.

Facio, E. 2014. Spirit Journey: "Home" as a Site for Healing and Transformation. In E. Facio and I. Lara (eds.), *Fleshing the Spirit: Spirituality and Activism in Chicana, Latina, and Indigenous Women's Lives* (pp. 59–72). Tucson: University of Arizona Press.

Flores, Y.G. 2013. Latina Sexuality: De (Re) Constructing Gender and Cultural Expectations in Midlife. *Women, Gender, and Families of Color*, 1(1), pp. 85–101.

Flores, Y.G. and Curiel, E. 2009. Conflict Resolution and Intimate Partner Violence among Mexicans on Both Sides of the Border. In Ramón Gutiérrez and Patricia Zavella (eds.), *Mexicans in California: Transformations and Challenges* (pp. 183–215). Urbana: University of Illinois Press. Fregoso, R.L. 2003. *MeXicana Encounters: The Making of Social Identities on the Borderlands* (Vol. 12). Oakland: University of California Press.

Gaspar de Alba, A. 1998. *Chicano Art Inside/ Outside the Master's House: Cultural Politics and the CARA Exhibition*. Austin: The University of Texas Press.

González-López, Gloria. 2006. Epistemologies of the Wound: Anzaldúan Theories and Sociological Research on Incest in Mexican Society. *Human Architecture: Journal of the Sociology of Self-Knowledge*, 4, pp. 17–24.

Griswold del Castillo, R.G., McKenna, T., Yarbro-Bejarano, S., and CARA National Advisory Committee. 1991. *Chicano Art: Resistance and Affirmations*. Wright Art Gallery, University of California, Los Angeles, p. 137.

Hurtado, A. 2003. *Voicing Chicana Feminisms: Young Women Speak Out on Sexuality and Identity* (Vol. 1). New York: New York University Press.

Jordan, M. 2018. "I Can't Go Without My Son," a Mother Pleaded as She Was Deported to Guatemala. *New York Times*, June 17.

Keating, A. and Anzaldúa, G. 2002. Charting Pathways, Marking Thresholds ... a Warning, an Introduction. In G. Anzaldúa and A. Keating (eds.), *This Bridge We Call Home: Radical Visions for Transformation* (pp. 6–20). New York: Routledge.

Kena, G., Hussar, W., McFarland, J., De Brey, C., Musu-Gillette, L., Wang, X., et al. 2016. *The Condition of Education 2016*. National Center for Education Statistics, NCES 2016-144.

Ladson-Billings, G. 1995. Toward a Theory of Culturally Relevant Pedagogy. *American Educational Research Journal*, 32(3), pp. 465–491.

Ladson-Billings, G., 2000. Fighting for Our Lives: Preparing Teachers to Teach African American Students. *Journal of Teacher Education*, 51(3), pp. 206–214.

Levitt, P. 2001. *The Transnational Villagers*. Berkeley: University of California Press.

Luibhéid, Eithne and Cantú Jr., L. (eds.). 2005. *Queer Migrations: Sexuality, U.S. Citizenship and Border Crossings*. Minneapolis: University of Minnesota Press.

Margolis, E. and Romero, M. 1998. "The Department is Very Male, Very White, Very Old, and Very Conservative": The Functioning of the Hidden Curriculum in Graduate Sociology Departments. *Harvard Educational Review*, 68(1), pp. 1–33.

Moll, L., Amanti, C., Neff, D., and Gonzalez, N. 2006. Funds of Knowledge for Teaching: Using a Qualitative Approach to Connect Homes and Classrooms. In *Funds of Knowledge* (pp. 71–87). London: Routledge.

Moraga, C. 1983. *Loving in the War Years: Lo que nunca pasó por sus labios*. Brooklyn: South End Press.

Niemann, Y.F. 1999. The Making of a Token: A Case Study of Stereotype Threat, Stigma, Racism, and Tokenism in Academe. *Frontiers: A Journal of Women Studies*, 20(1), pp. 111–134.

Orozco, C. 1984. Sexism in Chicano Studies and the Community. In T. Córdova (ed.), *Chicana Voices: Intersections of Class, Race, and Gender* (pp. 11–18). Albuquerque: University of New Mexico Press.

Pérez, E. 1999. *The Decolonial Imaginary: Writing Chicanas into History*. Bloomington: Indiana University Press.

Pérez Huber, L. 2017. Healing Images and Narratives: Undocumented Chicana/Latina Pedagogies of Resistance. *Journal of Latinos and Education*, 16(4), pp. 374–389.

Romero, S. 2019. Seesaws Straddle the Mexico Border, and Smiles Shine Through. *New York Times*, July 30. www.nytimes.com/2019/07/30/us/seesaws-border-wall.html

Rael, R. 2019. @Rrael. Video and images of the Teetertotter Wall. Instagram, July 29. www.instagram.com/p/B0fY2R6hfKr/?utm_source=ig_embed&utm_campaign=dlfix

Saldívar-Hull, S. 1991. Feminism on the Border: From Gender. In H. Calderón and J.D. Saldívar (eds.), *Criticism in the Borderlands: Studies in Chicano Literature, Culture, and Ideology*. Durham, NC: Duke University Press.

Sandoval, C. 1991. US Third World Feminism: The Theory and Method of Oppositional Consciousness in the Postmodern World. *Genders*, 10, pp. 1–24.

Sandoval, C. 2013. *Methodology of the Oppressed* (Vol. 18). Minneapolis: University of Minnesota Press.

Segura, D.A. and Facio, E. 2008. Adelante mujer: Latina Activism, Feminism, and Empowerment. In *Latinas/os in the United States: Changing the Face of América* (pp. 294–307). Boston: Springer.

Segura, D.A. and Zavella, P. (eds.). 2007. *Women and Migration in the U.S.-Mexico Borderlands: A Reader*. Durham, NC: Duke University Press.

Suárez-Orozco, C., Jin Bang, H. and Yeon Kim, H. 2011. "I Felt Like My Heart was Staying Behind": Psychological Implications of Family Separations & Reunifications for Immigrant Youth. *Journal of Adolescent Research*, 26(2), pp. 222–257.

Tillman, L.C. 2006. Researching and Writing from an African-American Perspective: Reflective Notes on Three Research Studies. *International Journal of Qualitative Studies in Education*, 19(3), pp. 265–287.

U.S. Department of Education. 1999. *Digest of Education Statistics*. U.S. Department of Education, Office of Education Research and Improvement NCES 2000-031.

Villenas, S. 1996. The Colonizer/Colonized Chicana Ethnographer: Identity, Marginalization, and Co-optation in the Field. *Harvard Educational Review*, 66(4), pp. 711–732.

Villenas, S.A. 2010. Thinking Latina/o Education with and from Chicana/Latina Feminist Cultural Studies: Emerging Pathways–Decolonial Possibilities. In Z. Leonardo (ed.), *Handbook of Cultural Politics and Education* (pp. 451–476). Leiden: Brill.

Yosso, T.J. 2016. Whose Culture has Capital? A Critical Race Theory Discussion of Community Cultural Wealth. In A.D. Dixson, C.K. Rousseau, and C.R. Anderson (eds.), *Critical Race Theory in Education* (pp. 113–136). London: Routledge.

Yosso, T., Smith, W., Ceja, M. and Solórzano, D. 2009. Critical Race Theory, Racial Microaggressions, and Campus Racial Climate for Latina/o Undergraduates. *Harvard Educational Review*, 79(4), pp. 659–691.

Zambrana, R.E. 2013. Toward Understanding the Educational Trajectory and Socialization of Latina Women. *Education Feminism: Classic and Contemporary Readings*, 75, pp. 75–86.

Zavella, P. 2003. "Playing with Fire": The Gendered Construction of Chicana/Mexicana Sexuality. In *Perspectives on Las Américas: A Reader in Culture, History, & Representation* (pp. 229–244). Oxford: Blackwell.

Zavella, P. 2020. *The Movement for Reproductive Justice: Empowering Women of Color through Social Activism* (Vol. 5). New York: New York University Press.

3 Interrogating the Image of the '21st Century Woman'

Laura Sjoberg

In 2013, the BBC published an article on 100 women's view of life in the 21st century, starting with the premise that "women's rights have progressed at an astonishing pace over the last hundred years" as an entry point into discussing the present and future. The article notes that "the responses revealed differences, including how female empowerment is defined around the world." It went on to detail universal commitments among women to the continued improvement of women's status, including a belief that education is "key to changing sexist attitudes and practices" in society. The article then features discussions of different women's perspectives on gender equality and life as a woman.

Yet vestiges of gender oppression are clear even in this article about the future of gender equality. For example, the women interviewees' marital status appears in the one-sentence bio that the BBC gives each featured woman more frequently than any other piece of information about the featured women. Looking a bit deeper, the language of marriage is used for non-heteronormative respondents even in places where same-sex marriage remains not a possibility. Across the '100 women' project, the idea of what a 'woman' is seems pre-given. There is no clear indication that any participant is trans* or nonbinary or woman-identifying. While there is no explicit indication that participants from a wide spectrum of gender identities are unwelcome, there are also no explicit suggestions of gender-inclusivity.

On top of these framing issues, the featured discussions with women about the status of gender equality are riddled with continued gender-based oppressions, despite (or even as evidence against) 'astonishing' progress. Even in the short preview of the project featuring only four women, the women discuss problems with sexual violence, physical safety, the lack of provision of education, the intersections of racisms and sexisms, unequal access to jobs and pay, continued pressure to engage in arranged marriage, emphasis on women's mothering responsibilities, stresses of work/life balance issues, chauvinism, and a wide variety of other continuing struggles.

This could be read as a question of progression, and it usually is. In this view, life is getting better for women around the world, if unevenly, and should and will continue to get better, if by struggle, in the future. This is

DOI: 10.4324/9781003281382-5

especially the case since it is generally understood that most people in most places are interested in a goal of gender equality. The '21st century woman,' then, lives in a world of unprecedented gender equality but continued gender oppression. 'She,' however, can see, live, and/or expect a future with even more gender equality and even more possibility. Still, women report that this positionality is more complex than feeling a triumph over the past and high expectations for the future. Instead, 'old' expectations about femininity are *added to* rather than *traded for* 'new' expectations about equality. Hidden, and even not so hidden, double standards, and continued violences, are often found in social and political life.

For example, I have written extensively (see, e.g., Sjoberg 2016; Gentry and Sjoberg 2015; Sjoberg and Gentry 2007) about media and academic coverages of women's political violence. Women's political violence is often treated as exceptional, even when political violence is not, and women are *in theory* equal to men. What one finds when one digs deeper is that even when women are understood as 'equal' to men, they are often understood as 'equal' without men's flaws. This constitutes a double standard, however desirable the trait of non-violence is, for women or more generally. Similarly, women are often 'added' to military missions, particularly peacekeeping missions (e.g., Kronsell 2012), to 'improve' (presumed male) soldiers' behavior. This move requires three problematic assumptions: that women necessarily behave better than men even when they are doing the same job; that women can positively influence men's behaviors; and that women can and should have those responsibilities added to their normal jobs without extra compensation. These externalities are not immediately obvious when we talk about women helping make peace, about women's inclusion in workplaces, or women's progress in the 21st century.

This complicates the idea of being a woman in the 21st century. As such, while it appears that many indicators of women's equality are improving in the early 21st century, 'progress' is uneven, and expectations of women are increasing in this new era of 'equality.' This chapter addresses three problematic dimensions of the image of the '21st century woman.' First, it looks at the uneven march of progress toward gender equality, where gender subordination remains, and is distributed differently on the basis of class, nationality, religion, ethnicity, gender identity, and sexualities, among other axes. Second, it addresses ways that policy, advocacy, and academic characterizations of women and gender equality tend to essentialize an image of 'a woman' who is engaged in the process of gender equalizing. Third, it argues that the image of 'the woman' in 21st century gender equality discourses carries with it a heavy weight of representation and expectation that harms women in a number of ways, including but not limited to being expected to do and be more than men are, and an instrumentalization of women's success that subordinates women to the goals for which they are being provided equality. In short, the presentation argues that the contemporary movement for gender equality has some real downsides for people imagined as women.

The Uneven 'Astonishing' Progress Toward Gender Equality

Though I used a BBC feature as a foil above, discussions of both amazing and continuing progress toward the equality of women have been a fairly constant feature of international political and social discourses for at least the last 30 years. Perhaps originating in the visibility of the 1995 Fourth World Conference on Women in Beijing (Phalen and Algan 2001) or in the groundbreaking jurisprudence that made wartime rape a war crime in its own right rather than relying on classification within other war crimes (Askin 1997), the idea that 'gender equality' is something which is both important and being progressed towards seems almost ubiquitous in many fora across global politics. This has manifested in a wide variety of (theoretical and practical) campaigns for 'gender mainstreaming' – the idea that leaders of any stripe (political, corporate, etc.) should consider the gender implications of each choice that they make before they make it to ensure that the most equitable choices are made (e.g., Caglar 2013; Moser and Moser 2005; Shortall 2015; Davids et al. 2013).

Alongside efforts towards, and rhetoric about, the progression of women's rights in the social and political world, even (and perhaps particularly) scholars of global politics who do not study gender have been proclaiming the success of gender equality in the 'world' as such and lauding its potential benefits or warning of its potential unintended effects. For example, Francis Fukuyama (1992), in declaring the "end of history" in global politics with the victory of Western, liberal democracy, flags gender equality and women's leadership as an inevitable externality of history's ending, bemoaning the potential uneventfulness of a gender-equal post-historic state of affairs in global politics.[1] Others have celebrated both increased gender equality in global politics and its potential unintended (or even intended and instrumentalized) side effects. For example, Ronald Inglehart and Pippa Norris (2003) argued that the "rising tide" of gender equality "lifts all boats" in terms of promoting cultural change that would benefit the whole of societies introducing gender-equitable measures and ensuring women's rights. This was shortly followed by Nicholas Kristoff and Sheryl WuDunn's (2009) *Half the Sky*, instructing readers "how to change the world" by providing measures for gender equality and women's empowerment, and highlighting issues as diverse as prostitution, maternal mortality, education, and microcredit.[2] This was followed by Steven Pinker's (2011) declaration that there is a decline of violence in the world generally, and that the decline co-varies with increases in social equality, including gender equality, extended explicitly to politics and international relations by Joshua Goldstein (2011).[3] Valerie Hudson, with co-authors and collaborators, has made an explicitly causal argument related to gender equality and interstate violence, suggesting that more gender equality makes states less violent.[4]

On the one hand, these arguments are intuitively appealing, especially to someone (like me) with a political interest in promoting gender equality. On the other hand, there are some important (if hidden) dangers in focusing on the benefits of gender equality other than gender equality itself, and even in the focus on progress of gender equality itself. The main dangers of focusing on the benefits of gender equality *outside* of gender equality as an end in itself (e.g., that gender equality leads to peace, or environmental protection) are in the instrumentalization of women and gender. If, for example, "women's rights are a national security issue" (Hudson and Cohen 2016), then the campaign for gender equality becomes important *because* of its security payoff rather than because of what happens to (or does not happen to) women in the process. The result *might* be good for women, but will not necessarily be – because the primary goal is national security, *through* women, rather than *for* women. This sort of instrumentalization also allows (and perhaps even encourages) oversimple accounts of what women and gender are, essential accounts of race and religion, and, as will be discussed below, narrowing images of 'women' to fit with narratives about the benefits of their equality.[5]

Even if the pitfalls of instrumentalization were carefully avoided, however, it does not take a lot of looking out in the world to see that the 'astonishing' progress made toward 'gender equality' is uneven at best. First, nowhere in the world can even a serious claim be made that 'gender equality' as such has been achieved. One can find gender-differential access and results almost everywhere in the world across a wide variety of areas, including but not limited to nutrition, health care, education, wages, legal protections, professional opportunities, and personal safety. Gender-based violence remains prevalent almost everywhere in the world. Even places where 'women' 'enjoy' relatively equal status, sexisms, heterosexisms, and cissexisms are nowhere near disappearing. Even countries whose gender-equality is well-reputed in their own or others' understandings continue to have real, serious, violent, and even deadly gender-related problems.[6] While no one would argue that the 'world' however defined is gender-equal, often stories about progress towards some idea of gender equality obscure continued (and even preserved) inequities. Moreover, as commonly referenced metrics like the 'gender pay gap' and measures of political representation 'improve', less visible axes of discrimination often do not get as much attention as the more surface-level problems once did.

Even if it were possible to suggest that these holdovers and setbacks were simply zig-zags on the path to the gender equality of the '21st century woman' as such, it *should* be impossible to ignore the uneven distribution of the benefits of 'gender equality' to those people that are understood as women. Though Kimberlé Crenshaw's (1990) term 'intersectionality' has become nearly ubiquitous in the 21st century, rarely are its implications fully grasped, and even more rarely is racialized gender inequity the subject of mainstream policy initiatives. Crenshaw's (1990: 1242) very basic suggestion that gender equality politics "frequently conflates or ignores intragroup differences" rings as meaningful now as it did more than three decades ago when she wrote it, and inadequate attention to violence against women of color *as such* remains a significant problem which is substantively different than violence against women and violence against people of color. One does not have to look far to see that, across different political and social situations in the world, different people understood as women have different levels of access to the things understood as gender equality.

This differential access can be found with respect to race, religion, national origin, economic class, heterosexuality, homonormativity, and gender identification among other, multiple, axes. For the '21st century woman', some of these axes of unequal access are public knowledge, and perhaps even over-publicized.[7] The front pages of almost all gender equality advocacy websites, for example, point out differences in access to gender equality in different places in the world. For example, the UN Women site singles out Viet Nam, Egypt, and Morocco (for the high economic cost of violence against women), 'Latin America and the Caribbean' (for 'no progress' on child marriage), 'West Africa' (for 'female genital mutilation'), and Pakistan (for harassment of women on the internet). The UNICEF gender equality front page, that page links to more in-depth discussions of manifestations of gender inequality like child marriage and female genital mutilation, where the children being married are racialized in pictures accompanying the story and the women being mutilated are identified as "more than half" from "Egypt, Ethiopia, and Indonesia."

I point out these discussions for three reasons. First, it is important to know that some people in some places have less access to gender equality and carry a higher burden of gender oppression than some other people in some other places. Even people who live in the same place have different access to gender equality based on particular situations or characteristics. Second, though, and equally important, there is a politics to who 'we' identify as having more or less gender equality, how 'we' define gender equality, and how 'our' and 'their' approaches to gender equality are understood. It is possible to see many (especially Western, liberal) discussions of 'gender equality' touting the 'progress' of Western, liberal democracy on gender equality without examining the complexities and problems with these claims. In a particularly stark example of this problem, *The First Political Order* (Hudson et al 2020) suggests that continued gender oppression is a 'syndrome' and that there are some states stuck in the 'syndrome' where others either have evolved away from it or are in the process of doing that evolving. This produces a (certainly unintentional but nonetheless visible) racialized and colonial 'map' of gender equality 'around the world.' Decolonial feminist thinkers (e.g., Lugones 2010; Rojas 2016; Motlafi 2018) identify the "coloniality of gender" "lies at the intersection of gender/class/race as central constructs of the capitalist world system of power" such that it is important to understand "the oppression of women who have been subalternized through the combined processes of racialization, colonialization, capitalist exploitation, and heterosexism" (Lugones 2010: 745, 746, 747). These decolonial approaches recognize *both* unequal access to 'gender equality' and the racialized and colonial construction of the idea itself as well as many readings of that idea.

Third, and relatedly, then, it is important to see the ways that different framings of what 'gender equality' *is* and who has access to it are political, rather than neutral or given. Political axes of the discussions of gender equality include, but are not limited to, racialized views of who the subjects of gender equality are,[8] racialized distribution of sexual- and gender-based violence and death,[9] heterosexist and trans* exclusive notions of who counts as 'women' who merit equality,[10] and the use of gender (and sexuality) equality as a measure of national superiority.[11] In these (and doubtless other, omitted) ways, the 'unevenness' of the distribution of access to gender equality is compounded and multilayered, where uneven access to 'gender equality' is compounded by and compounds itself, given the political significations of what 'gender equality' is and how it is understood in social and political presentations.

The Essential 'Woman' in the '21st Century Woman'

One of the social and political presentations of 'gender equality' is a set of essential assumptions about what 'women' are and how that entitles them to gender equality.

Though we now have the vocabulary to call out 'gender essentialism' (generally understood as the assumption that all people of a particular gender, used most often to refer to women, have certain common or essential characteristics), that has not made even the most simple essentialisms go away completely.[12] In many conversations, for example, the word 'gender' is used either in direct reference to or with a commonly understood meaning as referring to 'women' – where women are assumed to have a gender and men are assumed to be occupy the standard space.[13] Conversations about 'women' and women's needs often include certain assumptions about the things that women *are*, or the things that women have in common. For example, in the BBC story cited at the outset of this chapter, women's marital status and parental status seemed commonplace to discuss, though one would find that quite odd in short, one-sentence biographies of men. In addition to assuming that women will want to marry (men) and reproduce (children), many people in many contexts in the world continue to assume that there are personality traits that either all or most women necessarily share, including but not limited to pacifism, disinclination to commit (sexual) violence, empathy, care, passivity, and other ideas traditionally associated with femininity.

While there is significant pushback in the public sphere now about many gender essentialisms that may have been seen as commonplace or acceptable decades ago, this does not mean that the association of (perceived) maleness and femaleness with traits associated with masculinities and femininities have disappeared, much less assumptions about how 'men' and 'women' relate. Despite significant and continually growing evidence to the contrary, the notion that people are mostly heterosexual continues to dominate popular discourses – where ideas that men should pursue women remain rehearsed as much as they are questioned. While, many places in the world, it has become assumed that men will do part of the care labor for children, women's behavior continues, regularly, to be attributed to 'maternal instinct.'[14] A 2017 Pew survey of Americans suggested that these discourses are more than one-off or throw-away comments, where people (or at least Americans) continue to have different views of, and expectations of, men and women, such that "while many say that society values honesty, morality, and professional success in men, the top qualities for women are physical attractiveness and being nurturing and empathetic" (Parker et al. 2017).

Even reflectively abandoning simple gender essentialisms does not escape essentialism in the portrayal of the '21st century woman' as such, however. As I discussed in the introduction to this chapter, there are a number of assumptions that continue to be made about women's nature and women's capabilities even by people who are pursuing gender equality *as* they are pursuing gender equality. Whether it is the assumption that women are less able, less willing, or just less likely to commit political violence or the assumption that including women in politics will fix (some of) the problems men seem to have caused, there remains, deeply entrenched, in social and political life, the idea that there is something *different* about women as such. While some people see whatever that difference is as entirely attributable to socialization and others see it as rooted in some sort of biological mechanism, almost everyone shares, somewhere, some assumption that there is something (good or bad) distinct about being a 'woman' that makes the category meaningful as more than a relic.

Particular to the idea of 'womanhood' in 21st century global social and political life, images of women as capable of all of the traits and actions previously understood as masculine (and therefore reserved for men) *as well as* all of the traits and actions previously understood as feminine (and therefore reserved for women) have proliferated. At first glance, this sort of image of what a woman is seems to be positive: it removes (or appears to remove) the barriers that society (used to) set for those understood as women, to provide a path to become full members of 'society' as such.[15] Traditional notions of what it means to be a woman, then, have not disappeared – they have just been augmented by access to things which used to belong in the masculine sphere. As such, even many 'feminist' discussions continue to assume that women want the things that they were understood to want a hundred years ago in terms of husbands, children, and the provision of a stable home – they are just understood to *also* want more now. About a decade ago, Anne-Marie Slaughter (2012) espoused these assumptions pretty clearly in an article in *The Atlantic* which was heavily read and highly resonant, though it sparked significant debate.[16] Declaring that "it's time to stop fooling ourselves" because "the women who have managed to be both mothers and top professionals" (Slaughter's definition of 'having it all') "are superhuman, rich, or self-employed" while "all women" continue not to have access to the possibility of balancing "it all" (Slaughter 2012). Discussions of this article in public debate were very mixed – where some suggested that Slaughter had said what others had been thinking for a long time, while others suggested that it is indeed possible to 'have it all.' Fewer (though some) interlocutors questioned the remaining gender essentialisms in the idea of 'having it all.'

While the idea that what a 21st century woman 'is' is someone who wants (and can have) 'it all' in terms of a laundry list of previously sex-specific goals *for both sexes* is nowhere near unquestioned, it does, in many varied forums and in many varied conversations, remain either an explicit or implicit assumption. Some everyday examples make the easiest illustrations. At many workplaces, women have 'equal' expectations of the hours they will either be physically in an office or virtually connected to meetings for work, yet there are unequal expectations about preparation for being in those spaces, including things as complex as care responsibilities and things as seemingly trivial (but incredibly time consuming) as styling hair or applying makeup.[17] Whether at work or away from work, women are expected to move and function in the world much 'as men do' – even though many amenities in that world, from the ways that cars are built (e.g., Gupta 2021) to the cost of personal amenities (e.g., Narins 2015), and from likelihood to experience intimate partner violence (e.g., Zafar 2020) to vulnerability to poverty (Tavares and Martins 2020). The next section will discuss the impacts of some of these essentialisms – for now, the key thing to understand is that *an* essential idea of 'a woman' *remains* in the '21st century' as such, even if the idea of what 'a woman' is has changed since images of the '20th century woman.' The '21st century woman' who is seen to be shepherded by and at the same time shepherding this 'astonishing' progress on gender equality *remains* tied to many (though not all) traditional expectations of femininities, while *also* being associated with many of the traditional expectations of masculinities.

A 2008 *New Yorker* article about Hillary Clinton's candidacy for the United States presidency shows some of these dimensions well (Hertzberg 2008). Late in the 2008 Democratic primary season at a coffee shop in New Hampshire, in response to a question about how she stays 'upbeat' on the campaign trail, then-candidate Hillary Clinton could be seen with tears in her eyes as she talked about how important she thought her political goals were, and how she persisted in pursuing them despite being tired (Hertzberg 2008). Reminding us that "the media frenzy that followed had to be seen to be believed," Hertzberg noted that "the general assumption was that the incident would further damage Clinton's chances." Hertzberg (2008) discusses frankly that it is *advantageous* for men to cry in politics, as they will not appear too masculine, but *disadvantageous* for women to cry in politics, as they will appear too feminine. Even those (e.g, Breslau 2008) who suggested that the tears (or near-tears, depending on who is believed) would serve to show a warmer and more feminine side to Clinton, critiquing her campaign up to that point for over-emphasizing her masculine traits. While these articles *disagree* on how associations with femininities and masculinities matter both generally and in political campaigning, they *agree* that those associations continue to have (if more nuanced) salience. If the '19th century woman' would not have been a viable candidate for public office and the '21st century woman' *is*, that *does not* mean that gender has stopped mattering in the image of who should be chosen for public office and how, just that it matters differently. And *among* the ways gender continues to matter is continued (if more complex) associations with 'essential' gender tropes.

This means that the '21st century woman' seen to be living through this 'astonishing' time for gender equality is an image or trope which is *less stable* and *less precise* then perhaps previous images of femininity might have been. The decrease in stability and precision of 'essential' gender tropes, though, does not mean that there has been an accompanying decrease in the salience of gender-based images and expectations. Instead, proliferating and pluralizing views about gender create their own expectations, while age-old expectations have yet to fully loosen their grasp. This means, as I discuss below, that sometimes there are negative consequences of where 'we' are in terms of 'astonishing progress' for the '21st century woman.'

The Weight of '21st Century' Gender Expectations

As some of the examples above note, increasing 'gender equality' and the inclusion of more and more things traditionally reserved for men as among women's capabilities has made a real difference for the image of the '21st century woman,' making what it means to be a woman in the 21st century very different than perhaps that image has been in the past. This 'very different' image *does* include a wide variety of opportunities that were not previously available to women, accompanied often by increases in the availability of resources, decreases in unequal access to basic needs, and increased recognition of legal, social, and political rights and freedoms. This chapter is *not* arguing against the assumption that, in many ways and in many places and for many women, the traditional weight of gender inequality *is* decreasing, sometimes significantly.

It is the case, by almost every qualitative and quantitative measure possible and almost everywhere it is measured, that the gaps between the things available to men and the things available to women are lessening, that legal protections for women are increasing, and that women and men alike are more likely than ever before to see gender equality as a key social, political, and economic goal. This chapter is also *not* arguing for some sort of rewind button, to undo 'progress' toward 'gender equality.' Instead, it is suggesting that the linear view of that 'progress' toward gender equality most often featured both in media coverage and in everyday conversations is oversimple – that the 'road' toward 'gender equality' is not either fully clear nor equally accessible to everyone. If 'progress' toward gender equality is both unevenly distributed and subject to political manipulation, and the image of the '21st century woman' continues to contain significant (if evolving) gender essentialisms, however, this is important to recognize and to analyze.

Particularly, it is important to understand that images of the '21st century woman' *do* come with both the weight of past gender stereotypes and expectations *and* with the weight of new, contemporary, and potentially less visible expectations. While I have disagreed with and continue to disagree with both Slaughter's (2012) view of 'having it all' and her declaration of its impossibility, the article does recognize a general paradox of 21st century womanhood: a double standard that expects that women not only equal, but exceed, men. In the examples discussed in the introduction to this chapter, women were expected to be less violent than men, and were expected to be better-behaved peacekeepers than men at the same time capable of disciplining the men they bested. In the examples throughout other sections of this chapter, women are expected to navigate a world that is more dangerous for them than it is for men with similar (or, more likely, fewer) available resources, to rival men's political candidacies while remaining as feminine as the women to whom those positions used to be unavailable, and to pair what appear to be full-time parenting responsibilities with full-time work responsibilities.

The exact nature of these expectations varies in different political, economic, social, cultural, and locational contexts, but the emergence of a view of 'gender equality' that expects *more* of women can be found in many contexts and in many different places. Feminist theorists have suggested that this might be a problem embedded in the internal contradiction of the notion of 'gender equality' itself, where gender is used as a term to demarcate (perceived or actual) difference, and equality is achieved by sameness.[18] This difficulty was at the center of key legal and conceptual debates about the meaning of gender equality in the late 20th century, where legal theorists and activists alike wondered what it would mean to provide sameness to people whose situation was fundamentally different. For example, how might the law or even 'society' hold people who can or might become pregnant 'equal' to people who cannot or might not become pregnant with regards to pregnancy-specific rights and claims, including but not limited to pregnancy testing, the availability of means of abortion, prenatal health care, pregnancy-related accommodations at and/or leave from work, and a wide variety of other issues?[19] Talking about people as *equal* or *same* in this context does not make sense: there are people for whom these are or may be issues, and people for whom these are or may not be issues. While, recently, there has been a move away from associating pregnancy directly and only with women (see, e.g., Karaian 2013), paired assumptions that gender is *difference* and equality is *sameness* often produce difficult results like the entanglement of multiple gender-based expectations in ways that actually disadvantage people understood to be women.

As such, when I discuss the 'weight' of the image of the '21st century woman', I refer primarily to three things. The first 'weight' is that expectations of what women *ought to do* have increased significantly with the general broadening of views on women's capabilities, rather than new expectations *replacing* (all the) old ones. As such, what it means to be 'successful' as a '21st century woman' seems to have more, and more varied, expectations than one might initially think when one reads about the 'astonishing' progress of gender equality over the last century. As such, 'women' are frequently subjected to double requirements and/or double standards, because of a combination of increases in expectations and the (unevenly) incomplete delivery of the promise of 'equality' (in whatever form that might come). The second 'weight' is related, then – the idea that women are 'equal' to men *without their flaws*. This idea is rarely uttered but frequently implied, as a wide variety of advocates suggest that key institutions of social and political life would be 'better' if women were more represented in them, from legislatures to corporations, from peace processes to financial regulation, from manufacturing to programming. The suggestion that women *ought to be represented* simply *for the sake of representation* may not place a higher burden on women participants than on male participants,[20] but the suggestion that women ought to be represented *to improve the institution* does place that higher burden. The related higher burden is often ignored either because it is strategically advantageous for women to embrace that they would make the institution better or because it seems both politically difficult and potentially substantively trivial to criticize efforts to make institutions better.[21] The third, related, 'weight' of the image of the '21st century woman' is the weight of navigating what is expected in a rapidly changing world of gender expectations, where gender remains salient, the content of what that 'gender' means and what expectations it brings is shifting, and the intersection of genders and other positionalities cannot be ignored. The continued salience of gender categories creates both violences of *inclusion* – where being included in a gender category creates certain expectations that may or may not feel like they fit, and violences of *exclusion* – where people understood to be women and traits associated with femininity continue to be excluded from some of the practices and benefits of everyday social and political life. The shifting meaning and expectations related to the content of 'gender' and the related (new-ish) expectations of the '21st century woman' mean not only more to keep up with but uncertainty about where the metaphorical goalposts stand and how they might be reached. The unavoidability of the intersections between genders and other positionalities mean both that it is important to identify and deconstruct power and privilege *among* people understood to be women *and* that it is important to recognize not only a variety of different 'women's experiences' but the ways that those (gendered) experiences have political content *in and beyond* gender politics. This suggests that the weight of the trope(s) of the '21st century woman' are, with the 'astonishing' progress on gender equality, distributed unevenly in a way that merits both attention and redress.

Conclusion

The 'progress' that people understood to be women have seen over the last century is, in many ways, astonishing. In the archives at Royal Holloway, University of London, I saw a petition to admit women to British university medical schools that was scarcely a century older than the article discussed in the introduction to this chapter featuring women's views on 21st century gender equality. In this sense, the '21st century woman' lives in very different times, and with very different expectations both for her life and on her life than her predecessors did. The difference is *so* stark that it is sometimes difficult to see the continued, very real, role of both gender expectations generally and gender-based oppression specifically. When continued gender inequity is recognized for the '21st century woman', it is almost always framed either as the pesky but disappearing remainder of gender inequalities past *or* the problem of places in the world 'out there' treated as temporally 'behind' those places that have made more 'progress' toward an ultimate goal of equality.

This chapter has suggested that there is more to 'gender equality' in the 21st century, and that the image of the '21st century woman' as (past and future) victor over gender equality is oversimple and hides important remaining inequities as well as inequities created by the ways that gender equality is pursued in contemporary social and political contexts. The chapter started from the argument that, though, at first sight, one might think that gender-based expectations are dwindling as 'progress' toward gender equality is made, gender tropes are very much alive, thriving, and influential on people's lives worldwide. As such, it suggests that there is a trope of the '21st century woman' which has salience in social and political life, and brings with that salience a wide variety of gender-based problems.

As such, the chapter discussed the ways that the 'gender equal' trope of the '21st century woman' obscures both the very uneven distribution of whatever measure of gender equality one might choose and the weaponization of (perceived) superiority on issues of gender equality in processes of Othering in political and social life. While 'astonishing' progress on gender equality has indeed been made, it remains that a wide variety of situations, positionalities, and circumstances mean that people understood to be women have *very different* levels of access to gender equality, and that nowhere in the world can we look at a political or social situation and call it purely 'gender equal.' The chapter then explored one of the continuing axes of inequity that can be least visible: continued essentialist assumptions about what 'a woman' is, even as notions of womanhood have broadened so much that it is difficult to see remaining boundaries, however real they are. Using those two views of the situation of the '21st century woman,' the third section of this chapter explored various 'weights' that contemporary tropes of femininity *uniquely* place on those understood to be or imagined as women. Though those 'weights' are also distributed unequally *among* those understood to be women on a wide variety of axes, this chapter argued that they show (remaining) problems with the notion of the '21st century woman' and the mismatches between the life 'she' is told to expect and the life that 'she' lives.

This, of course, takes different forms for different people in different contexts. Some gender-based expectations might 'feel' like they 'fit' for some 'women,' and others might 'feel' like they 'fit' for others. But so long as there is a mold that one must 'try on' and learn to 'fit in,' gender-based expectations and the subordinations that come with them have not disappeared. If the current figuration of the '21st century woman' continues to come with the weights of (traditional and non-traditional) gender-based expectation, perhaps 'we' could aim to re-formulate the next figuration to recognize the continued subordinations, augmented expectations, and double standards that have come to be a quiet, but nonetheless present, part of womanhood as such in the 21st century.

Notes

1 See J. Ann Tickner's (1999) critique of this argument for detailed discussion.
2 See discussions of the limits of this metaphor in Shepherd (2011).
3 While I will discuss below some of the problems with this trend in work and this thesis specifically, for a direct critique of this work, see True (2015).
4 See, e.g., Hudson et al (2009); Hudson et al (2012); Hudson et al (2020); McDermott (2015). For a critique speaking explicitly to this argument, see, e.g., Kinsella and Sjoberg (2018).
5 See, e.g., discussion in Kinsella and Sjoberg (2018); Sjoberg et al (2018).
6 For a place that brags about its own gender equality (and uses it to shame other places regularly), the United States is a good example. For a sample of remaining (domestic) gender issues, see a recent *Marie Claire* article. Even in places held up by the international community as beacons of gender equality (e.g., Sweden), many inequities remain, including high levels of gender-based violence (Wemrell et al. 2019).
7 See, for example, arguments about intimate warfare, which suggest that the over-publication of 'wartime sexual violence' and 'rape as a weapon of war' serve to obscure the (high) prevalence of sexual- and gender-based violence in the 'everyday' as such (see, e.g., Pain 2015; Kirby 2013).
8 For example, many countries' 'National Action Plans' under United Nations Security Council Resolution 1325 (for 'Women, Peace, and Security') include *no* reference to the promotion of gender equality within their own borders, instead treating gender inequality as a foreign policy issue (see, e.g., Haastrup and Hagen 2020). Haastrup and Hagen suggest that race is dominant in "who the WPS agenda is *about*, and who it is *for*, on the international stage."
9 See, e.g., discussions of queer necropolitics, in, for example, Haritaworn et al. (2014).
10 See, e.g., Hines (2019); Da Costa (2021), which discuss cissexisms and racializations in definitions of who counts as a 'woman' – a problem also discussed by Lugones (2010) in racialized terms.
11 See, e.g., Langlois (2016); Rao (2016).
12 For a taxonomy of the kinds of gender essentialism, see, e.g., Witt (2010).
13 One can even find this is binary coding in many political science pieces that address gender, where people understood to be or self-identified as 'women' are given the score of '1' on the binary 'scale' of gender where people understood to be or self-identified as 'men' are given the score of '0' – suggesting, unintentionally though substantively, that women are those 'with' gender and men are not.
14 See, e.g., discussion in Gentry and Sjoberg (2015). For wider discussions of the continued relevance of the maternal in global politics, see Hall et al. (2019).
15 Writing this in these words reminds me of Catharine MacKinnon's (2006) wording of the question *Are women human?* as well as Maria Lugones' (2010) decolonial feminist understanding of a manufactured distinction between 'female' and 'woman' on racialized and colonial lines.

16 Among the 'debate' was my (2012) response on the *Duck of Minerva* blog.
17 For an in-depth and more nuanced discussion, see Dellinger (2002); Lipton (2021).
18 This 'paradox' of sorts is discussed in MacKinnon (2001), but my view of it comes more from the indirect but important discussion of it in Brown (1995).
19 My first exposure to this debate/discussion was in MacKinnon (2001), but, as that book shows, this debate had even at the time been going on for decades.
20 I say 'may not' because a significant literature suggests that participation in masculinized institutions itself creates a higher burden for women, and that the 'inclusion' of 'women' in these masculinized institutions does not automatically, necessarily, or often even functionally change the institutions' masculinized cultures. The work that has been formative to my thought on this includes Acker (1990) in organizational sociology and Enloe (1990) in politics and international relations.
21 The term 'strategic essentialism,' coined by Gayatri Spivak in a 1984 interview with Elizabeth Grosz, suggests that gender- and race-based tropes can (and might) be mimicked by those to whom they might be attached as expectations in order to gain advantage. While Spivak's initial discussion of the idea was much more focused on political action and protest than personal or political gain, the use of the term across gender, sexuality, and postcolonial studies has been much broader than the original articulation.

References

Acker, Joan. 1990. "Hierarchies, Jobs, Bodies: A Theory of Gendered Organizations." *Gender & Society* 4(2): 139–158.
Askin, Kelly Dawn. 1997. *War Crimes Against Women: Prosecution in International War Crimes Tribunals.* Leiden: Martinus Nijhoff Publishers.
Breslau, Karen. 2008. "Hillary Clinton's Emotional Moment." *Newsweek*, January 6, June 12, 2022 at www.newsweek.com/hillary-clintons-emotional-moment-87141
Brown, Wendy. 1995. *States of Injury: Power and Freedom in Late Modernity.* Princeton, NJ: Princeton University Press.
Caglar, Gulay. 2013. "Gender Mainstreaming." *Politics & Gender* 9(3): 336–344.
Crenshaw, Kimberle. 1990. "Mapping the Margins: Intersectionality, Identity Politics, and Violence against Women of Color."*Stanford Law Review* 43(6): 1241–1300.
Da Costa, Jade Crimson Rose. 2021. "The 'New' White Feminism: Trans-Exclusionary Radical Feminism and the Problem of Biological Determinism in Western Feminist Theory." In Kristi Carter and James Brunton, eds. *Transnarratives: Scholarly and Creative Works on Transgender Experience.* Toronto: Women's Press, 318–344.
Davids, Tine, Francien van Driel, and Franny Parren. 2013. "Feminist Change Revisited: Gender Mainstreaming as Slow Revolution." *Journal of International Development* 26(3): 393–408.
Dellinger, Kirsten. 2002. "Wearing Gender and Sexuality 'On Your Sleeve': Dress Norms and the Importance of Occupational and Organizational Culture at Work." *Gender Issues* 20(1): 3–25.
Enloe, Cynthia. 1990. *Bananas, Beaches, and Bases: Making Feminist Sense of International Politics.* Berkeley: University of California Press.
Fukuyama, Francis. 1992. *The End of History and the Last Man.* New York: Free Press.
Gentry, Caron and Laura Sjoberg. 2015. *Beyond Mothers, Monsters, Whores: Women's Violence in Global Politics.* London: Zed Books.

Goldstein, Joshua S. 2011. *Winning the War on War: The Decline of Armed Conflict Worldwide*. New York: Dutton Press.

Gupta, Alisha Haridsani. 2021. "Crash Test Dummies Made Cars Safer (for Average-Size Men." *New York Times*, December 27, accessed June 12, 2022 at www.nytimes.com/2021/12/27/business/car-safety-women.html

Haastrup, Toni and Jamie J. Hagen. 2020. "Global Racial Hierarchies and the Limits of Localization via National Action Plans." In Soumita Basu, Paul Kirby, and Laura J. Shepherd, eds. *New Directions in Women, Peace, and Security*. Bristol: Bristol University Press, 133–152.

Hall, Lucy B., Anna Weissman, and Laura J.Shepherd, eds. 2019. *Troubling Motherhood: Maternality in Global Politics*. New York: Oxford University Press.

Haritaworn, Jin, Adi Kuntsman, and Silvia Posocco, eds. 2014. *Queer Necropolitics*. London: Routledge.

Hertzberg, Hendrick. 2008. "Second those Emotions: Hillary's Tears." *The New Yorker*, January 13, accessed June 12, 2022 at www.newyorker.com/magazine/2008/01/21/second-those-emotions

Hines, Sally. 2019. "The Feminist Frontier: On Trans and Feminism." *Journal of Gender Studies* 28(2): 145–157.

Hudson, Valerie M. and Dara Kay Cohen. 2016. "Women's Rights are a National Security Issue." *New York Times*, December 26, accessed June 12, 2022 at www.nytimes.com/2016/12/26/opinion/womens-rights-are-a-national-security-issue.html

Hudson, Valerie, Donna Lee Bowen, and Perpetua Lynne Nielsen. 2020. *The First Political Order: How Sex Shapes Governance and National Security Worldwide*. New York: Columbia University Press.

Hudson, Valerie M., Bonnie Ballif-Spanvill, Mary Caprioli, and Chad F. Emmett. 2012. *Sex and World Peace*. New York: Columbia University Press.

Hudson, Valerie M., Mary Caprioli, Bonnie Ballif-Spanvill, Rose McDermott, and Chad F. Emmett. 2009. "The Heart of the Matter: The Security of Women and the Security of States." *International Security* 33(3): 7–45. Inglehart, Ronald and Pippa Norris. 2003. *Rising Tide: Gender Equality and Cultural Change around the World*. Cambridge: Cambridge University Press.

Karaian, Lara. 2013. "Pregnant Men: Repronormativity, Critical Trans Theory, and the Re(conceive)ing of Sex and Pregnancy in Law."*Social & Legal Studies* 22(2): 211–230.

Kinsella, Helen M. and Laura Sjoberg. 2018. "Family Values? Sexism and Heteronormativity in Feminist Evolutionary Analytic (FEA) Research." *Review of International Studies* 45(2): 260–279.

Kirby, Paul. 2013. "How is Rape a Weapon of War? Feminist International Relations, Modes of Critical Explanation, and the Study of Wartime Sexual Violence." *European Journal of International Relations* 19(4): 797–821.

Kristoff, Nicholas and Sheryl WuDunn. 2009. *Half the Sky: How to Change the World*. New York: Knopf.

Kronsell, Annica. 2012. *Gender, Sex, and the Post-National Defense: Militarism and Peacekeeping*. New York: Oxford University Press.

Langlois, Anthony. 2016. "A Fake and a Hysteric: The Captain of Team Australia." *Millennium: Journal of International Studies* 45(1): 98–104.

Lipton, Briony. 2021. "Academics' Dress: Gender and Aesthetic Labour in the Australian University." *Higher Education Research & Development* 40(4): 767–780.

Lugones, Maria. 2010. "Towards a Decolonial Feminism." *Hypatia* 25(4): 742–759.

MacKinnon, Catharine A. 2001. *Sex Equality.* New York: Foundation Press.
MacKinnon, Catharine A. 2006. *Are Women Human? And Other International Dialogues.* Cambridge, MA: Harvard University Press.
McDermott, R. 2015. "Sex and Death: Gender Differences in Aggression and Motivations for Violence." *International Organization* 69(3): 753–775. Moser, Caroline and Annalise Moser. 2005. "Gender Mainstreaming since Beijing: A Review of Success and Limitations in International Institutions."*Gender & Development* 13(2): 11–22.
Motlafi, Nompumelelo. 2018. "The Coloniality of the Gaze on Sexual Violence: A Stalled Attempt at a South Africa-Rwanda Dialogue?" *International Feminist Journal of Politics* 20(1): 9–23.
Narins, Elizabeth. 2015. "10 Things That Cost More for Women Than They for Men." *Marie Claire*, March 25, accessed June 22, 2022 at www.marieclaire.com/culture/a13816/things-that-cost-more-for-women/
Pain, Rachel. 2015. "Intimate War." *Political Geography* 44: 64–73.
Parker, Kim, Juliana Menasce Horowitz, and Renee Stepler. 2017. "On Gender Differences, No Consensus on Nature vs. Nurture." Pew Research Center Report, December 5, accessed June 12, 2022 at www.pewresearch.org/social-trends/2017/12/05/on-gender-differences-no-consensus-on-nature-vs-nurture/
Phalen, Patricia F. and Ece Algan. 2001. "(Ms) Taking Context for Content: Framing the Fourth World Conference on Women." *Political Communication* 18(3): 301–319.
Pinker, Steven. 2011. *The Better Angels of Our Nature: Why Violence Has Declined.* New York: Viking Press.
Rao, Rahul. 2016. "The Diplomat and the Domestic: Or, Homage to Faking It." *Millennium: Journal of International Studies* 45(1): 105–112.
Rojas, Cristina. 2016. "Contesting the Colonial Logics of the International: Toward a Relational Politics of the Pluriverse." *International Political Sociology* 10(4): 369–382.
Shortall, Sally. 2015. "Gender Mainstreaming and the Common Agricultural Policy." *Gender, Place & Culture* 22(5): 717–730.
Shepherd, Laura J. 2011. "Sex, Security, and the Superhero(in)es: From 1325 to 1820 and Beyond." *International Feminist Journal of Politics* 13(4): 504–521.
Sjoberg, Laura. 2012. "'Having It All' and A (Nonessentialist) Feminist Politics." *Duck of Minerva*, June 23, www.duckofminerva.com/2012/06/having-it-all-and-non-essentialist.html
Sjoberg, Laura. 2016. *Women as Wartime Rapists: Beyond Sensation and Stereotyping.* New York: New York University Press.
Sjoberg, Laura and Caron Gentry. 2007. *Mothers, Monsters, Whores: Women's Violence in Global Politics.* London: Zed Books.
Sjoberg, Laura, Kelly Kadera, and Cameron Thies. 2018. "Reevaluating Gender and IR Scholarship: Moving Beyond Reiter's Dichotomies Towards Effective Synergies." *Journal of Conflict Resolution* 62(4): 848–870.
Slaughter, Anne-Marie. 2012. "Why Women Still Can't Have It All." *The Atlantic*, July, accessed June 12, 2022 at www.theatlantic.com/magazine/archive/2012/07/why-women-still-cant-have-it-all/309020/
Tavares, Paula and Natalia MazoniSilva Martins. 2020. "We Can't End Poverty without Tackling Gender Inequality," *Let's Talk Development*, World Bank Blogs, October 16, accessed June 12, 2022 at https://blogs.worldbank.org/developmenttalk/we-cant-end-poverty-without-tackling-gender-inequality
Tickner, J. Ann. 1999. "Why Women Can't Run the World: international Politics According to Francis Fukuyama." *International Studies Review* 1(3): 3–11.

True, Jacqui. 2015. "Winning the Battle but Losing the War on Violence: A Feminist Perspective on the Declining Global Violence Thesis." *International Feminist Journal of Politics* 17(4): 554–572.

Wemrell, Maria, Sara Stjernlof, Justine Aenishanslin, Marisol Lil, Enrique Gracia, and Anna-Karin Ivert. 2019. "Towards Understanding the Nordic Paradox: A Review of Qualitative Interview Studies on Intimate Partner Violence Against Women (IPVAW) in Sweden." *Sociology Compass* 13(6): e12699.

Witt, Charlotte. 2010. "What Is Gender Essentialism?" In Charlotte Witt, ed. *Feminist Metaphysics: Explorations of the Ontology of Sex, Gender, and Self.* Dordecht: Springer, 11–25.

Zafar, Maria. 2020. "16 Shocking Facts about Violence against Women and Girls." *Reliefweb*, December 7, accessed June 12, 2022 at https://reliefweb.int/report/world/16-shocking-facts-about-violence-against-women-and-girls

Part II
Activating Rights and Securing Institutional Equality

Part II

4 Does Corporate Social Responsibility Matter to Gender Inequality During Times of Crisis?

Jinyoung Lee, C.K. Lee and Jane L. Parpart

In this chapter, we offer observations and commentary regarding the subject of corporate social responsibility (CSR) and the COVID-19 pandemic with particular attention to gender inequality in the workplace by building on our previous publication of 'Constructing gender identity through masculinity in CSR reports: The South Korean case' (Lee & Parpart, 2018). The most widely used definition of CSR, according to Matten and Moon (2008), is that it includes corporate policies and practices that demonstrate business responsibility for some aspects of the greater good of society. Beyond traditional philanthropy, economic, legal, and ethical business practices, CSR has broadened to include a wider range of issues. A series of changes brought about by the COVID-19 pandemic gave people the opportunity to rethink the concept of CSR. A number of recent studies have examined the effects of COVID-19 on organizations, including financial performance (Bae et al., 2021), and the responsibility issue of supply chains (Clean Clothes Campaign, 2020; Leitheiser et al., 2020). Furthermore, several studies explore the role of the COVID-19 pandemic at individual level. Research has shown that the COVID-19 pandemic reduces employee commitment and job satisfaction (Chanana, 2021), while Leitheiser et al. (2020) and Lund-Thomsen (2020) found that it is more an issue for those who are low-income, low-educated, and minorities.

Although the COVID-19 pandemic's impacts and businesses' responsibilities were discussed in the areas of CSR such as economic, legal, and ethical categories, CSR literature on issues related to gender is limited. This highlights a significant gap in the current discourse on CSR and the need for more attention to be given to gender-related issues in the context of the pandemic and beyond. It is crucial for businesses to address the gender inequalities that have been exacerbated by the pandemic and to implement policies that promote gender equality and inclusivity in the workplace. It is important to note that the COVID-19 pandemic exacerbated gender inequalities because social norms in many countries expect women to perform an overwhelming share of unpaid care work at home. According to the McKinsey Global Institute report on COVID-19 and gender inequality, women's jobs are 1.8 times more likely to be affected (Madgavkar et al., 2020). According to the

DOI: 10.4324/9781003281382-7

Bureau of Labor Statistics, there were still 1.4 million fewer employed adult women in the workforce in early February than there were employed adult men (Glynn, 2022). There has been a greater reluctance among women to return to work since the pandemic began. In short, there is no doubt that global pandemics are testing businesses' CSR strategies, policies, and actions, so businesses should pay special attention to the roles of women and men at work. Therefore, the purpose of this chapter is to revisit CSR before and after the COVID-19 pandemic, focusing particularly on gender inequality to satisfy stakeholder expectations. This highlights the need for more research and attention to be paid to the intersection of CSR and gender, particularly in the context of the COVID-19 pandemic. It is important to recognize and address the unique challenges and impacts that women and other marginalized groups may face during this time, and to develop strategies for promoting gender equality and social responsibility in business practices.

The structure of our work is as follows. First, a theoretical section draws on men and masculinity studies to identify the most promising approach to understanding gender and CSR, particularly in regard to the visibility and silence surrounding gender concerns. Second, we describe an empirical case section which explores the South Korean context and masculinity in chaebols (large industrial South Korean conglomerates). Then, we examine how chaebols' CSR reports portray gender from the viewpoint of men and masculinities based on our review of 15 CSR reports from Korean multinational enterprises (MNEs) as a primary source of data on corporate policies and discourse regarding gender equality at work. Lastly, we conclude with the need for CSR initiatives that specifically focus on gender equality and ensure that women are not further marginalized in times of crisis.

Theoretical Underpinnings: Corporate Social Responsibility and Gender Research from the Perspective of Men and Masculinity

A masculinity lens offers a theoretical framework for examining men's and women's relationships within culturally gendered practices in specific societies. Our study focuses on the power processes embedded in the gender relations that underlie gender inequality in South Korea. Masculinity studies have increased significantly in the past few decades, resulting in much more sophisticated empirical and conceptual work that rejects binary gender roles and emphasizes power, multiplicity, and hegemony (Davis & Connell, 2014). The concept of masculinity provides an analytical framework for assessing gender in CSR texts by revealing the aspects of gendered hierarchical relations that are present, but unrecognized, in CSR texts. This framework is particularly important for identifying the attitudes and practices among men that perpetuate gender inequality, masculine domination over women (except for a few women who identify successfully with masculine power), and the power of certain men over other men (Davis & Connell, 2014).

Drawing on a Gramscian understanding of hegemony (i.e., particular sets of ideologies about the ideals of maleness that support patriarchal social relations) (Connell, 1977), Connell and Messerschmidt (2005) emphasize that multiple masculinities and hierarchies of masculinities often define hegemonic masculinity (Connell & Messerschmidt, 2005). For example, hegemonic masculinity takes shape through its association with subordinated masculinities, such as the hyper-masculine, sexist, authoritarian masculinities attributed to some men of color and working-class men (Kim & Pyke, 2015). Accordingly, different forms of masculinity are embedded in power relations, and particular forms of masculinity may be characterized as 'hegemonic' or 'subordinate' in relation to each other (Connell & Messerschmidt, 2005). In turn, these masculinities are not fixed, but instead continually evolve.

While the concept of hegemonic masculinity has been widely used in the past decades, Connell poses the questions from the postcolonial or Southern perspectives by criticizing the dominance of the global North scholarship with regard to hegemonic masculinity (Connell, 2007, 2014; Roberts & Connell, 2016). In a similar vein, these concerns have recently emerged in research on CSR and gender. The CSR and gender literature is also largely Western-dominated in ways that crucially shape the form and content of what counts as knowledge (Grosser et al., 2017; Karam & Jamali, 2015). Consequently, when scholars engage with the global South, they adopt a methodology based on North–South gender binaries (Gugler & Shi, 2009; Schleifer, 2016). For example, the emphasis on Western MNEs as the primary agent of CSR initiatives reflects the neoliberal perspective of scholarship that places the Western firm at the center of the global economy (Khan & Lund-Thomsen, 2011). Since this binary and top-down discourse legitimates the need for creating CSR and codes of conduct, many discussions of CSR assume that 'gender' issues are about women and frame Third World women as a problem or as victims of globalization. For example, women laborers in the horticulture sector in Africa exporting to European markets during the 1990s are portrayed by Barrientos et al. (2003) as victims of insensitive gender codes of conduct (Barrientos et al., 2003). While the postcolonial approaches have clearly delivered many important criticisms of Western-dominated CSR scholarship, questions nonetheless remain as to how foundational postcolonial thought has been deployed regarding the category of gender. In this view, there is a greater need to critically examine how MNEs in the global North take for granted accepted dominant constructions, powers, and authorities of men in relation to women and minority men.

In light of the postcolonial critique outlined above, the idea of hegemonic masculinity must be applied in the global South. Gender concepts and hegemony should always be understood historically and in terms of social production. Consequently, we use the concept of 'hegemonic masculinity' to explore the dominant masculinism in local MNEs' CSR texts, which marginalize women and to a lesser extent subordinate men. Drawing on feminist social constructivism, specifically a perspective that foregrounds issues of 'doing gender' (West & Zimmerman, 1987), we analyze gender representations in CSR reports by deconstructing the texts to reflect on their implicit assumptions about gender roles, particularly how a masculine image of the ideal worker is reinforced and sustained. In contrast to previous strands of positivist and normative approaches to gender and CSR, the social constructionist feminism originates in social theories about knowledge and examines the social construction of gender as the dynamic practice of differences between women/femininity and men/masculinity by seeking insights into power processes and the ongoing creation of gender inequalities in the workplace (Benschop & Verloo, 2015).

We focus on how textual representations communicate specific relations of femininity and masculinity. In the masculinity literature, for example, being visible is associated with being 'different,' and being different from masculinist norms renders one marginalized (Simpson & Lewis, 2005). Men often maintain their powerful position as their identities are both explicit and implicit. As Connell (1995) argues, men are often seen as the normative standard, equated with being human. Consequently, as Collinson and Hearn (1994) noted:

> The categories of men and masculinity are frequently central to analysis yet they are taken for granted, hidden and unexamined. Men are both talked about and ignored, rendered simultaneously explicit and implicit. They are frequently at the centre of discourse but they are rarely the focus of interrogation.
> (Collinson & Hearn, 1994: 4–5)

At the same time, the concept of silence is critical to understanding the sources of resistance to gender equality from dominant and hegemonic groups in societies (Parpart, 2010). From this standpoint, Kronsell (2006) and Simpson and Lewis (2005) argue that to remain powerful and privileged, dominant discourses of masculinity must be able to silence other contradictory or competing meanings. As Kronsell (2006) indicates, studying silence requires a deconstruction of texts and the ability to recognize what is missing within the text and its implications for understanding the invisible gendered nature of the hegemonic masculinity so dominant in corporations and other institutions. In this way, the concept of silence is particularly apt in the CSR and gender literature as it facilitates investigations into the gendered nature of privileged access to resources and power. The point here is not only to note the absence of gender in many CSR discourses but also to unveil how these discourses limit our overall understanding of corporate silence and missing subjects, and how resistances to the dominant masculinities can have the potential to promote gender equality as a CSR goal.

Empirical Context and Methodology

Korean Chaebol Masculinity

Korean chaebols are predominantly male because Korean men created these corporations and adopted militarized management practices that align with the needs, values, and experiences of men (Kim, 2001). For example, since most men are required to serve in the military system for two years before entering the labor market, male employees are well-versed in militaristic approaches, which are integrated into the work ethic of the chaebols (Kim & Park, 2003). As a result, organizational operation is heavily influenced by the experience of living in military camps. A militarized management culture at work influences men's behavior, promoting hierarchical command, competitiveness, and a can-do attitude (Cho & Yoon, 2001). Thus, most chaebols have masculinist corporate cultures that rarely accept gender equality, which is considered a threat to the masculine identity, success, and competitiveness of a corporation.

Cultural factors also play a role in this gender imbalance in the workplace. Korean corporate culture is built on traditional cultural practices, which are embedded mainly in Confucian values and notions of hierarchy (Won & Pascall, 2004). Confucianism, which determines social hierarchy based on class, gender, seniority, and official status, continues to dictate the male-oriented political and corporate culture in South Korea (Kim & Park, 2003). Korean women are often viewed as docile, caring, sympathetic, kind, helpful, and cheap to employ, whereas Korean men are characterized as independent, responsible, aggressive, and forceful. The chaebols have used these gendered images and ideologies of femininity and masculinity to construct 'desirable' workers and encourage gendered job segregation in chaebols (Kim & Park, 2003).

Notably, in the Korean context, the ideal corporate form of Korean masculinity derives from a standard associated with the salarymen, who were middle-class men and full-time salaried employees during the 1945–1970 period (Taga, 2005). Salarymen were viewed as the ideal practitioners of hegemonic masculinity, a culturally dominant masculinity that is based on patterns of practice that legitimate men's dominance over women and subordinate men (Connell & Messerschmidt, 2005). The burden of sustaining the hegemonic masculinity of the salaryman falls primarily on the Confucian daughter/wife. The ideology of the salarymen remains powerful in South Korea today; the discourse on salarymen continues to frame public understanding, both publicly and privately, by reinforcing the link between full-time labor and normative ideals of masculinity rooted in productive patriarchy and dominance in the household (Kim & Pyke, 2015).

After the 1997 Asian economic crisis, when men lost jobs, many men could not fulfill the breadwinning role, and masculinity went into crisis (Kwon & Roy, 2007), leading to increased rates of depression, alcoholism, and suicide among men (Khang et al., 2005).

As a result of the Asian Financial Crisis in 1997, the Korean government liberalized its labor market, which had an impact on people's jobs, incomes, and health. During economic difficulties, men and women experience different types of job insecurity. In particular, women are more vulnerable and exposed to sudden economic recessions. It is common for Korean women to find themselves in precarious and irregular jobs with low wages, unsafe working conditions, and little respect for their labor union rights. Existing research indicates that CSR standards are inadequately addressing gender issues (Barrientos et al., 1999; Elias & Stevenson, 2009; Fuchs & Kalfagianni, 2010). CSR standards have a much greater effect on male workers than on female workers, which is a significant shortcoming. By undermining feminized employment in informal and domestic sectors, Elias and Stevenson (2009) emphasize how the CSR labor standard benefits full-time employment where mostly males prevail. Accordingly, Elias and Stevenson (2009) criticize CSR labor standards as favoring a small part of employment compatible with neoliberalism.

Yet little attention has been paid to the chaebols' role in and responsibility for gender inequality in the workplace. Research to date has largely focused on governmental intervention and responsibility (Kim, 1994; Sung, 2003; Won & Pascall, 2004). Chaebols have not only shaped macro-level economic development policies but also played a key role in shaping the micro-level inequality of women's and men's lives. Clearly, attention to local corporate power and gender dynamics is also crucial.

To make such an assessment, we selected 15 South Korean MNEs listed among the Fortune Global 500 companies in 2015 based on their labor market power and their contribution to the South Korean GDP and the global marketplace. The descriptive statistics of the sample are presented in Tables 4.1–4.4 in the Appendix. To select the texts and systematically investigate gender disclosure in our sample of CSR reports, we used thematic content analysis including targets, quantified data, descriptions of performance, and outcomes of gender issues. We coded the content of CSR reports by following the gender-specific guidelines called "The Women's Empowerment Principles (WEP): Reporting on Progress" produced by UN Women and UN Global Compact (Miles, 2012), to which gender-related texts regularly refer. The WEP's guidelines align with the most prominent sustainability reporting framework, the GRI (Miles, 2012). Drawing upon the WEP's guidelines on how to report gender-sensitive data, we categorized the 11 GRI disclosure points into four themes for gender analysis: (1) Leadership-Promoted Gender Equality (G4-38a, G4-40a); (2) Equal Opportunity, Inclusion, and Non-discrimination (G4-LA1, G4- LA12, G4-LA13, G4-EC5, G4-LA3); (3) Health, Safety, and Freedom from Violence (G4-HR3, G4-LA6); and (4) Education and Training (G4-LA9, G4-LA11) (see Tables 4.5–4.8 in the Appendix). Each category is linked with GRI 4 gender-related disclosure, including workforce, part-time work possibilities, childcare, facilities, the flexibility of working hours, pregnancy, maternity, and parental leave of absence, career development, equal pay, aspects of governance, promotion, recruitment, and training and education.

In the second step, we used discourse analysis, which is a useful tool for studying language in action and identifying the roles of silences as well as a voice within particular texts to explore how the knowledge of employees is constructed with respect to gender (Kelan, 2008). While reading the texts in the context of the WEP's guidelines, we coded these issues to gain a deeper understanding of the concepts and thematic gender issues in CSR documents, particularly how language and text privilege certain types of men and what it means to be male or female/masculine or feminine in South Korean chaebols. We also closely examined what was said and not said as well as the possibility that silences and missing texts may reinforce gender inequality (Kronsell, 2006; Lewis & Simpson, 2012; Simpson & Lewis, 2005).

Analyzing CSR Discourses: Discovering the Paradox of (In)Visibility from Masculine Discourse Analysis

Diversity Equals Masculinist Discourse

The government recognizes that bringing more women into the workforce is critical to the well-being of the national economy. As the country's first female leader, President Park Geun-Hye (2012, cited in Woo, 2013) noted: "More participation of women in the economy is the core engine for the nation's growth, and work-life balance is no longer just a women's issue but the country's." She attempted to address this issue to create 1.65 million new jobs for women by February 2018 (Kim & Seo, 2014). According to our analysis, to respond to the government and public pressure, all the corporations we examined considered gender inequality a social issue. The companies attempted to include and demonstrate awareness of gender diversity in their CSR statements. All of them had clear and explicit policy statements, of which the following is fairly typical:

> [Corporation 1] also respects employee diversity and places a priority on protecting the rights of our employees and prohibiting and discrimination by race, age, gender, sexual orientation, ethnicity, disabilities, pregnancy, religion, political inclinations, union membership, nationality or marital status.
>
> (Corporation 1 CSR report, 2015)

These gender-related policies reflect the corporate vision, as effectively communicated through CSR reports and websites. However, we constituted and reconstituted language of diversity through gendered discourse analysis. The diversity statement has been accepted as 'taken-for-granted.' For example, the CSR reports do not necessarily translate into practice, nor are they embedded within company cultures; there is a big difference between descriptive policies and realities in the workplace. Although CSR reports encourage positive societal views of particular companies, they also reveal the inferior position of women in their workforces and women's need for special assistance. For example, the marginal number of women in management indicated in CSR reports confirms that men dominate in managerial and leadership positions, whereas women dominate in lower-level positions. The two disclosures of G4–38a (report the composition of the highest governance body and its committees) and G4–40a (report the nomination and selection processes for the highest governance body and its committees and the criteria used for nominating and selecting highest governance body members) from WEP 1 reveal the low diversity of gender composition in the highest governing body and the commitment of leadership to gender diversity. Although two companies report on the members of the board by gender (G4–38a), only Company 11 has three female representatives at the board-member level. Regarding the disclosure of G4-LA1 (total number and rate of new employee hires and employee turnover by age group, gender, and region) and G4-LA12 (composition of governance bodies and breakdown of employees per employee category according to gender, age group, minority group membership, and other indicators of diversity) from WEP 2, the companies disclose the number of workforce members by gender. Overall, the low rate of female employment in the workplace is noticeable, except in retail (Company 11) and banking companies (Company 14).

In other words, the CSR reports demonstrate that gender discrimination in these workplaces prevails, thereby limiting opportunities for women and contributing to gender inequality in both employment and society. Dominant masculinity and the entrenched privileges of men are accordingly sustained by the discourses celebrating the diversity that do little to change existing gender patterns of inequality and remain largely unrecognized. Paradoxically, despite the companies' pledges to promote gender equality as part of their social responsibility, the CSR reports support Banerjee's (2008) argument that corporate statements provide opportunities for corporations to legitimate dominant masculinity practices of inequality rather than foster the promised gender equality. Thus, their reporting has failed to present the performance or impact of their commitment to gender equality. Instead, the CSR reports reveal how female labor has been exploited and marginalized. Although the CSR reports have been described as using gender-neutral objective language, gender features in CSR are far from neutral, and gender equality remains elusive.

Work–Life Balance and Feminine Discourse

In general, the context framing women in CSR reports focuses on work and life balance disclosure (G4-LA3 from WEP 2), which reveal gendered stereotypes and divisions of labor that continue to identify women/housewives as laborers whose primary motivation for working is presumed to be less important than that of men. This is particularly true for corporate discussions about their childcare policy for employees. For example:

> To this end, we support our female employees to achieve work-life balance and encourage them to benefit from our childcare leave program to avoid career disruption from childcare issues.
> (Company 5 CSR report, 2015)

These texts illustrate the corporations' logic on gender, which assumes that women alone are responsible for childcare, an assumption that reflects the cultural codes in South Korea. The text, with its heavily patriarchal gender bias, echoes Connell's (1995) argument that hegemonic masculinity in patriarchal settings provides a successful strategy for the subordination of women. In this context, CSR disclosures privilege the dominant masculine culture of corporations in South Korea. Furthermore, most of the companies reported their maternity and paternity return rates when providing retention data (G4-LA3 from WEP 2). Women employees take up more than 80 percent of leave opportunities, whereas male employees take up less than 10 percent. Very few men accept this offer. According to the Organization for Economic Cooperation and Development (OECD) family database, in 2014, 53 weeks of paid leave was reserved for fathers in Korea, the longest leave period of all OECD member states; in contrast, the Netherlands reserves 26.4 weeks (Kim, 2015). Despite the government's incentives and subsidies, only 4.5 percent of parents who took leave in 2014 were men (Kim, 2015). Male employees do not take paternity leave because they are afraid of losing their jobs, suggesting a bias against men who take on what is considered to be "feminine work" such as childcare (Kim & Kim, 2016). This is not surprising, as Confucian culture regards caring for children at home as a sign of either femininity or marginalized masculinity. The text and figures on maternity leave implicitly represent men who take on family responsibilities as abnormal and extraordinary, thus reinforcing established gender hierarchies. As the gendered assumptions about the domestic and secondary role of women appear in the CSR reports, these reports reveal the underlying ideology of gender relations and hierarchies by normalizing an inferior role for women and supporting a patriarchal society and workplace.

Women's Career Development in the Context of Chaebols' Hegemonic Masculinity

While corporations' attempts to legitimate the promotion of more women to higher managerial positions represent an important first step (Mun & Jung, 2017), improving the position of women in management does not necessarily translate into policy initiatives on gender equality. Among reporting companies, 40 percent indicated they were actively promoting career development programs specifically for women (G4-LA11 from WEP 4). As one company reported:

> At the same time, we continue to raise the portion of the female workforce across all levels of the organization. In 2015, female employees made up only 2.8%, or 966 people, of our total domestic workforce, but that percentage has been steadily rising each year.
>
> (Company 6 CSR report, 2015)

Of course, it is possible for corporations to enhance gender equality through implementing CSR initiatives or hiring more women. However, as Bexell (2012) notes, simply adding more women to existing structures is unlikely to challenge the fundamental gender inequality in masculine-dominated organizations. Likewise, we argue that this 'solution' to gender discrimination is often superficial; it tends to legitimate existing masculine leadership while failing to explore deep flaws in corporate gender practices and structural gender discrimination. One of the consequences of the continued patriarchal bias in corporations is that women in corporations often must go through a process of masculinization to be accepted as legitimate leaders. This process normally encourages individuals to conform to the idealistic and normative social behavior of corporate cultures, defined by dominant men (Moss Kanter, 1977). As a result, many women in corporate leadership positions believe that they must avoid marriage and childbearing to compete with male workers (Patterson & Bae, 2013). Therefore, women managers stand out and become highly visible in male-dominated roles. This 'solution' to improving women's participation in corporate leadership reinforces a social order whereby men support men in a highly masculine corporate sector and ignore the discrimination against women who are trying to move up the corporate ladder.

The Silence of Disclosure as a Form of Hegemonic Masculinity and the Marginalization of Subordinate Masculinity and Femininity

Now that we have discussed how Korean women's experiences at work have become more visible through CSR reports, this section addresses the silences and resistances of disclosure by investigating the relationships between women's and men's identities. By exploring what is omitted, neglected, disregarded, or avoided, we aim to break the silence and to develop new perspectives, understandings, and approaches that can more adequately analyze the discourse of CSR from a gender perspective. As mentioned previously, the gender pay gap and irregular employment are the main sources of gender inequality in Korean corporations. We now turn to an example that attempts to illustrate, more specifically, the strange silence in chaebols' organization, namely, discussions about the gender pay gap (G4-LA13 and G4-EC5 from WEP 2) and irregular worker disclosure.

The Women in Chaebols Challenge Hegemonic Masculinity through Equal Pay

In their efforts to embrace CSR and to respond to public pressure on gender inequality in South Korea, most of the corporations have committed to enforcing equal pay and promotion for both women and men. For example, the CSR reports of Company 5 state the following:

> [Corporation 5] practices no gender bias in the payment of basic salaries and maintains transparency in its performance reward system. We also

operate transparent evaluation and performance-based reward systems to ensure fair evaluations and rational compensations. We motivate employees to improve their individual competencies by applying performance evaluation results to the salaries of employees above the manager level.

Contrary to their claims of promoting equal pay, none of the companies identified disclosed their gender pay gap. Regarding the ratio of basic salary and remuneration of women to men by employee category (G4-LA13) and the ratio of standard entry-level wage to local minimum wage by gender (G4-EC5), none of the corporate CSR reports disclosed these inequalities. Women are portrayed as having equal chances for training and promotion opportunities as well as all subsidies. If this assertion is correct, why do women still earn less than men for similar work and face a stubborn glass ceiling? South Korea has the worst gender wage gap in the OECD countries. According to OECD reports, in Korea, women earned 36.7 percent less than men in 2014 (OECD, 2016). Gendered income inequality is taken for granted and very little has been said to justify the high pay that men receive. This absence of gender-equal pay disclosures in the CSR reports is not surprising, given the historical model of economic growth in South Korea, which is based on a pervasive gender wage gap (Seguino, 1997).

Historically, Korean women were disadvantaged and socially marginalized in the workplace. Immediately following the Korean War in 1953, South Korea was a poor country that relied on export-oriented industries with low salaries, such as clothing and textiles, where the majority of women were working as the primary sources of their earnings (Kim & Voos, 2007). As a result of a growing middle class and investments in the education of women during the 1980s and 1990s, women have gradually entered the highly masculine chaebol workforce for professional and managerial employment (Seguino, 1997). Despite women's efforts and access to higher levels of education, female employment rates still remain about the same as two decades ago (Kang & Rowley, 2005). As discourses have evolved over time, the norms of hegemonic masculinity have been contested (Connell, 1995). In this context, although hegemonic masculinity has been challenged by the advancement of Korean women's education and increasing salaries over time, masculine dominance has actually become more powerful because of its ability to adapt and to resist change. The silence on equal pay review disclosure provides an example of how masculine discourse within chaebols have continued to protect privileges and the pursuit of increasing salaries within a largely male managerial workforce. As Connell notes, hegemonic masculinity does not require any special policies as it is often simply reproduced through daily activities (Connell, 1995). Therefore, the silence on the gender pay gap suggests that the norms of hegemonic masculinity are embedded in the studied chaebols and their related gender policies.

Deconstructing the 'Silence' on Gender Relations Regarding Irregular Workers

Although an increasing number of irregular positions occupied by women is regarded as one of the main reasons for the widening of the gender wage gap in South Korea (Gress & Paek, 2014), the CSR reports contain little information on part-time or irregular employment. According to the National Human Rights Commission of Korea (NHRCK), women comprise 57.5 percent of the irregular workforce, whereas men comprise 37.2 percent (Seo, 2014). Additionally, female part-time workers are paid only approximately 35.2 percent of the wages that full-time male workers are paid and 53.2 percent of the wages of full-time female workers (Seo, 2014). The silence on data by gender regarding irregular positions also demonstrates masculine resistance to changes in gender hierarchies in the chaebols. Implicitly, maintaining full-time employment is regarded as essential for buttressing masculine identities, whereas irregular employment positions for women are regarded as normal. This silence reveals a broad acceptance of the notion that male employees are expected to be full-time employees, while women are expected to perform contract positions and focus on their domestic responsibilities. As Connell (1995) notes, women's issues are silenced in order to maintain the power of dominant masculinism by denying the existence of points of view that could disrupt existing power relations. As masculinity become meaningless without a complementary construction of femininity (Kronsell, 2006), the feminized part-time labor of women is utilized as the backdrop against which the masculinity of salarymen can be constructed and defined as a hegemonic norm. On this basis, we view the types of contracting employment as the major source of gender inequality in Korea that disrupts efforts to achieve gender equality.

Furthermore, while all men benefit from masculinity discourses, they do not do so in the same way. As Kimmel (2013) notes, access to gender privileges is not evenly distributed among men. Differences in power allow some men to become more hegemonic, while other men are more subordinate or marginalized (Cheng, 1999; Kimmel, 2013). Given the high unemployment rates and the economic recession during the Asian Financial Crisis in 1997, Korean men have faced significant pressure to remain marketable and employable. The salaryman form of Korean hegemonic masculinity has been disrupted by neoliberal labor reforms, which have introduced a more precarious and flexible employment system. This system is considered potentially unmanly, exhibiting the failure of subordinate masculinities to achieve hegemonic status (i.e., full-time positions). Irregular male employees are creating a new type of masculinity that defines them in opposition to the hegemony of the 'salaryman.' Accordingly, our 'knowledge' of salarymen embodies the qualities of the full-time employment, security, and cultural competence associated with hegemonic masculinity (Taga, 2005). This position is predicated on the silence around irregular work (marginalized masculinity) and a desire for security. As Korean hegemonic masculinity perpetually and competitively drives men to obtain full-time jobs and attain higher managerial positions to secure their status as men, disclosing the gendered part-time employment data to reduce gender inequality has the exact opposite effect.

Discussion

Women in the World: Promoting a New CSR Business Paradigm

Will a COVID-19 pandemic push business to resume the gender equality policy? Considering employee and labor relations are a key component of CSR, reducing gender inequality at work is of vital importance to the success of a company. The COVID-19 pandemic exposed and exacerbated gender inequalities to a profound degree. This discussion section is not intended to provide a comprehensive list of recommendations for businesses. However, based on the findings from the previous article, we identified five key areas where business action is urgently necessary to create more gender equality post-pandemic recovery: gender discrimination; work–life balance; career development; equal pay; and gendered irregular workers.

Gender Discrimination

In South Korean labor markets, the COVID-19 pandemic revealed gender inequalities in the workplace. The extent of gender inequality during the COVID-19 pandemic is striking. The results of a recent study indicate that women are forced to leave their jobs, while men continue to work during the COVID-19 pandemic (Ham, 2021). For example, it is estimated that approximately 5.5 percent of women were fired from work, which is more than double the rate of men, at 2.5 percent (Ham, 2021). Further, in the case of married women workers, the likelihood of unemployment is 3.7 times higher than that of unmarried men, which is 70.5 percent lower (Ham, 2021). In short, the results indicate that married male workers are even less likely than women to suffer from unemployment during the pandemic. These studies infer that there may have been direct or indirect discrimination that disproportionately impacted women. Consequently, women's employment is at risk at an unprecedented level, and the consequences will likely be devastating both short-term and long-term. For this reason, it is extremely important that firms prevent women from losing their jobs, keep women in the labor force, and establish a system for assisting women in re-entering the workforce as early as possible. The company should evaluate its gender diversity statement by setting clear goals to reduce gender discriminatory practices in the workplace to retain its female employees during and after a crisis. Retrenchment decisions should be considered carefully since studies indicate that gender equality is associated with higher profitability and productivity (Maji & Saha, 2021; Martí-Ballester, 2022).

Work–Life Balance

Following the COVID-19 pandemic, the Korean government implemented a number of social distancing interventions in order to slow down the transmission of the disease, including the closure of schools and nurseries (Yu et al., 2021). There has been a significant impact on families with children in terms of both the demand for home childcare and the changes in the nature of work life. According to the study, Korean women are responsible for the majority of childcare duties at home and the division of labor is similar to that which existed before the crisis (Ham, 2021). Particularly, women aged 30–45 tend to have a higher rate of leave of absence during the pandemic compared to Korean men, since women are responsible for childcare. Women are still viewed as having primary responsibility for their children by society (Akerlof & Kranton, 2000; Bertrand et al., 2016). While 14.8 percent of married women who took leave during the pandemic stated 'for childcare' as the reason for their absence, only 5.2 percent of their male counterparts did so (Ham, 2021).

As a part of their CSR initiatives during the COVID-19 pandemic, companies have demonstrated a strong commitment to the employee's work–life balance, including onsite daycare facilities, mental health benefits, flexible work schedules, caregiver support, and satellite offices. It has been demonstrated in recent literature that flexible work and remote work can contribute to gender equality. Research has shown, for example, that fathers take on more domestic duties during pandemics, likely reducing the gender disparity (Chung et al., 2021; Craig & Churchill, 2021). As a result of Korean men's low involvement in household chores, as well as their long working hours, considered indicators of masculinity, performance, commitment, and motivation, an increased remote working policy may shift gender roles such that fathers become increasingly involved in childcare (Lim et al., 2020). The corporate policies on work and balance could therefore serve as a mediator between CSR and gender diversity and assist women in keeping their jobs by incorporating work schedules (e.g., schedule flexibility, flexible work hours) and work locations (e.g., remote working, distributed working).

Career Development

In South Korea, women face discrimination and the threat of unemployment due to a combination of increased domestic responsibilities and workplace burnout during the COVID-19 pandemic (Jang, 2021). As a result of parental leave and reduced working hours, women experienced different types of disadvantages as a result of using childcare systems at work during the COVID-19 pandemic. Because women are responsible for childcare, men are often assigned to more important departments/tasks than women, resulting in women having a more difficult time getting promoted. A woman took an average of 1.3 years longer to reach the same rank as a man, and the higher the rank, the longer it took to reach the same rank as a man (Kim, 2021).

The difficulty of being promoted may result in women achieving a lower final rank in their current job than men. Only 29.5 percent of women expect to reach a managerial level or higher, compared to 46.6 percent of men (Kim, 2021). There is a possibility that this outcome is the result of women having insufficient time to engage in career development or training. In turn, this may contribute to the gender wage gap, since women may earn lower wages than men. To prevent discrimination against women in career advancement and promotion, corporations should implement a transparent HR policy to ensure that childcare usage does not inhibit the advancement of both marginalized men and women. Additionally, companies should monitor representation and promotion results more closely. Because the disadvantages associated with the use of childcare systems at work are considered individual issues, corporations are unlikely to intervene to resolve the problem. Nevertheless, according to a McKinsey report (Madgavkar et al., 2020), companies would benefit if they tracked hiring and promotion rates for women and men. By providing a variety of CSR programs, including career development programs, mentoring, and virtual support groups, companies can increase female employee participation and boost their retention.

Equal Pay

The COVID-19 pandemic caused the economy to stagnate, company performance to decline, and wage freezes and cuts have become increasingly common. In addition, performance-based bonuses are declining in South Korea. The gender pay gap in South Korea has not diminished, however, with men continuing to earn higher wages than women. In the period prior to the COVID-19 pandemic, the average monthly wage for men was 4,216 million Korean won, whereas, after the COVID-19 pandemic, the average monthly wage increased by 37,000 won to 4,253 million won. While the average wage for women was 4,078 million won before the COVID-19 pandemic, it decreased by 0.4 percent to 4,061 million won after the COVID-19 pandemic (Jang, 2021). According to recent research by the Korea CXO Research Institute, women will still earn almost 38 percent less than men by 2020 (Lee, 2022).

For the purpose of reducing the gender pay gap, companies should provide more detailed transparency regarding gender pay gaps at an organizational level (Westcott, 2021). As mentioned above, none of the companies disclose the gender pay gap, which makes it more difficult for them to identify and analyze the gap. Korean women's issues are silenced since dominant forms of masculine power deny the existence of gender inequality, which, if exposed, could disrupt existing gendered power relationships. In order to determine compensation for comparable roles, corporations should collect sex-disaggregated data and share that information. Several recent studies have shown that there is a positive correlation between financial performance and the disclosure of gender pay gaps (Austin et al., 2021). According to a study of how disclosure of gender pay information influences investor judgments, investors are more likely to invest in a company that discloses gender pay equity information (Austin et al., 2021).

Gender Relations Regarding Irregular Workers

Due to the relatively high percentage of non-regular employees, such as temporary, part-time, and daily dispatched workers, Korean female workers have been most affected by the COVID-19 pandemic (Aum et al., 2021). As a result of the COVID-19 pandemic, irregular workers accounted for the largest proportion of total wage workers, exceeding eight million for the first time in history (Dong A Newspaper, 2021). Among non-regular workers, the gender ratio was 55.7 percent for women and 11.4 percent for men (Dong A Newspaper, 2021). One of the main explanations for the gender gap is the uneven distribution of part-time employment. Compared with other OECD countries, Korean part-time workers receive relatively low post-employment social benefits (such as unemployment benefits and livelihood benefits), and there is a significant gap between regular and non-regular workers (Hwang, 2022). When the COVID-19 pandemic began, non-regular workers experienced an increase in involuntary unemployment that was more than twice as high as regular workers. However, non-regular workers received only half the number of unemployment benefits after involuntary unemployment (Hwang, 2022). The data indicates that the unemployment benefit receipt rate for the involuntary unemployed in 2020 was 40.2 percent for regular workers and 21.2 percent for non-regular workers (Hwang, 2022). Gender inequality manifests itself in ideological hegemonies that re-emphasize and normalize the privilege of full-time workers over irregular workers, as we have outlined above. The Korean culture regards full-time employed men as representatives of hegemonic masculinity, whereas irregularly employed women are considered subordinate, further establishing a hierarchical system between them.

A strong trend in CSR literature is addressing the needs of women's marginalized status in society, including irregular workers, as part of business social responsibility (Pearson, 2007; Prieto-Carrón, 2008). The business community can play a positive role in supporting, assisting, and developing the skills of irregular workers so they will be able to generate income and overcome the current economic crisis. Companies should use their CSR policies to improve irregular workers' attitudes at work by establishing a clear and distinct HR policy regarding how irregular workers are treated and perceived. The practices may include providing proper feedback, recognizing good performance, providing opportunities to improve skills, and providing effective dispute resolution mechanisms. To protect irregular workers in the context of the COVID-19 pandemic crisis, civil society and the government must work in cooperation. It is important to establish mechanisms that provide the necessary information to facilitate the implementation of social protection policies for irregular workers.

Conclusion

Even though CSR plays an important role in strategy, employee relations, and supply chain management, research on the impact of CSR on gender inequality is still limited. Due to a lack of research in this field, this chapter revisits an original article about CSR disclosures relating to gender in South Korea before and after the COVID-19 pandemic and offers observations and commentary about CSR and the COVID-19 pandemic, focusing particularly on gender inequality by highlighting five key areas after the pandemic. The COVID-19 pandemic has had significant implications for gender inequality. Women, particularly working mothers, and marginalized men are disproportionately affected by COVID-19 in South Korea and internationally. In this regard, the COVID-19 pandemic questions the core purpose of firms and what role they should play in tackling gender inequality. To prevent gender inequality from worsening, corporations should re-evaluate their current gender policy, with special consideration given to women's and marginalized men's roles in the workplace. As discussed in our original article, one way to move forward in understanding gender relations and inequalities in CSR is to focus on men, the construction of masculinities and gender relations in CSR (Lee & Parpart, 2018). By deconstructing the CSR text, we challenge and problematize the masculinity that is widely accepted and viewed as natural. Furthermore, this original article points to how multiple masculinities are required for the hierarchical structure of the chaebol to function. The masculinities of salarymen are more socially central, and more associated with authority and local power, than others (Lee & Parpart, 2018). Moreover, the concept of hegemonic masculinity presumes the subordination of marginalized masculinities such as women and part-time men. This original article reveals that the hierarchy of masculinities is a pattern of hegemony, not a pattern of simple domination based on force (Lee & Parpart, 2018). In closing, the CSR gender policy post-COVID-19 pandemic recognizes the need to prioritize cultural processes and adapt to the constantly evolving gender relations. The CSR policy also acknowledges the role of women's resistance to patriarchy and the emergence of alternative masculinities in challenging hegemonic masculinity. By doing so, companies can contribute to the larger societal shift towards gender equality and help create a more just and equitable world.

References

Akerlof, G. A. & Kranton, R. E. (2000) Economics and identity. *The Quarterly Journal of Economics*, 115(3), 715–753.

Aum, S., Lee, S. Y. T., & Shin, Y. (2021) COVID-19 doesn't need lockdowns to destroy jobs: The effect of local outbreaks in Korea. *Labour Economics*, 70, 101993.

Austin, C. R., Bobek, D. D., & Harris, L. L. (2021) Does information about gender pay matter to investors? An experimental investigation. *Accounting, Organizations and Society*, 90, 101193.

Bae, K.-H., El Ghoul, S., Gong, Z. J., & Guedhami, O. (2021) Does CSR matter in times of crisis? Evidence from the COVID-19 pandemic. *Journal of Corporate Finance*, 67, 101876.

Banerjee, S. B. (2008) Corporate social responsibility: The good, the bad and the ugly. *Critical Sociology*, 34(1), 51–79.

Barrientos, S., Dolan, C., & Tallontire, A. (2003) A gendered value chain approach to codes of conduct in African horticulture. *World Development*, 31(9), 1511–1526.

Barrientos, S., McClenaghan, S., & Orton, L. (1999) Gender and codes of conduct: A case study from horticulture in South Africa.

Benschop, Y. & Verloo, M. (2015) Feminist organization theories: Islands of tresure. In Mir, R., Willmott, H., & Greenwood, M. (Eds.), *The Routledge Companion to Philosophy in Organization Studies* (pp. 100–112). London: Routledge.

Bertrand, M., Cortés, P., Olivetti, C., & Pan, J. (2016) *Social Norms, Labor Market Opportunities, and the Marriage Gap for Skilled Women*. Cambridge, MA: National Bureau of Economic Research.

Bexell, M. (2012) Global governance, gains and gender: UN–business partnerships for women's empowerment. *International Feminist Journal of Politics*, 14(3), 389–407.

Chanana, N. (2021) The impact of COVID-19 pandemic on employees organizational commitment and job satisfaction in reference to gender differences. *Journal of Public Affairs*, 21(4), e2695.

Cheng, C. (1999) Marginalized masculinities and hegemonic masculinity: An introduction. *The Journal of Men's Studies*, 7(3), 295–315.

Cho, Y.-H., & Yoon, J. (2001) The origin and function of dynamic collectivism: An analysis of Korean corporate culture. *Asia Pacific Business Review*, 7(4), 70–88.

Chung, H., Birkett, H., Forbes, S., & Seo, H. (2021) Covid-19, flexible working, and implications for gender equality in the United Kingdom. *Gender & Society*, 35(2), 218–232.

Clean Clothes Campaign (2020) *Un(der) Paid in the Pandemic: An Estimate of What the Garment Industry Owes its Workers*. https://cleanclothes.org/filerepository/underpaid-in-the-pandemic.pdf/view

Collinson, D. & Hearn, J. (1994) Naming men as men: Implications for work, organization and management. *Gender, Work & Organization*, 1(1), 2–22.

Connell, R. (2007) *Southern Theory: Social Science and the Global Dynamics of Knowledge*. Oxford: Polity.

Connell, R. (2014) Using southern theory: Decolonizing social thought in theory, research and application. *Planning Theory*, 13(2), 210–223.

Connell, Robert William (1977) *Ruling Class, Ruling Culture*. Melbourne: CUP Archive.

Connell, Robert W. (1995) *Masculinities*. Berkeley: University of California Press.

Connell, Robert William & Connell, R. (2005) *Masculinities*. Berkeley: University of California Press.

Connell, Robert W. & Messerschmidt, J. W. (2005) Hegemonic masculinity rethinking the concept. *Gender & Society*, 19(6), 829–859.

Craig, L. & Churchill, B. (2021) Dual-earner parent couples' work and care during COVID-19. *Gender, Work & Organization*, 28, 66–79.

Crane, A. & Matten, D. (2020) COVID-19 and the future of CSR research. *Journal of Management Studies*, 58(1), 280.

Davis, I. D. & Connell, R. (2014). The study of masculinities. *Qualitative Research Journal*, 14(1), 5–15.

Dong A Newspaper (2021) The number of irregular workers surpassed 8 million for the first time following Corona. *Dong A Newspaper*, October 16. www.donga.com/news/Society/article/all/20211026/109915346/1

Elias, J. & Stevenson, H. (2009) Women workers in the global economy: A feminist critique of the core labour standards. *Ethics, Law, and Society*, 4, 331.

Fuchs, D. & Kalfagianni, A. (2010) The causes and consequences of private food governance. *Business and Politics*, 12(3), 5.

Glynn, S. J. (2022) Black women's economic recovery continues to lag. https://blog.dol.gov/2022/02/09/black-womens-economic-recovery-continues-to-lag

Gress, D. R. & Paek, J. (2014) Differential spaces in Korean places? Feminist geography and female managers in South Korea. *Gender, Work & Organization*, 21(2), 165–186.

Grosser, K., Moon, J., & Nelson, J. A. (2017) Guest editors' introduction: Gender, business ethics, and corporate social responsibility: Assessing and refocusing a conversation. *Business Ethics Quarterly*, 27(4), 541–567.

Gugler, P. & Shi, J. Y. J. (2009) Corporate social responsibility for developing country multinational corporations: Lost war in pertaining global competitiveness? *Journal of Business Ethics*, 87, 3–24. https://doi.org/10.2307/40294951

Ham, S. (2021) Explaining gender gaps in the South Korean labor market during the covid-19 pandemic. *Feminist Economics*, 27(1–2), 133–151.

Hwang, S. W. (2022) The inequality of job loss experiences during the Corona crisis. *Labor Today Newspaper*, June 24. www.labortoday.co.kr/news/articleView.html?idxno=209390

Jang, M. (2021) The impact of COVID-19 on female workers in South Korea. Seoul: Federation of Korean Trade Union Research Center.

Kang, H.-R. & Rowley, C. (2005) Women in management in South Korea: Advancement or retrenchment? *Asia Pacific Business Review*, 11(2), 213–231.

Karam, C. M. & Jamali, D. (2015) A cross-cultural and feminist perspective on CSR in developing countries: Uncovering latent power dynamics. *Journal of Business Ethics*, 1–17.

Kelan, E. K. (2008) The discursive construction of gender in contemporary management literature. *Journal of Business Ethics*, 81(2), 427–445.

Khan, F. R. & Lund-Thomsen, P. (2011) CSR as imperialism: Towards a phenomenological approach to CSR in the developing world. *Journal of Change Management*, 11(1), 73–90.

Khang, Y.-H., Lynch, J. W., & Kaplan, G. A. (2005) Impact of economic crisis on cause-specific mortality in South Korea. *International Journal of Epidemiology*, 34(6), 1291–1301.

Kim, A. E. & Park, G. (2003) Nationalism, Confucianism, work ethic and industrialization in South Korea. *Journal of Contemporary Asia*, 33(1), 37–49.

Kim, A. & Pyke, K. (2015) Taming tiger dads: Hegemonic American masculinity and South Korea's father school. *Gender & Society*, 29(4), 509–533.

Kim, B. (2015) Korean fathers shun longest paid paternity leave in OECD. *Korean Times*, December 2.

Kim, H. & Voos, P. B. (2007) The Korean economic crisis and working women. *Journal of Contemporary Asia*, 37(2), 190–208.

Kim, K. H. (2001) Work, nation and hypermasculinity: The "woman" question in the economic miracle and crisis in South Korea. *Inter-Asia Cultural Studies*, 2(1), 53–68.

Kim, R. (1994). Legacy of institutionalized gender inequality in South Korea: The family law. *Boston College Third World Law Journal*, 14, 145–162.

Kim, S. H. (2021) 71% of female workers worry about being disadvantaged at work as a result of use of family care system during Covid. *Women News*, March 18. www.womennews.co.kr/news/articleView.html?idxno=208509

Kim, S. & Seo, E. (2014) South Korea shun moms at peril as workforce shrinks. *Bloomberg*. www.bloomberg.com/news/articles/2014-01-23/south-korea-shuns-moms-at-peril-as-workforce-shrinks

Kim, T. & Kim, M. (2016) The recognition and demand of the worker about the use of the "childcare leave system" of "male." *Korean Early Childhood Education and Child Welfare Research*, 20, 613–653.

Kimmel, M. S. (2013) Masculinity as homophobia: Fear, shame, and silence in the construction of gender identity. In Gergen, M. M. & Davis, S. N. (Eds.), *Towards a New Psychology of Gender: A Reader* (pp. 223–242). London: Routledge.

Kronsell, A. (2006) Methods for studying silences: Gender analysis in institutions of hegemonic masculinity. In Ackerly, B. A., Stern, M., & True, J. (Eds.), *Feminist Methodologies for International Relations* (pp. 108–128). Cambridge: Cambridge University Press.

Kwon, Y. I. & Roy, K. M. (2007) Changing social expectations for work and family involvement among Korean fathers. *Journal of Comparative Family Studies*, 38(2), 285–305.

Lee, J. & Parpart, J. L. (2018) Constructing gender identity through masculinity in CSR reports: The South Korean case. *Business Ethics: A European Review*, 27(4), 309–323.

Lee, J. Y. (2022) Korean women still earn 38% less than men. *The Korea Herald*, March 8. www.koreaherald.com/view.php?ud=20220307000655

Leitheiser, E., Hossain, S. N., Sen, S., Tasnim, G., Moon, J., Knudsen, J. S., & Rahman, S. (2020) Early impacts of coronavirus on Bangladesh apparel supply chains. RISC Briefing, April.

Lewis, P. & Simpson, R. (2012) Kanter revisited: Gender, power and (in) visibility. *International Journal of Management Reviews*, 14(2), 141–158.

Lim, Y., Park, H., Tessler, H., Choi, M., Jung, G., & Kao, G. (2020) Men and women's different dreams on the future of the gendered division of paid work and household work after COVID-19 in South Korea. *Research in Social Stratification and Mobility*, 69, 100544.

Lund-Thomsen, P. (2020) Corporate social responsibility: A supplier-centered perspective. *Environment and Planning A: Economy and Space*, 52(8), 1700–1709.

Madgavkar, Anu, White, Olivia, Krishnan, Mekala, Mahajan, Deepa, and Azcue, X. (2020) COVID-19 and gender equality: Countering the regressive effects. New York: McKinsey and Company.

Maji, S. G. & Saha, R. (2021) Gender diversity and financial performance in an emerging economy: Empirical evidence from India. *Management Research Review*, 44(12), 1660–1683.

Martí-Ballester, C.-P. (2022) Examining the effect of gender leadership and workforce equality on thematic mutual funds financial performance. In *International Conference on Gender Research* (Vol. 5, pp. 139–147). Academic Conferences and Publishing Limited.

Matten, D. & Moon, J. (2008) "Implicit" and "explicit" CSR: A conceptual framework for a comparative understanding of corporate social responsibility. *Academy of Management Review*, 33(2), 404–424.

Miles, K. (2012) *Women Empowerment Principal's Reporting Guidance*. http://weprinciples.org/Site/WepsGuidelines/

Moss Kanter, R. (1977) *Men and Women of the Corporation*. New York: Basic Books.

Mun, E. & Jung, J. (2017) Change above the glass ceiling: Corporate social responsibility and gender diversity in Japanese firms. *Administrative Science Quarterly*, 0001839217712920.

OECD (2016) *Gender Pay Gap*. Paris: OECD. www.oecd.org/els/LMF_1_5_Gender_pay_gaps_for_full_time_workers.pdf

Parpart, J. (2010) Choosing silence: Rethinking voice, agency and women's empowerment. In Ryan-Flood, R. 7amp; Gill, R. (Eds.) *Secrecy and Silence in the Research Process*. London: Routledge.

Patterson, L. & Bae, S. (2013) Gender (in) equality in Korean firms: Results from stakeholders interviews. *Journal of Organizational Culture, Communication and Conflict*, 17(1), 93–154.

Pearson, R. (2007) Beyond women workers: Gendering CSR. *Third World Quarterly*, 28(4), 731–749.

Prieto-Carrón, M. (2008) Women workers, industrialization, global supply chains and corporate codes of conduct. *Journal of Business Ethics*, 83(1), 5–17.

Roberts, C. & Connell, R. (2016) Feminist theory and the global South. *Feminist Theory*, 17(2), 135–140.

Schleifer, P. (2016) Private governance undermined: India and the roundtable on sustainable palm oil. *Global Environmental Politics*, 16(1), 38–58.

Seguino, S. (1997). Gender wage inequality and export-led growth in South Korea. *The Journal of Development Studies*, 34(2), 102–132. https://doi.org/10.1080/00220389708422513

Seo, A. (2014) *National Human Right Commission of Korea Report Reveals Gender Inequality in the Workforce*. Human Rights Korea Organization, November 16. http://www.humanrightskorea.org/2014/nhrc-report-reveals-gender-inequality-workforce/.

Simpson, R. & Lewis, P. (2005) An investigation of silence and a scrutiny of transparency: Re-examining gender in organization literature through the concepts of voice and visibility. *Human Relations*, 58(10), 1253–1275.

Sung, S. (2003) Women reconciling paid and unpaid work in a Confucian welfare state: The case of South Korea. *Social Policy & Administration*, 37(4), 342–360.

Taga, F. (2005) East Asian masculinities. In Kimmel, M. S., Hearn, J., & Connell, R. W. (Eds.), *Handbook of Studies on Men and Masculinities* (pp. 129–140). London: SAGE.

West, C. & Zimmerman, D. H. (1987) Doing gender. *Gender & Society*, 1(2), 125–151.

Westcott, M. (2021) Women specialist managers in Australia–Where are we now? Where to next? *Journal of Industrial Relations*, 63(4), 501–521.

Won, S. & Pascall, G. (2004) A Confucian war over childcare? Practice and policy in childcare and their implications for understanding the Korean gender regime. *Social Policy & Administration*, 38(3), 270–289.

Woo, J. (2013) Tapping at South Korea's glass ceiling. *The Wall Street Journal*, June 18.

Yu, H. M., Cho, Y. J., Kim, H. J., Kim, J. H., & Bae, J. H. (2021) A mixed-methods study of early childhood education and care in South Korea: Policies and practices during COVID-19. *Early Childhood Education Journal*, 49(6), 1141–1154.

Appendix

Table 4.1 Characteristics of the Selected Companies

	Male employees	Female employees	Total employees	Sector (ranking in the Fortune Global 500 companies in 2015)
1	74%	26%	319,000	Electronics (13)
2	95.2%	4.8%	65,614	Automobile (84)
3	87%	13%	41,949	Energy (172)
4	94.8%	5.2%	17,045	Steel (173)
5	84%	16%	37,904	Electronics (180)
6	97.2%	2.8%	33,984	Automobile (208)
7	94%	6%	27,409	Industrial machinery (237)
8	87%	13%	2,490	Energy (277)
9	94.5%	5.5%	4,174	Energy (294)
10	89%	11%	8,672	Motor vehicles and parts (310)
11	34%	66%	27,880	Retail (414)
12	74%	26%	32,610	Electronics (429)
13	90.0%	9.1%	3,079	Energy (431)
14	56%	44%	5,339	Financial (439)
15	90.1%	9.9%	3,497	Energy (464)

Source: Lee & Parpart (2018)

Note: Companies 3 and 15 are not chaebols but state-owned companies.

Table 4.2 Modes of Reporting

Mode	% of companies using this mode	% that reported gender equality by this
CSR report	100	100
Website		

Source: Lee & Parpart (2018)

Table 4.3 Mode of Guidelines and Third-Party Assurance

	% of companies
GRI G4 Guidelines	100
Third-Party Assurance	100

Source: Lee & Parpart (2018)

Table 4.4 The Total Pages of CSR Reports

Company number	Total number of pages
1	213
2	142
3	84
4	160
5	98
6	100
7	111
8	82
9	110
10	86
11	95
12	81
13	51
14	85
15	95

Source: Lee & Parpart (2018)

Table 4.5 WEP 1 – Leadership Promotes Gender Equality

GRI performance indicators	N	%
G4–38a. Report the composition of the highest governance body and its committees by: executive or non-executive, independence, tenure on the governance body, number of each individual's other significant positions and commitments and the nature of the commitments, and gender.	11 (not by gender)	73
G4–40a. Report the nomination and selection processes for the highest governance body and its committees and the criteria used for nominating and selecting highest governance body members, including the following: whether and how diversity is considered; whether and how expertise and experience related to economic, environmental and social topics are considered; and whether and how stakeholders are involved.	7 (not by gender)	46

Source: Lee & Parpart (2018)

Table 4.6 WEP 2 – Equal Opportunity, Inclusion and Nondiscrimination

GRI performance indicators	N	%
G4-LA1. Total number and rate of new employee hires and employee turnover by age group, gender, and region.	13	86
G4-LA12. Composition of governance bodies and breakdown of employees per employee category according to gender, age group, minority group membership, and other indicators of diversity.	12	80
G4-LA13. Ratio of basic salary and remuneration of women to men by employee category by significant locations of operations.	2 (not by gender)	13
G4-EC5. Ratios of standard entry-level wage by gender to local minimum wage at significant locations of operations.	0	0
G4-LA3. Return to work and retention rates after parental leave by gender.	11	73

Source: Lee & Parpart (2018)

Table 4.7 WEP 3 – Health, Safety and Freedom from Violence

GRI performance indicators	N	%
G4-HR3. Total number of incidents of discrimination and corrective actions taken.	7 (not by gender)	46
G4-LA6. Types of injury and rates of injury, occupational diseases, lost days, and absenteeism and total number of work-related fatalities by region and by gender.	6 (not by gender)	40

Source: Lee & Parpart (2018)

Table 4.8 WEP 4 – Education and Training

GRI performance indicators	N	%
G4-LA9. Average hours of training per year per employee by gender and by employee category.	0	0
G4-LA11. Percentage of employees receiving regular performance and career development reviews by gender and employee category.	6 (not by gender)	40

Source: Lee & Parpart (2018)

5 The Untapped Potential of the Human Security Paradigm for Indian Women Construction Workers

The Gender, Agency, Human Security Nexus

Chantal A. Krcmar

Key Words: Human Security; gender; agency; informal economy; South Asia

Magnitude of the Problem

My research concern is the Human Security of Indian women construction workers. Human Security, a ground-breaking paradigm developed by the United Nations Development Program (UNDP) in 1994, is a people-centered approach which is meant to shift the focus from state security to individual security in global affairs. The seven main components of Human Security, as designated by the UNDP, are economic, food, health, environmental, personal, community, and political. It is amply utilized in development programs and policy-making across the globe.

While not a perfect fit, the Human Security paradigm and feminist approaches in some fundamental ways fit hand-in-hand, and have the potential to enhance one another. They both are people-centered and they have emancipatory aims. Critical scholar, Oliver Richmond, argues that in taking a "bottom-up approach [which] means that individuals are empowered to negotiate and develop a form of Human Security that is fitted to their needs … [it] is therefore focused upon emancipation from oppression, domination, hegemony, as well as want" (2010, p. 58). In that vein, "[t]he ultimate aim of feminist research is to 'capture women's lived experiences in a respectful manner that legitimates women's voices as sources of knowledge'" (Liamputtong, 2007, p. 10, as cited in White et al., 2009, p. 19). Feminist and gendered approaches can push Human Security in much-needed radical directions (Marhia, 2013; Reardon & Hans, 2018; Tripp et al., 2013; Nuruzzaman, 2006; Wibben, 2016; Cohn, 2013; Sjoberg & Gentry, 2007). In turn, Human Security can push feminism to more deeply interrogate one of the most valued aspects of people's lives: their own security.

Despite the potential of the Human Security paradigm to enhance people's lived experiences, a number of scholars offer pushback against it. Some criticisms include whether or not Human Security is (or ever was) radical enough, whether it is too rooted in Western, liberal notions of security, whether it has been too co-opted by neoliberal capitalist enterprises, and whether broad or narrow definitions are more useful for policy-making (Nunes, 2012; Richmond, 2011; Chandler & Hynek, 2010; Glasius, 2008; Tadjbakh & Chenoy, 2007; Paris, 2001). Postcolonial critiques of Human Security go even further, making the case that Human Security is imperialistic – not simply neutral but harmful.

> From a post-colonial perspective, it is argued that Human Security can be seen as the latest installment of the "civilising mission" of nineteenth-century imperialism in that it seeks to universalise a Eurocentric conception of the "human" as a rational, autonomous agent.
> (Shani, 2017, p. 277)

Since Human Security, however, is utilized as a tool for development across the globe, interrogating and improving it is necessary. Critical scholar Jao Nunes (2012) reminds us: "Overall, security is just too important – as a concept and a political instrument – to be simply abandoned" (p. 355).

The Human Security of Indian women construction workers matters because of the sheer size of this laboring population, as well as the intensity of their marginalization. Deemed by the International Labor Organization (ILO) as one of the most dangerous jobs in the world, construction work is a large source of global employment, but it is not a source of much security. There are 180 million construction workers worldwide, 50 million of which are in India (Srivastava & Jha, 2016). Construction is the second largest labor sector in India (after the agricultural sector). Dangerous and unsanitary work conditions, wage withholding, little to no compensation for medical care and no work contracts, drinkable water, safety gear or toilets, are all rampant in the construction industry (Barnabas et al., 2009; Rai & Sarkar, 2012; Bhattacharyya & Korinek, 2007). Additionally, though the government of India does not keep reliable statistics on fatalities of construction workers, journalists and NGO staff claim they are common (Shah, 2019; Rebbapragada, 2018; Jain & Matharu, 2017; Express News Service, 2017).

Against this backdrop, we see that the security of women laboring on construction sites is especially compromised. Indian women make up a substantial portion of construction laborers (30–40 percent). For comparison, in the United States, about 1 percent of those who labor on construction sites are women. Indian women construction workers earn roughly half of what men earn doing similar work on sites, have low educational and literacy outcomes, are from Scheduled Tribes and Scheduled Castes, and face a number of specific health challenges, including sexual and gender based violence, as well as poor gynecological and maternal health outcomes. The majority of women workers are under the age of 35, and therefore of childbearing age (Srivastava, 2014). They get no maternity leave and very few construction sites have childcare facilities. As a result, infants and young children are often at the construction site, too. Accounts of children being tethered to a corner of a construction site for their own safety, or dying due to accidents, highlight some of these everyday dangers.

Finally, a key piece of this puzzle is that most Indian construction is in the informal economy. Indeed, 97 percent of Indian construction workers are informal laborers. "Informal employment is ... usually defined by the absence of social protection (mainly health coverage) or the absence of a written contract" (Charmes, 2012, p. 106). This problem does not stop with the construction industry. Informality around the globe is increasing. More than 60 percent of the world's employed persons work in the informal economy (Bonnet et al., 2019). Due to the emancipatory aims of the Human Security paradigm, and the fact that this population of informal laborers is so marginalized, understanding what Human Security means to them is critically important.

Fieldwork in Mumbai and Navi Mumbai, India

To interrogate how Indian women construction workers conceptualize and experience Human Security, I conducted qualitative fieldwork including in-depth semi-structured interviews, focus groups, and observations in Mumbai and Navi Mumbai from August 2019 until September 2020 (in-person until March 2020 when India was put in nationwide COVID-19 lockdown and then via WhatsApp). I worked closely with Mumbai Mobile Creches (MMC), an NGO which provides childcare and educational services to children living on construction sites, and with Youth for Unity and Voluntary Action (YUVA), which engages in advocacy and relief efforts for informal laborers, including construction workers, domestic servants, and street vendors. They helped me access participants who can be categorized as *naka* laborers and proper company workers (labels used by the laborers).

Though both kinds of workers are informal, there are distinctions. *Naka* laborers are paid low daily wages; often do not know from one day to the next if they will get work; none had contracts, bank accounts, retirement savings, or paid sick leave, and almost none were compensated for medical care even if injured at work; live in *bastis* (slums) in homes constructed mostly with plastic tarps, sheets of corrugated metal, and sometimes concrete. Proper company workers are paid lower daily wages than *naka* laborers, but get free (substandard) housing on the construction site in temporary shelters much like those in *bastis* or in unfinished buildings; they do not have formal contracts, but they have verbal agreements to work for the same company on the same site for a period of months (sometimes years), and often go work on another site run by that same company when they complete a project; most have bank accounts (though as one of my participants joked with me, "Yeah, but I have no money in it") but no retirement savings or paid sick leave; more often than not, medical care was paid for by the company.

I interviewed 20 female *naka* laborers, 13 female proper company workers, one female Safety Officer (very rare), ten male *naka* leaders (volunteer liaisons between YUVA and construction workers in the community [all men]), six staff from YUVA, five staff from MMC, one executive, one site manager, three engineers, and one architect at SP, India's second largest construction company, one of the architects of the Building and Other Construction Workers Act, and one union official. I logged countless hours of observations in *bastis, nakas*, and construction sites, too.

Human Security Defined

While there are many definitions of Human Security, the one which resonates with a project seeking to find the ways in which it is conceptualized and experienced on the ground requires a broad definition so as to not limit participants' perspectives. Hence, this definition is my starting point:

> [H]uman security, in its broadest form, consists of three components which simultaneously delineate its scope: freedom from fear (conditions that allow individuals and groups protection from direct threats to their safety and physical integrity, including various forms of direct and indirect violence, intended or not); freedom from want (conditions that allow for protection of basic needs, quality of life, livelihoods and enhanced human welfare) and freedom from indignity (conditions where individuals and groups are assured of the protection of their fundamental rights, allowed to make choices and take advantage of opportunities in their everyday lives).
>
> (Tadjbakh & Chenoy, 2007, p. 44)

Agency Defined

The concept of agency is utilized in a variety of Social Science fields; hence, there are many, and sometimes conflicting, definitions (Campbell & Mannell, 2016; Hojman & Miranda, 2018; Kabeer, 1999, 2016; Hennink et al., 2012; Klein, 2014; Okkolin, 2016; Samman & Santos, 2009). As defined in Anthropology, agency is "the socio-culturally mediated capacity to act" (Ahearn, 2001, p. 112). Economists tend to conceptualize agency as the ability to participate in financial decision-making in the household and markets (Gammage et al., 2016). According to Kabeer, a well-known feminist economist who has more expansive notions of agency and empowerment, "agency [is] the ability to define one's goals and act upon them" (Kabeer, 1999, p. 438). Further:

> Sociologists (e.g. Giddens, 1979; Mead, 1934) speak of agency in the context of the structure-agency relationship. They recognize the constraints of social relations (structure) on individual action, and their moulding influence on the individual, whilst also insisting that individuals are often able to resist or reshape the social contexts in which they find themselves (agency).
>
> (Campbell & Mannell, 2016, p. 2)

Feminist and postcolonial approaches which assert that agency does not only look like a Western, enlightened model resonate deeply with my work (Kabeer, 1999, 2008, 2016; Sen, 1999; Hynes et al., 2016; Madhok & Rai, 2012; Shefer, 2016; Denov & Gervais, 2007; Hanmer & Klugman, 2016; Nair, 2018; Epstein, 2014; Geeta & Nair, 2013; Dutta & Basu, 2013; Mahmood, 2001, 2009, 2011; Jabri, 2013; Mohanty, 1988; Loomba, 2015; Loomba & Lukose, 2012). Scholars such as Madhok and Rai (2012) and Khader (2016) are especially critical of the Western liberal notion that equates agency with autonomy. They make the case that in many cultural contexts, autonomy is not conceived of or valued. This can certainly be the case in a society like India where individuality is subsumed in the group – family most often being the most important group. While India is extremely ethnically and religiously diverse, the norms of communalism over individualism are strong across most groups. Also, Mohanty (1988) cautions us against homogenizing the "Third World Woman" and only seeing her as a victim who does not fit the Western model of empowerment. Feminist postcolonial approaches focus on the expansiveness of agency as it is practiced on the ground. According to Parpart and Parashar (2019), agency can look different, and have different meanings, in different contexts. Having the ability to act and speak out may be one way of exercising agency; coming up with one's own thoughts and ideas may be another.

Gender Defined

Gender is a key theoretical lens which helps shed light on micro and macro features of Indian women construction workers' Human Security. Cohn (2013) argues that gender is an analytical tool – not simply a category. We cannot understand the ways in which Human Security, gender, and agency connect without knowing the gendered inequities of the political economy that constrain Indian women construction workers. From a sociological perspective, gender is not only an individualistic trait, but also a structural trait. As Kimmel argues, "the social institutions of our world — workplace, family, school, politics — are also gendered institutions, sites where the dominant definitions are reinforced and reproduced, and where 'deviants' are disciplined" (Kimmel, 2000, p. 16). Regardless of individualistic characteristics (i.e., skill level, years of experience, physical strength), Indian women are always paid less than men doing the same jobs on construction sites, and they almost never get an opportunity to work in higher skilled jobs on sites. That disadvantage is structural in nature. "Gender is a system maintenance mechanism of patriarchy as manifest in the state" (Reardon, 2018, p. 12). In her chapter on gendered conflict processes, El-Bushra states that "gender [is] a major axis of power" (2000, p. 80). I see gendered power operating in multiple realms in the lives of Indian women construction workers – from hiring practices to family relations all the way down to access to toilets.

The Human Security/Gender/Agency Connection

The connection between Human Security, gender, and agency is critically important for my work. A number of scholars focus on the Human Security/agency connection (Innes, 2016; Tripp, 2013; Tadjbakh, 2013; Kostovicova et al., 2012; Detraz, 2013; Glasius, 2008; Grayson, 2008; McCormack, 2008; Thakur, 2004). Few scholars, however, focus on the Human Security/gender/agency connection, and it was that connection which rose to prominence in my fieldwork. Regarding the Human Security/agency connection, Glasius (2008) argues, "human security should be concerned both with vulnerability *and with agency* [emphasis mine] into a double mandate for protection and empowerment" (Glasius, 2008, p. 44). The research done by Kostovicova et al. (2012) on the agency/Human Security connection in the Kosovo context resonates with my work on the agency/Human Security connection amongst women construction workers in Mumbai and Navi Mumbai. They state:

> [W]e are interested in the "actorness" of individuals in dangerous and difficult environments in terms of how they confront dilemmas of survival and develop a role in articulating (in)security that provokes others to act to assist them. By putting "the individual at the centre of debate, analysis and policy" (Thakur, 2004: 347–8; see also Tadjbakh and Chenoy, 2007: 13), human security can be said to articulate an agential view of security. Indeed, for some, empowerment and emancipation constitute the whole point of offering a radical reworking of traditional security approaches, although the extent to which agency is incorporated into human security is frequently not spelled out.
>
> (Kostovicova et al., 2012, pp. 570–571)

In that vein, Tadjbakh (2013) makes the case that "[w]hen agency is returned to people, it is the localized, subjective sense of the security of individuals that in the last analysis is of paramount importance" (p. 46). Localized understandings of agency can strengthen the Human Security paradigm. Localized understandings of agency and gender can strengthen the Human Security paradigm even more. Gendered inequities in Mumbai and Navi Mumbai's construction sector impact agency and, therefore, Human Security.

The Ways in Which Indian Women Construction Workers Exercise Agency to Enhance Their Human Security

As already discussed, there are enormous gendered constraints in Mumbai and Navi Mumbai's construction industry which negatively impact women construction workers' Human Security. There were also a number of ways that my participants exercised agency to try and enhance their Human Security, including: by being as financially self-sufficient as possible; by nurturing aspirations for their children; by focusing on what they do get out of their work; and by choosing to participate in family decision-making (if given the chance).

Exercising Agency by Being Financially Self-sufficient

Far and away the predominant way my participants conceptualized Human Security was economic security. Regardless of their caste, religion, native place, position as *naka* laborer or proper company worker, or years doing construction work, they wanted to talk to me about economic security almost to the exclusion of all else. One major way my participants exercised agency to enhance that component of their Human Security was by being as financially self-sufficient as possible. This included working as much as they could, participating in informal financial arrangements with neighbors called *bishees*, not relying on an unreliable (and mostly absent) state, and demanding stolen wages. All the women I spoke to experience financial hardship, but some more than others. *Naka* laborers who only get day jobs had the least financial stability. The women who work more consistently for a company and live on the construction site had a bit more. The companies they worked for mostly paid for medical care if injured on the job and opened bank accounts for them (for direct deposit of their paychecks). But as one participant joked with me, "I have a bank account but there's no money in it."

Working as Much as They Could

Time and time again, the women with whom I spoke told me that they tried to maintain economic security by working as much as they could. Finding employment on construction sites was their priority. And when they could not get construction work, they did whatever other work they could. While they all identified as construction workers, some did occasional domestic work and/or sex work. My participants made it very clear to me that they had no choice but to be utterly self-sufficient.

> There's never been any external support for any sort of health or children's education or family wellbeing. Whatever we need, the responsibility is on us. Again, at times you get work and at times you don't. Only when you work hard ... it's as simple as that.
> (Minita, *naka* laborer, *basti* near railway tracks in Navi Mumbai, January 10, 2020)

This mode of exercising agency is particularly circumscribed by gender. As mentioned, gendered wage inequality in the construction industry of India is rampant. Male construction workers also are underpaid for the work they do; however, women's work is even more underpaid.

Along with a desire for economic security came a desire for respect and acknowledgment of what they do for their family's security. Naznee, a proper company worker living on a construction site for residential high-rises in Dadar (a neighborhood in Mumbai), demonstrated this to me: "Alone my husband cannot earn enough especially for our kids' education. If he works it's only for the food, but then what about the children's education? Whatever work I do, it's for supporting the family" (interview, November 26, 2019). And many of my participants made it clear to me that they could physically handle the work, grueling as it was. As Mahek and Dipti, two proper company workers on a construction site in Agripada, a neighborhood of Mumbai, boasted, "Whenever we start working for the first time, it seems very difficult. But once we get used to the kind of work it becomes very easy" (interview, December 11, 2019). Work earned women construction workers more than just income.

Informal Financial Systems

While most of the women construction workers whom I interviewed and observed expressed that they only have themselves and their families to rely on (and sometimes not even their families if their husbands were incapacitated due to health issues), some did tell me about collective ways they tried to manage finances. To avoid borrowing money from money lenders who charge usurious fees, some participated in *bishee*, a collective, unofficial form of saving money in which women from the same neighborhood or community pool their money together, lend money out to those in the collective when they need it, and do not charge interest rates for repayment.

Demanding Stolen Wages

While most of my participants did not or could not demand unpaid wages, some of them did demand payment for work when contractors refused to pay them. When I probed about wage theft, often I was met with a shrug of the shoulders and "What can we do?" *Naka* laborers explained to me that they often do not have contact information for the *thekadar* and, even when they do, he often does not pick up his phone if they are trying to get paid. Because they had not gotten work that day, I was able to have a long conversation about *thekadar* "abuse" (as they called it) with women *naka* laborers who sat at home one day in their *basti* near the Nerul *Naka* in Navi Mumbai (January 10, 2020). The two who spoke the most were Minita and Sarita, both migrants from Karnataka. Minita, the *naka* laborer who told me that the onus was on each individual to care for themselves, told me that they knew of women construction workers from whom contractors or fellow laborers stole jewelry. Because the poor lack access to effective banking, their jewelry is a form of social security or savings. So losing one's jewelry to a thief is particularly problematic for poor women. Sarita nodded along with Minita and then added,

Once it's [the jewelry] gone, it's gone. And who's taken it nobody knows. And secondly the contractors, you have no proof of who the fellow is. This has not happened to us but to other people; we heard they went to the police but they could not do anything. So what's gone is gone.

I asked, "What would you do if you don't get your wages from the *thekadar*?" The reply from Minita and Sarita was: "Nothing we can do." The absence, or corrupt presence, of the police was a running theme in many of the conversations I had with construction workers. So it was not surprising that many said they would not approach the police in case of wage theft, or any other crime of which they were victims.

Related to this, these women also talked to me about other insecurities at the hands of contractors. Minita told me, "The issues [we face] have been firstly safety. There have been many times the contractors take the ladies but don't look out for their safety. Nothing has happened to us as such, but ..." her voice trailed off.

In speaking to YUVA staff, it was clear that this was a veiled way of talking about sexual and gender based violence on the worksites. It is such taboo that women were reluctant to talk about it openly; however, they did use euphemisms ("the contractors take the ladies") and often would say they heard about it happening to other women – never to themselves. Obviously, this type of abuse was a way of constraining agency.

This illustrates other aspects of the gendered political economy which negatively impacts women construction workers: the ineffectiveness of local authorities to protect these informal sector laborers, as well as the complications that arise from working in such a convoluted labor chain. I heard from all my participants that *naka* laborers do not know the name of the contractor who picked them up for work, nor do they know the name of the company that runs the construction site on which they are working. They simply work and hope that they will be paid the wages due them and that they will not be victimized by sexual and gender based violence or any other type of abuse.

Despite most of my participants telling me that they could not demand payment for wages if they were withheld, in some instances, women construction workers I spoke with did exercise agency by demanding wages owed to them. When I interviewed five *naka* laborers, all women who had migrated from Telangana, at Nerul *Naka*, they spoke to me about their strategies to combat wage withholding. They explained to me,

> Some contractors pay two days at a time or three days at a time, so we eventually don't go there. [They prefer daily payments for work so they don't get so easily cheated.] If they don't pay us, we collectively put up a fight and ask him to pay us.

They followed this with a raucous tale of physically threatening one of the *thekadars* who withheld their wages. When they succeeded in getting their wages, they felt delight in their success – as well as in their strategies. As they told me the story, all the women collapsed into fits of laughter. This same group of women also told me that if *thekadars* do not pay them then "We go to police but they don't take us seriously."

Exercising Agency by Focusing on What Work *Does* Provide Them

One of the ways in which many of the Indian women construction workers exercised agency is a direct challenge to the notion that agency is *resistance* and *action-oriented*. As previously mentioned, feminist postcolonial scholars remind us that agency may look different in different contexts, particularly for marginalized communities in the Global South. Agency may look more "passive" to a Global North audience. What I found is that many of the women construction workers in Navi Mumbai and Mumbai chose acceptance as opposed to resistance. They acted, but in a very subtle manner. They focused on the present. They chose to do what they felt they could do for themselves and their families.

This interview with Biju (December 11, 2019), a woman who was working at the MMC childcare facility on the Agripada construction site, but who used to do construction work before her 11-month-old was born, illustrated this strategy of exercising agency, and thereby enhancing, her own Human Security. I asked, "What would you hope for yourself? What would you want five years from now?"

Her answer was "I still have not thought that far."

So I followed with, "How about one year from now?"

"It's life," Biju said matter-of-factly. "You never know what's going to happen; you never know when a person's going to die. So we don't think that far. However life is, we take it." Her tone was not fatalistic; it was simply pragmatic.

In addition to focusing on the present as a way to exercise agency, some of the women construction workers told me they intentionally take a positive outlook. An older construction worker, Nirmala, with whom I spoke in the Belapur *Basti*, exhibited a commitment to positivity – despite the many setbacks she has faced in life. She came to Mumbai from Karnataka 50 years ago and started doing construction work as a ten-year-old child. Nirmala told me,

> We've been working in this field for a long time, so we started working because of our responsibilities. My husband did not even stay alive for more than ten years [after we got married] so I had to take care of my daughters. I had a lot of responsibilities there and I have been working because I had to work to feed my family.

Without missing a beat, she finished, "There are no negative things in that. I have to do it so rather than looking at negative things, we look forward to our work and do it and get whatever we can get out of it" (interview, January 31, 2020).

Admittedly, I found Nirmala's positive attitude hard to believe at first, but nothing about her tone, body language, or facial expressions led me to believe that what she said was anything but genuine. As Nirmala talked to me, her young grandchildren ran around the small hut in which we sat. She held one, her four-year-old granddaughter, in her lap for some time as we talked. This elderly, widowed, poor construction worker also told me that she helps take care of her grandchildren because one of her two sons-in-law is an alcoholic and can't take care of his family financially or in any other way. Her positive attitude was hard-won and intentional.

To be frank, when I first started doing interviews, I was surprised and dubious about the calm and accepting attitudes of many of the women that I encountered. I thought that some of them were just so oppressed that they could not think of ways to choose for or assert themselves. But the more I heard and observed in the field, the more I had to take notice of it as perhaps a sign of more than just being beaten down by life. Obviously, exercising agency in this fashion does not push the boundaries of oppression; it does not resist the many structural insecurities that women construction workers face. But it may enhance the mental and emotional well-being of the women who exercise agency in this fashion.

Exercising Agency by Nurturing Aspirations for Their Children

Another way in which women construction workers I spoke to exercised agency was by nurturing aspirations for their children. Many scholars are critical of lumping women and children into the category of "womenandchildren" as if women are not worthy of consideration in their own right. Cynthia Enloe (1990) brought our attention to this in her classic piece, "Womenandchildren: Making Feminist Sense of the Persian Gulf Crisis." Given my findings about how women construction workers include their children in their conceptualization of *their own security*, though, it was clear that their hopes for their children were their expression of what they thought of as a better life *for themselves*.

When I asked my participants aspirational questions, such as what would constitute the good life for you, or what would you want to make your life more secure, or what would you hope for one year or five years from now, I was most often met with very limited answers. In fact, many women told me they do not think that way. Ragnee, a proper company construction worker at the Agripada worksite in Mumbai (December 11, 2019) who migrated from Chattisgarh and has been doing construction for 14 years, captured the general sentiment. When I asked her, "Could you tell me what you think of as a good life for you and your family? What would that look like for you?" she answered, "I can't answer that."

But she could answer that for her four children, ranging from two years old to 13 years old. Ragnee said, "[I hope] that they're not poor, get a respectable position so when we introduce them we are proud of them and they have a better life than what they have right now so get proper education and grow up." She was not sure how they would achieve "respectable positions" but that was her hope. Indeed, in general when I asked my participants aspirational questions about their children, answers flowed in abundance. Not one woman with whom I spoke – not one – wanted her children to go into construction work (though some adolescent and adult children did for lack of other opportunities).

This interview at a construction site in Dadar, Mumbai (November 26, 2019) encapsulates the vast majority of my conversations with workers about this topic. I asked Ariana, a young mother of a three-year-old son and a proper company laborer, "When your children are adults would you want them also to do construction work or would you want them to do something different?"

She answered vehemently,

> Absolutely not. We would not want our kids to be working in the same conditions we work in and we would want them to have a better future. For us also the kids are the priority, and education is what we think should get better.
>
> (Interview, November 26, 2019)

Most of my participants have had no formal schooling, or only have up to middle school education. Unfortunately, their children's educational realities often do not match their aspirations. Many of the children go to local municipal schools (which offer sub-standard educational opportunities) and often must change schools when their parents migrate for work. Hence, their schooling is at the very least broken up and inconsistent. Some parents send children back to their home village when they reach school age, where they will go to the municipal school there. Educational outcomes in either case are typically not good.

Exercising Agency by Decision-making

Many of my participants also focused on enhancing their economic security by making decisions for their families, sometimes by choice and sometimes by necessity. To illustrate this mode of decision-making, Minita again told me,

> The general pattern is that my three kids earn and give it [their wages] to me, so I decide where the money is going to go. But families where they just earn and spend individually, those families do not stay together. ... Since I can make a lot of the decisions about finances, my family stays together.
>
> (Interview, January 10, 2020)

To her, making decisions on her own actually cemented family relations. She did not see her individualistic ways of making decisions as going against family ties, but rather as strengthening them. In her case, she told me she had no choice since her husband was incapacitated due to alcoholism, but she also preferred to make the decisions. Like nurturing aspirations for their children, this illustrates the fluid connections between notions of family and individual, between self and others.

The Impacts of the Pandemic on Human Security: A Demonstration of Our Changing World

The COVID-19 pandemic has dramatically illustrated the massive structural constraints on the ways in which Indian women construction workers exercised agency. Particularly, exercising agency by being financially self-sufficient and by nurturing aspirations for children were severely hampered. The limits of government in enhancing Human Security of Indian women construction workers were painfully clear before the pandemic even hit – and even more so once COVID-19 began.

COVID-19's Impact on Financial Self-sufficiency

The pandemic, ensuing nationwide lockdown, devastating second wave in India, and inconsistent recovery of construction jobs, has severely curtailed the ability of women construction workers to work to earn. Their predominant conceptualization of Human Security, economic security, was shattered by the pandemic. Not only were there major job losses, the state was largely absent in the beginning of the pandemic, and then sporadically and unpredictably present since then. The failure of the Building and Other Construction Workers Act (BOCW) of 1996, legislation designed to enhance the Human Security of construction workers, is an ideal illustration of the impotency of the Indian state. Though the BOCW Act demands that money is set aside for construction worker social security, including scholarships for children of the workers, medical care, and housing vouchers, it is not implemented. Of all my participants, only two had heard of the BOCW Act. By law, there is supposed to be informational signage on the BOCW Act at all construction sites. In all my time in the field, I never once saw such a sign.

All the cess (tax) money held by the BOCW state welfare boards could have been spent for relief efforts for construction workers when nationwide lockdown was hastily instated. But it was not. Using the idleness of the BOCW welfare board in Delhi during COVID-19 as a prime example, Subhash Bhatnagar, one of the chief architects of the BOCW, told me:

> Delhi government has 10 lakh workers to take care of. We have 3200 crore rupees [$42,593,122.54 USD] with the construction workers board for their welfare, which means 32,000 rupees per ten workers. But they have given money only to 40,000 workers. That's not even 4 percent, which is a small amount, and the rest of the 96 percent of workers they

are not giving anything. We are asking them [the welfare board] again and again and we are asking others to ask them but there is no impact. We also cannot physically reach them, so they are enjoying it. It's a very bad situation and we can't get answers.

(Phone interview, April 17, 2020)

It is beyond the scope of this chapter to discuss all the reasons that the BOCW Act has been such a failure in enhancing Human Security; but, put simply, it has been a tremendous loss to Indian women construction workers.

YUVA's interim report "Access to Entitlements and Relief: Among the Urban Poor in the Mumbai Metropolitan Region during COVID-19" (June 2020) and final report "Living with Multiple Vulnerabilities: Impact of COVID-19 on the Urban Poor in the Mumbai Metropolitan Region" (August 2020) details the profoundly weak reach of government assistance to the poor. Thirty-seven percent of the respondents could not access free grain rations, and 93 percent of households were not able to access free cooking fuel to which they were entitled. Regarding construction workers, in particular, only "5.29% reported being registered with the Building and Other Construction Workers (BOCW) Welfare Board, the first step to accessing cash transfer."

My observations during lockdown in Mumbai dramatically illustrated some of YUVA's findings. A building adjacent to the apartment building in which I lived in Mumbai was being renovated. When nationwide lockdown was announced (a mere four hours before going into effect), the 12 laborers (all men) were stuck living in the gutted building for the first six weeks of lockdown. I came to know that their employer paid them enough money to get basic food supplies, but not their wages to which they were entitled by Maharashtra law. Those who supported families back in their villages were unable to support them. Human Security of the laborers, as well as their families, was obliterated.

COVID-19's Impact on Children

COVID-19 deprived women construction workers of one of the main ways they want to experience Human Security: through their children. A clear illustration of one of the adverse impacts of COVID-19 on children's Human Security, and therefore on their mothers', comes from the closure of childcare centers on construction sites. While the vast majority of construction sites do not have childcare facilities, of the ones that do, the children and parents of construction workers rely on them. These childcare centers are run by MMC. Not only do the centers provide educational enrichment, they also provide safety from construction vehicles, debris, tools, and other hazards where the children stay, as well as food and regular medical attention.

To illustrate the before and after of COVID-19: Before March 2020, MMC had 20 childcare centers, out of which 17 were on construction sites, one on a brick-kiln site and two in slums. The number of children utilizing their services for 2019–2020 was approximately 1,073 for the 20 centers. And only for the month of February 2020, it was 1,192. They have a total of 63 teachers, and 14 supervisory staff (electronic communication with MMC, July 13, 2020). Between March 2020 and February 2022, all MMC childcare centers were closed. The loss to the children, and their parents, is enormous. I visited a number of MMC childcare sites in fall and winter 2019–2020, and I observed the children preparing for dance competitions and engaging in reading and art projects. I also observed a staff physician doing regular medical check-ups and making notes on each child in their files, as well as snacks given to the children.

Not only is the Human Security of the children of Mumbai and Navi Mumbai at high risk now, children in most regions of India are. Nutrition and vaccination campaigns had been sorely affected by lockdown (Johari, 2019; Akshatha, 2020; Mander, 2021). The National Programme of Nutritional Support to Primary Education (NP-NSPE), known more colloquially as the Mid-day Meal (MDM) Scheme, which was launched by the central government in 1995, has had to change. The world's largest school feeding program, this scheme ensured that children at primary and secondary government educational facilities would get a cooked lunch. With nationwide lockdown, and then subsequent more localized lockdowns, the central government instructed state and local municipalities to continue the MDM Scheme. The map drawn up by the International Food Policy Research Institute (IFPRI) (Scott et al., 2020) shows that the MDM Scheme became a patchwork of programs, with some states not providing MDM at all. The MDM Scheme in India just started again in April 2022 (Rajvanshi, 2022) and in Mumbai and Navi Mumbai, government schools only reopened in January 2022. Child malnutrition rates were on the rise since before the pandemic and are now even worse (Chatterjee, 2021; Gagdekar, 2021).

Conclusion

Through exploring Indian women construction workers' experiences and conceptualizations of Human Security, we see a strong gender, agency, Human Security connection. There are a number of ways that women who labor on construction sites in Mumbai and Navi Mumbai utilize agency to try and enhance their Human Security. Those strategies include being as financially self-sufficient as possible, nurturing aspirations for their children, focusing on what they do get out of their work, and choosing to participate in family decision-making. Indeed, a number of structural constraints, including the COVID-19 pandemic, limit their agency. Women construction workers in Mumbai and Navi Mumbai are particularly limited by gendered constraints in the construction industry. However, if the Human Security paradigm were deployed to improve their security in the ways they want, this group of marginalized laborers in the Global South would be less marginalized.

References

Ahearn, L. M. (2001). Language and agency. *Annual Review of Anthropology*, 30(1), 109–137.

Akshatha, M. (2020). No school, no mid-day meals or ration; COVID-19 deals double blow to kids in Karnataka. *The Economic Times*, October 16. https://economictimes.indiatimes.com/news/politics-and-nation/no-school-no-mid-day-meals-or-ration-covid-19-deals-double-blow-to-kids-in-karnataka/articleshow/78694080.cms?from=mdr

Barnabas, A., Anbarasu, D. J., & Clifford, P. S. (2009). A study on the empowerment of women construction workers as masons in Tamil Nadu, India. *Journal of International Women's Studies*, 11(2), 121–141.

Bhattacharyya, S. K. & Korinek, K. (2007). Opportunities and vulnerabilities of female migrants in construction work in India. *Asian and Pacific Migration Journal*, 16(4), 511–531.

Bonnet, F., Vanek, J., & Chen, M. (2019). Women and men in the informal economy: A statistical brief. International Labour Office, Geneva. www.wiego.org/sites/defa ult/files/publications/files/Women% 20and% 20Men% 20in% 20the% 20Informal

Campbell, C. & Mannell, J. (2016). Conceptualising the agency of highly marginalised women: Intimate partner violence in extreme settings. *Global Public Health*, 11(1–2), 1–16.

Chandler, D. & Hynek, N. (eds.). (2010). *Critical perspectives on human security: Rethinking emancipation and power in international relations.* Routledge.

Charmes, J. (2012). The informal economy worldwide: Trends and characteristics. *Margin: The Journal of Applied Economic Research*, 6(2), 103–132.

Chatterjee, P. (2021). India's child malnutrition story worsens. *The Lancet: Child & Adolescent Health*, 5(5), 319–320.

Cohn, C. (ed.). (2013). *Women and wars: Contested histories, uncertain futures.* John Wiley & Sons.

Denov, M. & Gervais, C. (2007). Negotiating (in) security: Agency, resistance, and resourcefulness among girls formerly associated with Sierra Leone's Revolutionary United Front. *Signs: Journal of Women in Culture and Society*, 32(4), 885–910.

Detraz, N. (2013). *International security and gender.* John Wiley & Sons.

Dutta, M. J. & Basu, A. (2013). Negotiating our postcolonial selves. In S. H. Jones, T. E. Adams, & C. Ellis (eds.), *Handbook of autoethnography* (pp. 143–161). London: Routledge.

El-Bushra, J. (2000). *States of conflict: Gender, violence and resistance.* London: Zed Books.

Enloe, C. (1990). Womenandchildren: Making feminist sense of the Persian Gulf crisis. *The Village Voice*, 25(9).

Epstein, C. (2014). The postcolonial perspective: an introduction. *International Theory*, 6(2), 294–311.

Express News Service (2017). Accidents at workplaces in India "under reported"; 38 per day in construction sector: Study. *The Indian Express*. https://indianexpress.com/article/india/accidents-at-workplaces-in-india-under-reported-38-per-day-in-construction-sector-study-4947079/

Gagdekar, R. (2021). Malnutrition is rising across India – why? *BBC News*, February 18. www.bbc.com/news/world-asia-india-56080313

Gammage, S., Kabeer, N., & van der Meulen Rodgers, Y. (2016). Voice and agency: Where are we now? *Feminist Economics*, 22(1), 1–29.

Geeta, C. & Nair, S. (2013). *Power, postcolonialism and international relations: Reading race, gender and class.* Routledge.

Glasius, M. (2008). Human security from paradigm shift to operationalization: Job description for a human security worker. *Security Dialogue*, 39(1), 31–54.

Grayson, K. (2008). Human security as power/knowledge: The biopolitics of a definitional debate. *Cambridge Review of International Affairs*, 21(3), 383–401.

Hanmer, L. & Klugman, J. (2016). Exploring women's agency and empowerment in developing countries: Where do we stand?. *Feminist Economics*, 22(1), 237–263.

Hennink, M., Kiiti, N., Pillinger, M., & Jayakaran, R. (2012). Defining empowerment: Perspectives from international development organisations. *Development in Practice*, 22(2), 202–215.

Hojman, D. A. & Miranda, Á. (2018). Agency, human dignity, and subjective well-being. *World Development*, 101, 1–15.

Hynes, M.E., Sterk, C.E., Hennink, M., Patel, S., DePadilla, L., & Yount, K.M. (2016). Exploring gender norms, agency and intimate partner violence among displaced Colombian women: A qualitative assessment. *Global Public Health*, 11(1–2), 17–33.

Innes, A. J. (2016). In search of security: Migrant agency, narrative, and performativity. *Geopolitics*, 21(2), 263–283.

Jabri, V. (2013). *The postcolonial subject: Claiming politics/governing others in late modernity.* Routledge.

Jain, S. & Matharu, S. (2017). Fatal heights: The untold death of India's construction workers. *NDTV*, August 5. www.ndtv.com/india-news/fatal-heights-the-untold-death-of-indias-construction-workers-1733974

Johari, A. (2019). The Modi years: How successful is the Swachh Bharat Mission or Clean India campaign?. *Scroll.in*, February. https://scroll.in/article/910562/the-modi-years-how-successful-is-the-swachh-bharat-mission-or-clean-india-campaign

Kabeer, N. (1999). Resources, agency, achievements: Reflections on the measurement of women's empowerment. *Development and Change*, 30(3), 435–464.

Kabeer, N. (2008). *Mainstreaming gender in social protection for the informal economy.* Commonwealth Secretariat.

Kabeer, N. (2016). Gender equality, economic growth, and women's agency: The "endless variety" and "monotonous similarity" of patriarchal constraints. *Feminist Economics*, 22(1), 295–321.

Khader, S. (2014). Empowerment through self-subordination. In D. T. Meyers (ed.), *Poverty, agency, and human rights.* New York: Oxford Academic.

Khader, S. (2016). Beyond autonomy fetishism: Affiliation with autonomy in women's empowerment. *Journal of Human Development and Capabilities*, 17(1), 125–139.

Kimmel, M. S. (2000). *The gendered society.* Oxford University Press.

Klein, E. (2014). Psychological agency: Evidence from the urban fringe of Bamako. *World Development*, 64, 642–653.

Kostovicova, D., Martin, M., & Bojicic-Dzelilovic, V. (2012). The missing link in human security research: Dialogue and insecurity in Kosovo. *Security Dialogue*, 43(6), 569–585.

Liamputtong, P. (2007). *Researching the vulnerable: A guide to sensitive research methods.* SAGE.

Loomba, A. (2015). *Colonialism/postcolonialism.* Routledge.

Loomba, A. & Lukose, R. A. (2012). *South Asian feminisms.* Duke University Press.

Madhok, S. & Rai, S. M. (2012). Agency, injury, and transgressive politics in neoliberal times. *Signs: Journal of Women in Culture and Society*, 37(3), 645–669.

Mahmood, S. (2001). Feminist theory, embodiment, and the docile agent: Some reflections on the Egyptian Islamic revival. *Cultural Anthropology*, 16(2), 202–236.

Mahmood, S. (2009). Agency, performativity, and the feminist subject. In *Pieties and gender* (pp. 11–45). Brill.

Mahmood, S. (2011). *Politics of piety: The Islamic revival and the feminist subject*. Princeton University Press.

Mander, H. (2021). A lesson in how to end the mass suffering unleashed by India's first lockdown. *Scroll.in*, May 14. https://scroll.in/article/994378/harsh-mander-a-lesson-in-how-to-end-the-mass-suffering-unleashed-by-indias-first-lockdown

Marhia, N. (2013). Some humans are more human than others: Troubling the "human" in human security from a critical feminist perspective. *Security Dialogue*, 44(1), 19–35.

McCormack, T. (2008). Power and agency in the human security framework. *Cambridge Review of International Affairs*, 21(1), 113–128.

Mohanty, C. (1988). Under western eyes: Feminist scholarship and colonial discourses. *Feminist Review*, 30(1), 61–88.

Nair, S. (2018). Postcolonial feminism. In *Handbook on the international political economy of gender*. Edward Elgar.

Nunes, J. (2012). Reclaiming the political: Emancipation and critique in security studies. *Security Dialogue*, 43(4), 345–361.

Nuruzzaman, M. (2006). Paradigms in conflict: The contested claims of human security, critical theory and feminism. *Cooperation and Conflict*, 41(3), 285–303.

Okkolin, M. A. (2016). Who decides? Tanzanian women's narratives on educational advancement and agency. *Gender and Education*, 28(7), 886–902.

Paris, R. (2001). Human security: Paradigm shift or hot air?. *International Security*, 26(2), 87–102.

Parpart, J. L., & Parashar, S. (eds.). (2019). *Rethinking silence, voice and agency in contested gendered terrains: Beyond the binary*. Routledge.

Rai, A. & Sarkar, A. (2012). Workplace culture & status of women construction labourers: A case study in Kolkata, West Bengal. *Indian Journal of Spatial Science*, 3(2), 44–54.

Reardon, B. A. (2018). Women and human security: A feminist framework and critique of the prevailing patriarchal security system. In *The gender imperative* (pp. 7–36). Routledge.

Reardon, B. A. & Hans, A. (eds.). (2018). *The gender imperative: Human security vs state security*. Taylor & Francis.

Rebbapragada, P. (2018). No country for construction workers: Two decades after first legislation, fight for compensation and identification goes on. *FirstPost*. https://www.firstpost.com/india/no-country-for-construction-workers-two-decades-after-first-legislation-fight-for-compensation-and-identification-goes-on-5432901.html

Richmond, O. P. (2010). Post-colonial hybridity and the return of human security. In *Critical perspectives on human security*. Routledge, 51–63.

Richmond, O. P. (2011). Critical agency, resistance and a post-colonial civil society. *Cooperation and Conflict*, 46(4), 419–440.

Rajvanshi, A. (2022). Mid-day meal plan struggles to feed India's hungry students. *BBC News*, April 22. www.bbc.com/news/world-asia-india-61162642

Samman, E. & Santos, M. E. (2009). *Agency and empowerment: A review of concepts, indicators and empirical evidence*. Oxford Poverty & Human Development Initiative.

Scott, S., Menon, P., Yunu, S., and Parajuli, B. (2020). *Nourishing children and adolescents in India*. International Food Policy Research Institute (IFPRI), June 1. https://southasia.ifpri.info/2020/06/01/nourishing-children-and-adolescents-in-india-how-is-indias-mega-school-meal-program-coping-with-covid-19/

Sen, A. (1999). *Freedom as development*. Oxford University Press.

Shah, R. (2019). India's 80% construction sites "unsafe", death 20 times higher than those in Britain. *Counterview*. www.counterview.net/2019/05/indias-80-construction-sites-unsafe.html

Shani, G. (2017). Human security as ontological security: A post-colonial approach. *Postcolonial Studies*, 20 (3), 275–293.

Shefer, T. (2016). Resisting the binarism of victim and agent: Critical reflections on 20 years of scholarship on young women and heterosexual practices in South African contexts. *Global Public Health*, 11(1–2), 211–223.

Sjoberg, L. & Gentry, C. E. (2007). *Mothers, monsters, whores: Women's violence in global politics*. Zed Books.

Srivastava, R. (2014). Documenting the lack of labour rights in India's construction sector. Centre for Development Policy and Research, School of Oriental and African Studies at University of London, Development Viewpoint, 80. www.soas.ac.uk/cdpr/publications/dv/file93806.pdf

Srivastava, R. & Jha, A. (2016). *capital and labour standards in the organised construction industry in India*. CDPR, SOAS.

Tadjbakh, S. (2013). In defense of the broad view of human security. In *The Routledge handbook of human security*. Routledge.

Tadjbakh, S. & Chenoy, A. (2007). *Human security: Concepts and implications*. Routledge.

Thakur, R. (2004). Developing countries and the intervention—Sovereignty debate. In *The United Nations and global security* (pp. 193–208). New York: Palgrave Macmillan.

Tripp, A. M. (2013). Toward a gender perspective on human security. In A. M. Tripp, M. M. Ferree, & C. Ewig (eds.), *Gender, violence, and human security: Critical feminist perspectives* (pp. 3–32). New York University Press.

Tripp, A. M., Feree, M., & Ewig, M. (2013). *Gender, violence, and human security: Critical feminist perspectives*. New York University Press.

White, J., Drew, S., & Hay, T. (2009). Ethnography versus case study: Positioning research and researchers. *Qualitative Research Journal*, 9(1), 18–27.

Wibben, A. T. (2016). The promise and dangers of human security. In *Ethical security studies*. Routledge, 114–127.

6 What Blocks Equality for Women?[1]
Recollections from a Feminist Life

Galia Golan

When Prime Minister Trudeau of Canada was asked why he insisted on having an equal number of men and women in his cabinet he said simply because it's 2015. That's of course the case, but still the truth is that here we are, still asking why we don't have gender equality.

I think it's quite clear that in most countries, if not all countries, we do not have gender equality and there have been of course many explanations for this, from biological explanations to psychoanalytical explanations to social explanations. Feminists in the 20th century began to understand this as a result of patriarchy, because most of us live in societies where the institutions and the norms have been created by men according to their needs, interests, and inclinations. This isn't necessarily out of disdain for women, or even to preserve masculine power, but circumstances were such that most societies have been shaped by men and the result is patriarchy.

Patriarchy is, namely, a preference for men – entitlement if you want to call it that. It is the design of institutions and norms that suit men mainly. In many cases these designs aren't even seen as male-oriented institutions. Masculine norms are internalized and have been internalized for centuries, even by women, and viewed as natural.

How can we achieve gender equality and break down the barriers that stand before us? Equality is an ideal, not necessarily a reality. Obviously not all men are equal. In most countries there are many inequalities – by class, by race, by religion, by ethnicity. Even men are not all equal, but there are universal principles. There is equality before the law, equality of opportunity. From the Protestant Reformation we get equality as human beings. In the revolutionary movements of the late 19th and early 20th centuries, women tended to be Universalists like anarchist Emma Goldman (2019 [1917]) or Marxist Rosa Luxemburg (2012 [1903]). These social revolutionaries believed that revolution would end social classes and create equality for everybody. They espoused the idea that if there was no more exploitation social relationships would become equal. Although they did speak specifically of the rights of women, they also believed that equality would come about as part of an overall redemption and reorganization of society which would benefit everyone.

DOI: 10.4324/9781003281382-9

We have seen examples where revolutions led to a total reorganization of society and the expected equality didn't occur. I was a Soviet specialist for my first 20–30 years in academia, and I can assure you that the Revolution did not bring equality. Looking at first-wave feminists in the late 19th and early 20th centuries, including the suffragettes, not all of them demanded equality as a matter of principle. Many stated that women should have the vote because women would do things differently. This was a key idea, that women are more moral than men and would bring their nurturing qualities into the public sphere. But whether they demanded rights in the name of democracy, in service of a broader principle, or in the name of improvement, the idea was certainly to gain equality. From today's perspective, we would say that they were liberal feminists, saying let us in, and breaking down the barriers of the existing institutions. They sought to create equality from within.

Cynthia Enloe (1988, 2014) poses an important question when she asks, "Where are the women?" She asks us to ask that question all the time. Are they invisible, are they counted? What happens when women are left out of statistics in sociology, in medicine?

Carol Gilligan (1982) is also an important voice. In her work she sought to counter the claim, then prominent in psychology, that women were less moral than men. She didn't argue that women were more moral, just that they speak in a different voice. She wrote that women's experience was different from men, not necessarily better, not necessarily worse, but different.

Catharine MacKinnon (1987, 2017) reminded us that it's not an even playing field, that all things are not equal. This was the beginning of the core of radical feminism. MacKinnon argued that in terms of the patriarchy, you can't just join, you can't win at their game, you have to change it. One has to counter patriarchy head-on and rebuild society because the world is built according to their norms, their interests, their inclinations.

Birth of a Women's Studies Program

I had become a feminist in the early 1970s, once I married and became a mother. Fortunately for me my husband was already a feminist when we married, and he much preferred his cooking to mine. But it was my realization then that family and work, for women, are not easily juggled. Things like who stays home with a sick child, who can work late hours, and so forth, were too often taken for granted. In our case, as a doctor, David could not really cancel patients and stay home. But nor could I cancel a class to do so. It was matters like these that opened my eyes to women's issues.

My first step, in 1974, was to organize the women working at the Hebrew University, in Jerusalem, Israel. At our first meeting we elected a senior colleague, Alice Shalvi, to lead us in our demands to the university president. In addition to being a mentor for me, she was one of the few women professors, religious, and the mother of six – perfect for the position. We had very moderate work-related demands connected with equal conditions for pensions or travel, but we were totally unsuccessful. The university virtually dismissed us, dispatching us to our faculty trade union.

As a result of this failure, I decided to try another tack, the creation of a women's studies program. I researched such programs abroad and consulted with some of the women who were already teaching a course here or there on women, in particular Alice but also Amia Liblich in psychology and Rivka Bar Yosef in sociology, both of whom, like me, had tenure. Obviously, having tenure was important if we were going to make trouble. I then went to the Dean of the Social Science Faculty with a proposal to organize an MA seminar on women in the western world. For us, this was to be an initial step, to gauge interest and test the waters, so to speak. The Dean, economist Chaim Barkai, agreed, and I put together a team-taught course with Frances Raday from the Law Faculty, Yael Atzmon from sociology and Brenda Danet from communications, in addition to Alice, Amia, and Rivka. As a Soviet specialist, this was not my academic field at all, so I simply remained the coordinator. Basically, I saw myself as an 'entrepreneur' working as a feminist activist in academia.

We scheduled the seminar for 08:30am Tuesday mornings, but the first day of classes some 80 people showed up, mainly women, including some faculty and women who worked in administration, in addition to students from various departments. We had to shift rooms and convert this from a seminar to a course. Every class was electric, like a happening. Obviously, it was an enormous success, and we judged the time ripe for the creation of a program. We lobbied our colleagues, prepared a curriculum for the equivalent of a minor, and chose the non-feminist, hopefully non-offensive title of "Program in Sex Differences in Society." We got it passed in the Social Science Faculty Council, composed of all tenured faculty, with just two voting against, one of whom was a woman.

In 1981 I was able to announce the creation of the first women's studies program in Israel, even though this was not our official name. I made the announcement at an international women's studies conference in Haifa, organized by two feminist academics, Dr. Daphna Izraeli and Dr. Marilyn Safir. They had been active for some years but unsuccessful in their efforts to open similar programs at their universities (Bar Ilan and Haifa, respectively). Now that we had opened such a program at the Hebrew University, the oldest and most conservative of the country's seven universities, the way was open for them and others, which indeed did follow.

Our program was interdisciplinary, composed mainly of courses that I personally urged lecturers and department heads to offer in their departments. The program did not offer courses of its own and there was no faculty position specifically for a scholar in women's studies, much less the possibility of getting a department. The university did direct a donation to us that covered the costs of some of these department-based courses. In addition, a Jewish women's group in the US donated funds for a lecture series, to be conducted in town rather than inside the university itself so as to reach a broader public. In time that became an endowment from Virginia Snitow, allotted for a public lecture series in the women studies programs in a number of our universities. All this was progress, and positive, but our existence was fragile and our budgets terribly limited, especially since the university took a large overhead, as universities are wont to do. Moreover, there was nothing for research.

So, enter Fred and Barbara Lafer and the creation of the first Center for Women's Studies in Israel in 1991. We could insist on this title now, for Fred was treasurer of the Hebrew University trustees and if he wanted this title, and also lower overhead, he could get it. At the time, I was chair of the Soviet and East European Research Center so Amia Liblich agreed to be the first chair of the Lafer Center. We began as a research center, offering fellowships for graduate students and faculty. But the teaching program, still dependent on the generosity of various departments, was struggling. So a few years later, I was able to engage Fred to help us undertake a significant expansion, absorbing the teaching program and offering more scholarships and research money. He personally helped me (I was now chair of the Lafer Center) raise over a million dollars for this expansion. And I believe, with his generous personal assistance, we managed to put the Fred and Barbara Lafer Center on the map and women's studies at the Hebrew University on a sound basis.

For our next try, Amia and I, by now both full professors, lobbied for a tenured position in women's studies and also for an MA program. By the time I retired from the Hebrew University in 2000, we still had not achieved either of those things, while Tel Aviv University now had an undergraduate Department of Women's Studies and Bar Ilan had an MA, staffed by many of our former students. Today these programs, and also the Lafer Center, are called Gender Studies or Women's and Gender Studies. At some point in the late 1990s, I invited Daphna Izraeli and Marilyn Safir to meet with me at the Hebrew University to see about creating a feminist studies association in Israel to bring together all the women in the field. They both agreed and we took up the task with great energy, engaging our contacts abroad and the help of feminist scholars. In time we obtained Ford Foundation money for all the programs in the country and an organization of feminist studies. While I continued to view myself as an activist/entrepreneur in all this, my own interest in feminism led me to undertake a good deal of research. Eventually I began teaching a course on women and politics, initially with my colleague Naomi Chazan, and, when asked, writing. New to academic writing in that field, I often showed my drafts to former students for comments. I'm not sure I ever mastered the technique, particularly of what amounted to sociological studies, but much of my writing on the topic relating to women was and is based on my many years of experience as an activist and observer.

Legal Developments

Over the years, with increased gender awareness in the country as a whole, progress was indeed made in the legal area in Israel. But attitudes, including those of legislators, are hard to change. The first topic to receive broad attention and political support was the issue of battered women and the need for battered women's centers. This and similar legislation over the years was actually 'protective' legislation, that is, born of the traditional view of women as the weaker sex, the victim, to be protected. In fact, long before the feminism of the 1970s, Israel's socialist leaders in the early days of the state had introduced numerous measures designed to protect working women, for example. This underlying approach has not changed much to this day, even as women are allotted more and more non-traditional roles.

Around 20 years ago a younger female law professor, where I was teaching at the time, stopped me on the campus to say, "You know you didn't do us any favors." I didn't exactly understand what she meant, so she said

> You early feminists in Israel you got us to where we go out, and we work, and we can work in any profession but you didn't change anything else. We now have all the other stuff too; we've got the double burden. I'm sure most of you know you didn't change society. It wasn't built for us in Israel, the school day ends at one o'clock, what's a woman supposed to do if she has children? All kinds of things of this nature, even public transportation, women are the ones who mainly use public transportation, is it organized according to their needs?

These were the kinds of thing that she pointed out. For me it was like a light bulb going off, where all of a sudden I realized that she was absolutely right. It wasn't just 'let us in', 'let us be professors, let us be doctors'. Instead, we have to change society because society was not built for us.

This is not unique to Israel, but in Israel there is the additional, still unsurmountable problem of the political power held by the religious establishment. This power is largely due not to numbers of supporters but to the coalition system whereby smaller parties, such as the ultra-orthodox parties, can and do tip the scales for one leader or another, depending on what that leader is prepared to accord the religious sector in the way of benefits. This absence of division between religion and the state, the disproportionate power of the religious parties, and the conservative, retrograde character of these parties have all led to a contradictory situation. Independent courts, for example, have initiated progressive changes such as the ground-breaking ruling on equality in the military that came from the case of a women who wanted to be a pilot. Yet, the religious establishment has managed to bar legislation for affirmative action in political parties (a minimum quota system) and outside the Knesset actually managed to gain separate seating on buses in some areas and gender separation in certain university programs.

My feminist activity was not limited to the university or academic studies, and this issue of religious coercion as it affected women was one of the first battles I was involved in outside of academia. Working with some of the same women I had organized at the university, primarily Alice Shalvi – who remained our leader – we took up the issue of Jewish women who could not remarry because they could not obtain a divorce from their husbands. The issue itself reflected the basic problem of the absence of separation between religion and state: there was and is no civil marriage or divorce in Israel. The old system of the Ottoman Empire has been maintained, with family law in the hands of each religious community. And in Jewish law the husband, or wife, must grant a divorce (a *get*) to the spouse. The major problem here is that barring such agreement, a man may nonetheless remarry, a woman may not. There are other ramifications, and there are other examples of religious injustice, especially for women. But the issue of these thousands of women who could not remarry was, for us, a good place to start in trying to tackle not only laws but attitudes toward women in Israel.

We formalized this battle in 1984 by creating the Israel Women's Network (IWN), in Hebrew called the *Stula* or 'Lobby.' A liberal feminist advocacy organization (as distinct from the older radical feminist movement that had been leading the struggle against violence against women), we sought equality – in politics, in the army, in academia and so on. Heavy on a legalistic approach, our Legal Center was originally organized by Frances Raday. It was instrumental in bringing precedent-setting cases to the Supreme Court including the 1995 breakthrough Alice Miller decision on equality in the army. Miller was a young woman who had a civil pilot's licence and wanted to use it in her regular army service in Israel and go into pilot training. But they didn't let women into the pilot training course, they didn't take women into the Air Force as pilots in Israel. We took the case to the Supreme Court, and the court decided that yes, she had the right to take the course. The reason this case was so important was that the judgment concerned the principle of equality. The other reason the judgment was important was that it forced the army to change. The Court noted that while it was hard for the current system to accommodate a woman, the system had to change; the army couldn't bring her into a system that didn't really work well for a woman.

Another challenge came in what we call the third wave of feminism. This was an attack on essentialism, the recognition that not all women are the same and not all women have the same experiences. Women come from different classes, races, ethnic groups, religions – that's what we mean today when we talk about intersectionality. As an example, I was once on a panel and one of the other participants was an Arab woman, a Palestinian citizen of Israel. She explained her intersectionality in the following way: she was a woman in Arab society where women were not on an equal level, and she was an Arab in Israel, so she was, as she put it, right there at the bottom.

As the late Susan Okin (2005, 2013), accepting the idea that of course not all women are the same, pointed out, in every class, every ethnic group, any category whatsoever, women's experiences are different from men's. Although it may be entirely different from a woman from another class, or another race, or another ethnic group, a woman's experience will always be different from that of a man. It will be a gendered view in terms of how we interact with the world, and so a feminist approach to understanding women is one that breaks down a situation, an event, a law, and analyzes it from the point of view of social relationships and power relations.

Feminism examines where we are in these settings, and in analyzing women's places it tends toward a sensitivity to the marginalized – to what psychologists call an out-group. This makes women sensitive to hierarchy, and as Gloria Steinem (1995) said, it doesn't really matter if you call yourself a liberal feminist or a radical feminist – what's important is this gendered view. This is one of feminism's major contributions to modern philosophy, the idea of looking at gender relations and power relations. It is not only a question of analyzing a situation but also how to deal with the situation, how to transform the situation.

Alice Shalvi was the founding chair of the IWN and I became her deputy chair. But I did not want to take the position of chair when she resigned some years later. Out of various, mainly family considerations, I did not want to take on such a demanding task; I was content to be active but not take the responsibility for initiating campaigns and the like. One of the reasons for this is that when I do take responsibility for an endeavor, I tend to become obsessed with it. This has its advantages, in terms of the time and effort I am willing to put in, but this also means that, realizing this, I generally eschew the top role, preferring only to be active, second in command so to speak, while limiting – or harnessing – my initiatives and responsibilities to the degree possible. That is probably too rational an explanation, but I do try to prioritize even as I multi-task. I was and remain involved in many things, including research and writing as well, but only as labors of love, and self-expression.

After Alice's retirement, I gradually became less involved in the IWN and by the 1990s I had shifted from liberal to radical feminism. The main reason I became more radical was that despite the progress we had contributed to, basic attitudes had not really changed in Israeli society, and much remained to be done. Aside from the continuation of chronic issues like violence against women, wage inequality, etc., we still had even more religious intrusions into our lives, and a failure to implement many of the progressive laws we had (or had already been) put in place.

I came to the conclusion, perhaps a little late, that we had to do much more than simply promote women's participation and advancement. Societal change was, and is, needed. Present society had been created by and for men, albeit not necessarily out of hatred of women. But the meaning of patriarchy is that society, its institutions and norms, have been made by men, in keeping with their needs and their interests. Feminism is all about power relations, and I came to realize that joining the existing institutions would not change basic power relations. Society's institutions and norms had to be overhauled. This is a revolutionary task, a radical task, but necessary.

Women, War, and Peace

A strong element of the early feminists was anti-militarism and pacifism. Jane Addams and the women who came to the Hague to oppose World War One advocated for negotiations, mediation, and non-violence. They connected the pursuit of peace to their identity as women, arguing that war was a woman's worst enemy. Moreover, war gives value to power, to strength, to stereotypical male attributes. War is based on hierarchy, on orders and commands. Hannah Arendt used to say that for women power comes by working together, whereas command and control military institutions were seen by these early feminists as a major barrier to equality for women – women who were opposed to the exercise of power, to violence, to slavery, to male domination, to war and the idea of conflict between genders or between nations. For them the link between feminism and pacifism was not because women were peaceful by nature; their pacifism was the result of an everyday experience of oppression.

There were those who did claim that women were more peace-loving. Others sought equality in the name of motherhood. Women are nurturers, it was reasoned, they seek harmony. United Nations Resolution 1325 (UN Security Council, 2000) is an important resolution that demands that women be brought into the decisions of war and peace. But Resolution 1325 is based on three justifications: one is a rights argument, one is a victims argument, and the final is a nurturing argument. The rights argument states that it's our right that we be equal, to be part of such discussions. The victims argument states that wars affect us and so we should have a say. The nurturing argument says that we should be part of the decision-making because we are more peace-loving. This is the old stereotype at work again.

Gender norms are socially constructed, and girls are socialized to be more peace-loving, so what happens in a society that's at war? In a society involved in armed conflict over many years, will we find a gender gap concerning views about war? A study conducted by Professor Michal Shamir (Shamir et al., 2020; Shamir and Gedalya-Levy, 2017) from Tel Aviv University found that women were more hawkish than men on certain issues. In other issues, such as border security, she found no gender gap; indeed, most studies from Israel find no gender gap on issues concerning war and security. But, when Professor Shamir asked people to put their preferences in a hierarchy of priorities – democracy, peace, settlements, a Jewish majority, peace – women more than men put peace at the top.

The reasons for the difference in priorities remains unclear, and it leads us to other questions. What about actions? What happens if women are in power? What happens if women are at the peace table?

We have some research on what happens when women are at war. Orna Sasson-Levy (2006; Lomsky-Feder & Sasson-Levy, 2018) looked at women in the military and found that women who went into combat positions became like men. They lowered their voices, stood differently, adopted a male way of acting. We also know women can be violent. Women perpetrated violence in Rwanda; there are women terrorists.

The Council on Foreign Relations did an enormous study on women and peace that looked at all the conflicts between 1992 and 2011 (Bigio & Vogelstein, 2016). They found that societies that have higher gender equality or gender harmony also have lower rates of violence and lower possibilities of actual wars, whether internal or inter-state. High percentages of women in legislatures was associated with fewer state conflicts. They also found that peace agreements tended to last longer if more women were involved. Mariam Anderson's (2015) study of 181 peace agreements since 1989 also found that when women participated in peace talks the agreements lasted longer, an average of 15 years. One explanation was that women tend to be involved in growing a civil society, have grassroots connections, and may be more willing to work with different people. Another reason given is that women tend to bring issues of human security to bear – that is to say, issues of getting food on the table, shelter, and so on. An additional explanation argued that the involvement of women conferred a certain legitimacy to the peace agreements.

One fascinating piece of research took a group of military men and presented them with a peace proposal for the Israeli-Palestinian conflict. The men were told the peace proposal was written by a man, and the proposal was rejected. An additional group of military men were shown the same proposal and were told it was written by a woman, and the proposal was accepted. During questioning, the military men who accepted the proposal stated that the proposal seemed fair and trustworthy, stereotypical ideals associated with femininity.

Marian Anderson also found that women's presence in peacemaking not only made for more lasting peace agreements but shaped the nature of the agreement itself. She looked at 195 agreements between 1975 and 2011 and found that when women were involved, 40 percent of them had clauses linked to the status of women and women's rights. I did research which examined legislators in Israel over the years and looked at proposed laws dealing with women's rights. I discovered it wasn't about how many women were in the Knesset or Parliament at the time, but whether those there were feminists.

To some extent, the evolution of my thinking regarding feminism and women's rights mirrored my political evolution. There is the saying (belief?) that generally one is radical as a young person and with maturity becomes conservative. It has definitely been the other way around for me, at least since immigrating to Israel. In the run up to the 1992 elections a new saga began for me when I announced that I was interested in being nominated to run for the Knesset. The problem was that another woman had already decided to run and had begun to work at getting the nomination and we were too much alike – both professors, active feminists, active peaceniks; we even taught courses together. The concern was that we would cancel out each other since party members were not likely to put both of us in realistic positions. This was before we had minimum quotas for women – something we were fighting for and eventually achieved as the first party to require 40 percent gender representation. The party's decision was that the other candidate should be the one to run. With regret, I dropped out of the race, but with the idea of running the next time around.

Part of my calculation was also that I had seen close up just how unpleasant politics in the Knesset could be. I saw that much of the time was spent making compromises and answering party members' requests, i.e., politics, rather than the lofty task of policy-making. I think it was a combination of all of these things that led me to decide, finally, that this was not for me. I'm not self-confident or thick-skinned enough nor confrontational enough for politics. I am far more comfortable in extra-parliamentary activity, without the competition and infighting of party politics.

My peace activism had begun in earnest with the creation of Peace Now in 1978. Already a regular demonstrator, on an *ad hoc* basis, I had not sought a place in any of the few, quite small peace groups already in existence. But in March 1978, in the middle of difficult Israeli-Egyptian peace talks, an open letter of 148 reserve officers and soldiers appeared in the press urging the government to take a more flexible position and not let the opportunity for peace, now, to be missed. They more than implied that their future service might be in doubt if they did not believe that the government was doing everything in its power to make peace. Since they added an address for expressions of support, my husband – who was a reserve combat medical officer – sent in his name. Shortly thereafter the movement contacted me to give a speech at a small demonstration, and so both of us joined the group, building Peace Now into Israel's first and only mass peace movement.

The secret of the group's mass appeal was the security-related character of the letter's signatories, as distinct from the intellectual or extreme left-wing nature of previous groups. As combat reservists, their loyalty was above suspicion, providing them the legitimacy as well as presumed experience to express such opinions. These were highly valued credentials in a society engaged in prolonged armed conflict. A motif employed in order to gain legitimacy within the public, indeed prompting mainstream support for just this reason. That this was deliberate exploitation of the public trust in the military – that is the male military, was demonstrated by the refusal of the group to include the signature of the one woman among the initiators (who had been a lieutenant when she did her obligatory service). The use of military motifs was typical of many peace groups that emerged over the years, a natural phenomenon for a militarized society perhaps, and an exclusion of women from public representation that was only gradually altered over the years.

While one might view the religious move into (some might say takeover of) the army as a further sign of the militarization of Israeli society, it would appear to be, rather, a sign of the greater religiosity of an already militarized society. Yet this development, an apparent contradiction to the trend toward greater gender equality both in the army and in Israeli society, can be expected to contribute further to the militarization of Israeli society given the strong link between these religious groups and militaristic *policies* (settlement building, continuing the occupation). Their religious beliefs tie them to territorial domination (sentiment such as *"eretz Israel"* equaling God-given lands to Abraham) while their political beliefs are based on the conviction that Israel is fated to live by the sword ("Arabs/Islam will never accept Israel in the region"). And as they take control of the sword, gender will be further affected through the influence of the army. Thus, the patriarchal nature of the army has now been compounded and strengthened by the influx of this other patriarchy. In fact, the issue of separating men and women in public, even official, events and (public) transportation, has become a major issue in Israel with a distinct blurring of the military and civilian spheres. Thus, the swing toward greater religiosity in Israel may be seen as still another change impacting on militarization, with the accompanying effects on gender.

Gender Asymmetries

The question I pose is: would looking at gender composition change or in any way affect the role of asymmetry? There is by now a vast literature on gender differences, along with feminist theory not only on the construction of gender, but also the problem of essentialism and the need to understand differences within genders. Literature on gender and negotiation tends to be essentialist, focusing on differences between men and women in the way in which they negotiate, the skills they bring to negotiation, the way in which they perceive such matters as peace or security or power, and how they perceive their own relative power (Boyer et al., 2009; Tickner, 1992; Cockburn, 1998; Golan, 1997, 2004; Kray et al., 2001; Tessler & Warriner, 1997). Indeed, research has shown gender differences in all of these areas, in some cases providing varied explanations ranging from gender role socialization to situational power (access to power such as resources) to combination of gender and situation (power affecting each gender differently) to expectation (with regard to each gender and self) (Stuhlmacher & Walters, 1999; Walters et al., 1998; Watson, 1994; Kray et al., 2001). Yet, it is clear that while many of the factors raised by these explanations may be operative, there are different degrees of power amongst women (as there are amongst men) and different ways of using or responding to power in a negotiating situation.

While some researchers (for example, Watson, 1994) maintain that asymmetry of power (situational asymmetry) is more important a factor than gender with regard to negotiating style (collaborative or competitive), it has been found that while a woman with power (defined in terms of control of resources, status, numbers) may be more assertive in negotiation, she will have a harder time controlling the negotiation than a powerful man negotiating with a woman. Namely a woman's power is diminished when she negotiates with a man, indicating greater importance of gender than power (Watson, 1994, 120, citing Berger et al., 1977). Moreover, according to other studies, even a powerful woman employing an assertive negotiating style will be viewed as less effective than a male (Watson, 1994; Karakowsky & Miller,

2006). Sell et al. (1993) too found that women's power was diminished and the man's power was enhanced in mixed groups, but only when gender identity was known (Sell et al., 1993; Sell, 1997).

One explanation for such findings is connected with the matter of expectations, namely, knowledge of and therefore reaction or adaptation to gender stereotypes (Sell, 1997; Kray et al., 2001). Begging the question of whether or not the expectation is justified, it derives from the stereotypical (if not proven) view of women as less assertive, competitive, or confrontational than men. Supported by psychological studies such as Gilligan's (1982) ground-breaking work, women are said to be empathetic, compassionate, relational or other-oriented, and communicative (Markus & Kitayama, 1991; McCarthy 1991; Babcock & Laschever, 2003; Cross & Madison, 1997; Kolb & Coolidge, 1991). In negotiation, it would follow, women would be expected to give greater attention to process and preservation of relationship (preference for harmony) than to be goal-oriented, with a greater degree of risk-aversion than men and less concern for one's own interests. To some degree these hypotheses were proven, particularly by testing in which there was stereotype activation (Kray et al., 2001). Yet, the matter of asymmetry (of power) was not involved, unless, that is, one were to attach concepts of 'weak' or 'powerful' to these different forms of behavior or styles – thereby adhering to stereotypical views of women as weaker, less effective. Obviously less effective would depend upon the type of negotiation – collaborative negotiation being one in which women would be expected to be more 'effective' (Karakowsky & Miller, 2006; d'Estree & Babbitt, 1998; Watson et al., 1996).

A better measure of the relationship between gender and asymmetry may be found in looking at same-sex negotiation, particularly all-female. Kray et al. (2001) found that as distinct from mixed dyads, same-sex dyads did not respond to stereotype activation. Presumably, as Watson posited,

> gender is not expected to have any impact on the power of negotiators in same-sex pairs of negotiators. ... Being a woman should not eliminate your power when you face another woman, nor should being a man enhance your power when you face another man.
> (Watson, 1994, 124)

Indeed, Watson found that a high-powered woman did not become cooperative when dealing with a less powerful woman. Similarly, Sell found that women were not more cooperative in all-female groups than they were with men, though her more complex study did find that greater female cooperation resulted when the women were aware (but only when they were aware) of the gender of the whole group and the strategy adopted by both sides in the negotiation (Sell, 1997). Even studies of same-sex, all-female groups in collaborative negotiations found no significant gender effects (Boyer et al., 2009), or, as Stockard put it, "males and females usually reacted in similar ways to conditions which were designed to promote cooperative behavior" (Stockard et al., 1988, 161, cited in Sell et al., 1993, 211). Only the Watson study cited above, however, examined for gender and asymmetry, finding that asymmetry of power was not affected by gender.

So, of course we must ask, which women? Who are we bringing in? It's not biology, it's a consciousness of power relations, a consciousness of what is at stake. Arguably, there is a tendency for a woman to be more be aware of these things. This awareness is at the heart of feminism. Feminism is a way of looking at the world, looking at our day-to-day reality in a different way. When this reality is brought to the table, literally and figuratively, it can literally create new paths for peace.

Note

1 Pieces of this chapter were previously published in: Golan, G., 'Autobiographical Note' in *Galia Golan: An Academic Pioneer on the Soviet Union, Peace and Conflict Studies, and a Peace and Feminist Activist* (PAHSEP, Vol. 22), published 2018, Springer International Publishing, reproduced with permission of SNCSC. The author is grateful to the publisher for permission to reuse the material, which is still copyright protected and owned by the publisher.

References

Anderson, M.J. 2015. *Windows of opportunity: How women seize peace negotiations for political change.* Oxford: Oxford University Press.

Babcock, L. and Laschever, S. 2003. *Women don't ask: Negotiation and the gender divide.* Princeton, NJ: Princeton University Press.

Berger, J., Fisek, H., Norman, R. and Zelditch, M. 1977. *Status characteristics and social interaction: An expectation states approach.* New York: Elsevier.

Bigio, J. and Vogelstein, R. 2016. *How women's participation in conflict prevention and resolution advances US interests.* Council on Foreign Relations.

Boyer, M., Urlacher, B., Hudson, N., Niv-Soloman, A., Janik, L., Butler, M. and Brown, S. 2009. Gender and negotiation: Some experimental findings from an international negotiation simulation. *International Studies Quarterly* 53: 23–47.

Cockburn, C. 1998. *The space between us: Negotiating gender and national identities in conflict.* London: Zed.

Cross, S. and Madison, L. 1997. Models of the self: Self construals and gender. *Labor Bulletin* 22: 5–37.

d'Estree, T. and Babbitt, E. 1998. Women and the art of peacemaking: Data from Israeli-Palestinian interactive problem-solving workshops. *Political Psychology* 19(1): 185–209.

Enloe, Catherine. 1988. *Does khaki become you.* London: Pandora.

Enloe, C. 2014. *Bananas, beaches and bases: Making feminist sense of international politics.* Berkeley: University of California Press. Gilligan, C. 1982. *In a different voice.* Cambridge, MA: Harvard University Press.

Golan, G. 1997. Militarization and gender: The Israeli experience. *Statsvetenskaplig Tidskrift* 100: 115–122.

Golan, G. 2004. The role of women in conflict resolution. *Palestine-Israel Journal* 11 (2): 92–96.

Goldman, E. 1917. *Anarchism and other essays*. Third revised edition. New York: Mother Earth Publishing Association. Goldman, E. 2019 [1917]. Anarchism: What it really stands for. In *Ideals and ideologies* (pp. 305–313). London: Routledge.
Karkowsky, L. and Miller, D. 2006. Negotiator style and influence in multi-party negotiations: Exploring the role of gender. *Leadership & Organization Development Journal* 27(1): 50–65.
Kolb, D. and Coolidge, G. 1991. Her place at the table: A consideration of gender issues in negotiation. In *Negotiation theory and practice*, edited by W. Breslin and J. Rubin. Cambridge, MA: Harvard Program on Negotiation.
Kray, L., Thompson, L., and Galinsky, A. 2001. Battle of the sexes: Gender stereotype confirmation and reactance in negotiations. *Journal of Personality and Social Psychology* 80(6): 942–958.
Lomsky-Feder, E. and Sasson-Levy, O. 2018. *Women soldiers and citizenship in Israel: Gendered encounters with the state*. New York and London: Routledge.
Luxemburg, R. 2012 [1903]. *Marxist theory and the proletariat*. Berlin: Vorwärts.
MacKinnon, C. 1987. *Feminism unmodified*. Cambridge, MA: Harvard University Press.
MacKinnon, C. 2017. *Butterfly politics*. Cambridge, MA: Harvard University Press.
Markus, H. and Kitayama, S. 1991. Culture and the self: Implications for cognition, emotion, and motivation. *Psychological Review* 98: 224–253.
McCarthy, W. 1991. The role of power in getting to yes. In *Negotiation theory and practice*, edited by W. Breslin and J. Rubin. Cambridge, MA: Harvard Program on Negotiation.
Okin, S.M. 2005. *Justice, gender, and the family*. London: Routledge.
Okin, S.M. 2013. *Women in western political thought*. Princeton: Princeton University Press. Sasson-Levy, Orna. 2006. *Identities in uniform: Masculinities and femininities in the Israeli military*. Jerusalem: Eshkolot Series, Magnes Press, and Tel Aviv: Migdarim Series, Hakibutz Hameucahd Press (Hebrew).
Sell, J. 1997. Gender, strategies, and contributions to public goods. *Social Psychology Quarterly* 60(3): 252–265.
Sell, J., Griffith, W., and Wilson, R. 1993. Are women more cooperative than men in social dilemmas? *Social Psychology Quarterly* 56(3): 211–222.
Shamir, M. and Gedalya-Lavy, E. 2017. A gender gap in voting? Women and men in the 2013 Elections. In *The elections in Israel 2013* (pp. 231–256). London: Routledge.
Shamir, M., Herzog, H., and Chazan, N. 2020. *Political gender gaps in Israel*. Jerusalem: The Van Leer Institute and Am Oved (Hebrew).Steinem, G. 1995. *Outrageous acts and everyday rebellions*. New York: Macmillan.
Stockard, J., van Kragt, A., and Dodge, P. 1988. Gender roles and behavior in social dilemmas: Are there sex differences in cooperation and its justification? *Social Psychology Quarterly* 52: 154–163.
Stuhlmacher, A. and Walters, A. 1999. Gender differences in negotiation outcome: A meta-analysis. *Personnel Psychology* 52: 653–677.
Tessler, M. and Warriner, I. 1997. Gender, feminism, and attitudes towards international conflict. *World Politics* 49(2): 250–281.
Tickner, A. 1992. *Gender in international relations*. New York: Columbia University Press.
UN Security Council. 2000. *Security Council resolution 1325 (2000)* [*on women and peace and security*], October 31, S/RES/1325.

Walters, A., Stuhlmacher, A., and Meyer, L. 1998. Gender and negotiator competitive-ness: A mega-analysis. *Organizational Behavior and Human Decision Processes* 76: 1–29.

Watson, C. 1994. Gender versus power as a predictor of negotiation behavior and outcomes. *Negotiating Journal*: 117–127.

Watson, R., Haines, M., and Bretherton, D. 1996. Effects of interpersonal communication process on outcomes in international conflict negotiation simulation. *Journal of Social Psychology* 136(4): 483–489.

Part III
Challenging Boundaries, Subverting Expectations, and Emphasizing Potential

Part III

7 Shifting Perceptions of Women in the World

The Implications of Place, Space, and Time

Kate Seaman and Hoda Mahmoudi

> No individual woman's identity ... will escape the markings of gender, but how gender marks her life is her own
>
> (Iris Marion Young, 1994: 734)

Introduction

How do we imagine a better world for all women? Not only imagine it, but make it a reality? While in many areas the progress which women have made would seem remarkable to those living only a few decades ago, and some women today have more choices than their predecessors, the reality of women's individual lived experiences demonstrate that there is still a long way to go. Every woman will have a story, or more likely stories, of ways in which she has made herself smaller, ways in which she has adapted, to make herself fit into spaces and places that were not designed for, and do not adapt to, women. While men are "the group that sets the standard" (MacKinnon, 2017: 115) individual women who excel are still seen as the exception to the rule in a patriarchal world.

On a daily basis, women are navigating a world designed to limit them, their agency, their choices, their mobility, and their actions. The existing institutions that govern our daily lives are manmade, and no matter how many women enter these institutions, the underlying structures remain unaltered. Women are forced to navigate these systems and structures while simultaneously pushing for change, attempting to break down barriers, and shatter glass ceilings. The spaces we operate in are male defined and our place within them is determined by our gender. It is therefore not possible for these institutions and structures to operate in a gender neutral manner, as Tickner (1997: 614) notes, "all too often, claims of gender neutrality mask deeply embedded masculinist assumptions which can naturalize or hide gender differences and gender inequalities." In order to unmask these differences and inequalities, feminists have focused on how gender interacts with other power relations. This complexification enables a conceptualization of power in terms of multiple axes of interconnected and mutually transformative relations (Gilbert, 1998).

By drawing on scholarship from the fields of feminist international relations, and feminist geography, both of which are inherently interdisciplinary, this chapter examines how these complex power relations intersect with the concepts of space, place, and time, and how these interactions either reduce or increase the barriers to women's agency. The chapter begins with an exploration of agency, and how socially constructed structures such as gender constrain women's exercise of their agency. The remainder of the chapter is divided into three sections, the first examines the concept of place, the second, space, and the third, time. Throughout the three sections runs a thread examining the role of relationships/solidarity and the connection these have with the cultural changes required in each of these three concepts to truly create a world of equality and change in the future.

Gender, Power, and Agency

As Catharine MacKinnon (2017: 227) states: "Feminism starts with the simple observation that women are people. It moves into the more complex observation that they have been denied that simple recognition to their disadvantage. Then it gets complicated." The complications are what this chapter explores. We are interested in how the role of women has been constructed throughout history, and how this impacts on women's ability, as diverse subjects, to act on their own desires, and to define and pursue their goals.

The starting point for our examination of agency, gender, and power is the socially constructed division between the public sphere and the private. Deconstructing this artificial divide is a key part of the feminist project, and its goal of expanding the definition of politics and political acts. As Tickner (2005) argues, the absence of gender equality "cannot be understood without reference to historical, gender-laden divisions between public and private spheres." The separation between public and private also includes a division between 'rational' activities reserved for the public sphere, politics, economics, law, and 'natural' activities relegated to the private sphere, family responsibilities, child care, caring responsibilities (Peterson, 1992). This division of activities confines women to the private sphere, the familial sphere (Benhabib, 1998) while simultaneously providing an explanation and ideological foundation for women's oppression (Davidoff, 1998).

Rationality and objectivity are equated with the masculine and the universal, again contained within the public space, whereas the private space becomes synonymous with the particular (Pateman, 1989). As Tickner (2005) elaborates, the foundations for this can be found in modern Enlightenment science (see also Keller, 1985) and also in the foundations of the modern western state, which "set up hierarchical gendered structures and role expectations, that impede the achievement of true gender equality, even in states where most legal barriers to women's equality have been removed." These foundational structures did not recognize women as citizens, removing them from both the public political arena, and the economic sphere of production

(Peterson, 1992). This also served to deny women status as full legal citizens, with access to all of the rights this entails.

The social advantage of the association of the male/masculinity with the universality of humanity requires an association of the female/femininity with the opposite, the particular. As MacKinnon (2017: 227) argues, feminism "reveals that women have a universality that has been denied, as well as a contribution to make to universality that has been overlooked" and "men have a particularity that they have denied in themselves in defining that particularity as the universal." This exposes the socially and culturally constructed characteristics of gender and the relational nature of both masculinity and femininity (Tickner, 1997). The introduction of power – dominance and subordination – into the equation demonstrates the inequalities of the gender hierarchy. While there is variation in gender relations across cultures, the inequalities inherent in the hierarchical gender structure are near universal, meaning that gender, as a structure, provides a crucial insight into relationships of power (Scott, 1986: 1069).

Gender as a structure impacts on the entirety of human experience (Flax, 1987), with boys and girls effectively growing up in entirely different social contexts, with vastly different norms, expectations, and agency (Tannen, 1990). For this reason, while the focus on the female experience is important and necessary, we must also not neglect the male experience, as the activities of all are shaped through the interaction between the social context, norms, and power relations (Cope, 2004; Cohn, 1993).

In the current system "Power takes a male form, specifically a white one" and "powerlessness takes a female form" (MacKinnon, 2017: 29), however in this chapter we want to push back against that dichotomy in order to complexify power relations. As Cope argues, nobody

> is without power altogether, but each person's power constellation consists of many different sets of relations that take shape in a variety of spaces (and times), and which can occur simultaneously and even contradictorily. Thus, power is not just a dominant/subordinate relationship between individuals, groups, or institutions; it is also a set of mutually conditioning or contradicting relationships.
>
> (Cope, 1996: 186)

Therefore, in our approach, we seek to understand not just a single dynamic of power, but rather the webs of power within social relationships. Following Staeheli et al. (2004) we conceptualize power as multifaceted, diffuse, and relational. Women's agency is directly linked to and limited by the power structures and relations of gender, what Folbre (1994) identifies as gender structures of constraint, and it is the variation in these constraints, and how this impacts on women's agency, which this chapter will examine next.

Agency is defined as the "ability to define one's goals and act on them" (Kabeer, 1999). The rules and norms governing social interactions restrict women's ability to both define their goals and act on them. As Hanmer and Klugman (2016) argue, "Agency invokes an ability to overcome barriers, to question or confront situations of oppression and deprivation, and, as individuals or together with others, to have influence and be heard in society." Agency, therefore provides the possibility of transforming power arrangements (Martin, 2004). In order to transform these arrangements Martin (2004) goes on to argue that the political must be located within discursive practices, with an understanding of how these practices set relationships between people. Language has to be linked to materiality, in order to expose the ways in which ideas of legitimacy and truth are produced in contexts of unequal power distribution. The inequality of power distribution here is key, especially in the manner in which it constrains women's options.

Herein is the catch-22 for feminists in relation to women's agency, as Meyers (2002: 4) argues:

> With regard to women's agency, it seems that if women are systematically subordinated, their ability to choose and act freely must be gravely compromised. Yet, if feminist theorists are to respect women's dignity and if they are to defend women's capcity to emancipate themselves, it seems they must counter that women's agency has been concealed or overlooked, not diminished.

As MacKinnon (2017) notes, in this case in relation to consent, which she argues relies on the illusion of women's agency within what is an intrinsically unequal concept. Consent, she argues, presupposes an actor and acted upon, whereby the power of the 'acted-upon' is acceding to (consenting to) the actor's actions – in other words doing what you are told – with no guarantee of equality of circumstance. Consent therefore relies only on an illusion of 'women's agency' within this context of inequality, ignoring the reality that women cannot be free without being equal.

To further unpick this, we need to be clear about, and conscious of, the constraints in and positions from which women are operating. As Narayan (2018) emphasizes, we have to acknowledge the ways in which women's responses, and choices in how to respond, to the patriarchal system and the associated cultural practices, are constrained, but we also need to recognize the choices that are available within those constraints as this influences the different kinds of policies feminists should support. These choices are also connected to individual experiences and a feminist approach therefore requires a focus on 'situated knowledges,' what Haraway (1988: 580) calls a "reliable account of things ... an earth-wide network of connections, including the ability partially to translate knowledges among very different – and power-differentiated – communities."

We must also recognize the ways in which gender and the patriarchal system have been internalized. From a young age women learn to perceive themselves as objects, their identities become both gendered and individualized, and as Meyers (2002) highlights, the individualized experience of women does not protect their agentic capacity from damage, rather the reality that "women's identities are gendered in patriarchal cultures does impede women's ability to function as self-determining agents" (Meyers, 2002: 5). This damage to agentic capacity is attributed to women's internalized oppression, whereby the subordination assigned to women as a gender is internalized, and becomes integrated into each woman's identity – but to each individual woman in a different and unique way as the opening quote from Young identifies. Women will self-limit, will choose the path of least resistance based on their internalized recognition of the inherent inequalities of the current patriarchal society. This reality can be seen in the ways in which women who have managed to beat the odds, and have gained access to the public sphere, tend to have done so by playing by the male rules (Duncan, 1996: 2).

The subordination of women within the current system is both socially and legally institutionalized, as MacKinnon (2017: 36) argues, this reality "systematically deprives women of human dignity, respect, resources, physical security, credibility, full membership in our communities, speech, and power." This system is not natural, however. Rather, as Harding (1986) suggests, there are three processes involved in the creation of our current gendered social life: gender symbolism – the assignment of dualistic gender metaphors to perceived dichotomies (male/female, public/private, strong/weak, etc.); gender structure – utilizing those dualisms to organize social activities between males and females; and individual gender – the division of social activities between the different groups of humans. These three processes contribute to the complex socially structured regime of gender difference that is systematically reproduced across all areas of social life, politics, economics, culture, and institutions. However, as Young (1990) argues, difference is both fluid and relational, you cannot have one side of the dichotomy without the other. The inequality between the genders is therefore not a single variable, "rather, it is a historically contingent, complex confluence of socio-cultural power relationships, including associated subjective understandings" (Tickner, 2005: 17).

This is why the reliance on claims to legal and political rights are insufficient in attempting to transform the current gender based power systems, because as Brown (2000) argues, they do not eliminate the underlying structures, mechanisms of production, the dominant gender regime, or male dominance. As Olufemi (2020: 4) argues, "Liberal feminism's obsession with getting women 'to the top' masks a desire to ensure that the current system and its violent consequences remain intact." It is reliant on maintaining the current systems, which rely on the invisibilization of women of color, lower classes, migrants, and those whose suffering ensures the success of those at the top. As she goes on to argue, "A feminism that seeks power instead of questioning it does not care about justice" (Olufemi, 2020: 5). Instead Olufemi asks us to practice radical compassion, and to examine what our politics can help articulate, and the violence it can expose.

Instead of attempting to work within the system, we need to subvert it, as Olufemi states:

> History allows us to see that subversion and, more importantly, resistance has always existed. Feminist activists have always pushed boundaries set by the state, by men, by the powerful, and in doing so, laid the foundations for a new world.
>
> (Olufemi, 2020: 11)

It is these foundations that we must build upon in order to radically alter the spaces accessible to women, and the places women can operate from and engage with. The following sections of this chapter engage with the concepts of place, space, and time to explore more deeply how these intersect with power relations, to impact women's agency.

Place, Creation, Growth

We begin this next section with an examination of what we mean by place, As Massey (2013: 1) notes, the term place

> can raise an image of one's place in the world, of the reputedly ... deep meanings of 'a place called home' or, with much greater intimations of mobility and agility, can be used in the context of discussions of positionality.

For our purposes we are interested in the idea of positionality, of women's place within the power relations and systems of patriarchy, and with "the intricacy and profundity of the connection of space and place with gender and the construction of gender relations" (Massey, 2013: 2). Any examination of women's place requires an understanding of the bodily, lived experiences of place and space for women (Hyndman, 2004). What does place mean to women? How does it shape their daily lives, and their sense of self? How does it limit or encourage their agency?

For us, place is not only a territorially bounded notion, it is also a position within a network of social relationships, a position which influences the capacity of individual women to define their goals and act on them (agency). Whilst in this chapter we draw on the work of feminist geographers, this concept of place is also important for interdisciplinary feminists too and can be utilized in other fields of scholarship. Here we build on Massey (2013) and her disaggregation of the views of place as bounded, fixed, singular, a conception of space as stasis versus places as a particular articulation of social interrelations at all scales, in the context of space and time. As Massey (2013) argues, this increases the uncertainty about the meaning of places, and how we relate to them, especially in relation to local, particular places. This stands in contrast to earlier understandings of place, where, as Giddens (1990: 12) argues, "[i]n premodern societies, space and place largely coincided, since the spatial dimensions of social life are, for most of the population ... dominated by 'presence' – by localised activity." As Conway (2008) notes, 'local' implies a proximity, a sense of everyday life more easily embodied and understood, however any 'local' is in reality constituted by numerous processes and practices occurring across multiple scales. This then requires us to view places, as open and porous, as unfixed, contested, and multiple (Massey, 2013).

As we noted earlier, the default for places and spaces is male. We are therefore interested in how women adapt themselves to places, and contest spaces, that were not designed for them, and that in many ways accommodate them only as 'special cases' which deviate from the norm read 'male' (Duncan, 1996: 3). As Staeheli et al. argue, "The experience of women as women, and men as men, in all its multiplicity and variety, exists in social space in the real world" (2004: 228). So how do women's and men's experience of place differ? Gilbert (1998) notes that women's sense of place can be more limited, that women's daily activities often occur in a more spatially limited way then men's, and that this can be attributed to the patriarchal system which influences the built environment to instigate the separation of public and private spheres (Wajcman, 1991). This gendered separation can be seen in the historical division between home and workplace, and even in the ways in which our homes have been constructed to create these separate environments (Flanagan, 2018). The influence of this environment can be both direct and indirect in the ways it limits both the options women have, and the choices women make. Going further, however, Gilbert (1998) also highlights the ways in which spatial boundedness can have a positive effect for women, in terms of their ability to create 'place-based' personal networks to help ensure their health, safety, and security, as well as that of their families. As Katz and Monk argue,

> the inverse of mobility is not always immobility; there are positive polarities as well. For example, rootedness offers many women personal satisfactions and rewards, as well as the possibilities for social life and the sharing of burdens in productive and reproductive spheres.
>
> (1993: 271)

To understand women's experiences of place, it is therefore necessary to avoid separating the sites, scales, and spheres of activity into political and non-political, to avoid simplifying dualisms such as public/private, and to move towards a more complex understanding of how political action can take many forms (Fincher, 2004). Building on Staeheli et al. (2004: 6, see also Cope, 2004) we view the political as "a struggle for inclusion in a wide range of settings, acts, perspectives, and embodied experience" rather than being "tethered to particular sites or institutions." This requires, as Staeheli et al. (2004: 3) outline, understanding the political across three overlapping approaches. First, politics as distribution, including access to power, resources, privilege, and the determination of who gets what. Second, politics as antagonism, including processes of interest formation, coalition building and place making, in other words the shape of political struggle. Third, and finally, politics as constitutive, meaning the political as an ongoing process in which societies are made, through struggle, including the formal spaces of state, space of home, the recognition of personhood, and debates about what this means for how society functions in a just and democratic manner.

For our purposes, the most important pieces of this understanding are the notions of place making (antagonism), the determination of access (distribution), and the recognition of personhood. Place making in societies today is complexified by the influence of globalization – as Massey (1995: 212) argues:

> Places are constantly being produced through social relations and practices, which are inherently dynamic and conflictual. Especially under conditions of globalization, places can no longer be conceived of as pre-given or bounded locals. Places are being constituted in significant ways by forces and conditions arising beyond the place, including the globalization of production, trade, and finance, international migration, environmental crises, and transnational social movements.

These external factors therefore influence the ways in which women's perceptions of their interests are formed, and the ways in which women are able to build coalitions across borders. These factors also influence the distribution of power and influence within societies, by determining who has access to resources, and by continuing to build upon the colonial, patriarchal, power systems which determine privilege based on both whiteness and maleness. The inbuilt inequalities in the global system today also serve to limit whose personhood is fully recognized and protected.

As Massey (2013: 5) notes:

> Since the late 1980s the world has seen the resurgence of exclusivist claims to places – nationalist, regionalist and localist. All of them have been attempts to fix the meaning of particular spaces, to enclose them, endow them with fixed identities and to claim them for one's own.

This can be tied to what Kobayashi (1997) terms differencing, which involves complex sociospatial processes designed to empower some, and marginalize and oppress others, based on the differences they embody. For women, this is particularly dangerous given that, as Chouinard (2001) notes, "[a]s women ... we are caught up in relationships to state power through multiple identities, roles, and embodiments of differences such as class and race." Even more so when we put this idea in conversation with Anderson's (2000) understanding of nation building as a sociospatial process of putting differenced citizens, whether by gender, race, class, ableness, etc. into relatively more and less empowered places. In this case, legal rights, and the recognition of women's legal rights, is not sufficient to transform the gendered power systems, because as Brown (2000) argues, "they do not eliminate the dominant gender regime, its mechanisms of production, or even male dominance." As Lorber (1994) notes, we also need to monitor how the granting of new rights to women based on their gender only serves to mark 'women' as a distinct or different group, further reinforcing the idea that because men and women are fundamentally different, the subordination of women is somehow predetermined or natural.

Rather than relying on an outdated understanding of citizenship which relies solely on access to legal rights, what we need is a feminist reformulation of citizenship, one which relies on both official political status (rights) and the practice of citizenship (participation) (Lister, 1997). We need to recognize a more relational model of citizenship, that explores more deeply the changing geography of citizenship, and the multiplicity of ways in which the global and the local interact to shape how we understand our place in the world (Martin, 2004). This requires a recognition that "political identities are gendered but in diverse, embodied, and spatially uneven ways" which allows us to focus "attention on people's diverse locations within relations and practices of citizenship" (Chouinard, 2001). We need to open up women's access to political space, and explore further how space, place, and gender interrelate. As Massey (2013: 2) argues:

> space, place and gender are interrelated: that is, in their very construction as culturally specific ideas – in terms both of the conceptual nature of that construction and of its substantive content – and in the overlapping and interplaying of the sets of characteristics and connotations with which each is associated. Particular ways of thinking about space and place are tied up with, both directly and indirectly, particular social constructions of gender relations.

In the following section we will explore this interrelation from the perspective of space, and the ways in which women can both reclaim space, shape space, and remove restrictions to their access to space.

Space, Reclaiming, Unrestricting

In the following section we again utilize the work of Massey (2013: 3), and her argument that we think of space, not as an absolute, an independent dimension, but instead as constructed out of social relations. This requires a recognition of what Massey (1994: 156) terms "power geometry" because "[a]s a result of the fact that it is ... created out of social relations, space is by its very nature full of power and symbolism, a complex web of relations of domination and subordination, of solidarity and cooperations." For women, their power geometry is limited, based on both identity and space, for Massey (2013: 179) this is most clearly identifiable in the west, with the specific distinction between public and private spheres, and the attempts to confine women to the domestic sphere as a both "a specifically spatial control, and through that, a social control on identity." This builds on our earlier exploration of the social and spatial differences experienced by subjects of the state, particularly those whose claim to legal rights of citizenship and other associated benefits are tenuous (Chouinard, 2004). For women in particular there is a continuous and pervasive gap between "the rights and frameworks that exist on paper and the reality of many women's daily lives" (Berry, 2017: 833).

Women have been limited in their ability to move between spaces, the restriction of women's mobility, as Massey (2013: 179) notes, has been in some cultural context as crucial means of ensuring their subordination. This subordination has been dependent on limitations on both identity and space, and as she goes on to argue "the two things – the limitation on mobility in space, the attempted consignment/confinement to particular places on the one hand, and the limitation on identity on the other – have been crucially related" (Massey, 2013: 179). This is why feminist movements have focused on breaking down the dichotomies between the public and private spheres, and between formal and informal politics. As Cope (2004: 73) argues:

> because women often are constrained from participating fully in formal political structures (voting, holding office) and are often limited in their access to public spaces, it is important to acknowledge many different actions that are constituted as political and the diverse locational contexts in which they occur.

Further, Staeheli (1996) also argues that the content of political actions should be separated from the space in which they are performed, allowing for the efficacy of an action to be disconnected from determinations of success bounded by the public sphere. This then allows for examination of the ways in which women actively create new and different spaces for political action (Cope, 2004). It also allows for challenges to the notion that the private sphere, or the home, is restricted to and dominated by particular concerns that do not translate to the universal (Alcoff, 1996). Throughout the history of feminist movements, women's activism has relied on the reclamation and redefinition of public spaces (Enke, 2003).

Women's collective and political action also more often occurs outside of the formal political sphere, and tends to be in more fluid and diffuse organizations (Ferree, 1992; Taylor, 1999; Tilly, 1981). What is also interesting to note is the ways in which these less formal organizations, and newly created spaces, also "took shape around privileges and exclusions of race, class, parental status, age, etc., and thus even women's spaces could never be just about gender or women as a pre-existent, unified group" (Enke, 2003: 638). As hooks (1989: 18) asks, do women share a common vision of what equality means? And how does this determine the ways in which spaces for women are created and maintained?

As Berry (2015: 5) argues:

> While oppression is pervasive across all of these divisions, the construction of women as a single entity assumes that the powerlessness and subjugation of all classes of women is rooted in the same structures. This creates a simplistic understanding of women as oppressed, which fails to see that some women are situated at the intersection of several oppressions at once.

This can then lead to, as Berry (2017) argues, the fracturing of women's organizing which limits the prospects for inclusive or intersectional emancipation. The space for solidarity is limited.

This brings us back to Haraway's (1988) argument for situated and partial knowledge. For Haraway, situated knowledge does not mean relativism but shared conversations leading to "better accounts of the world" (Haraway, 1988: 580). As Nielsen (1990: 26) argues, feminist inquiry is a dialectical process which requires listening to women and understanding how the subjective meaning they attach to their lived experiences is so often at variance with meanings internalized from society at large. What we therefore need to do is open up the space for these conversations to happen, as Watson and Heath (2004) argue, we have to think about how we grow up the space in which we talk to each other. This requires a recognition of the inherent power inequalities between different women, and a recognition that holding a conversation with

> someone that you wield power over is always going to be a partial conversation. ... There's only so much of a conversation that someone you're oppressing wants to have with you. No matter your individual goodwill, your participation in that larger structure of power prejudices the capacity for the conversation to mean much or to go anywhere.
> (Watson and Heath, 2004: 109)

Instead, as Tickner (1997: 626) argues, we need to be sensitive to the history and context in which our conversations take place, and we must seek understanding "through dialogues across boundaries and cultures in which the voices of others, particularly those on the margins, must be seen as equally valid as one's own." To be successful in this endeavor we need to recognize the interrelations in the ways our space is constructed (Massey, 2013). Each of us is involved in our own individual "enterprise of negotiating a space from which to speak and in which to live" (Kinser, 2004: 139) and we need to be hyper aware of the ways in which our individual gains may come at the expense of another's. As Berry (2017: 849) argues, "women's gains are not a linear, uniform process, but should be better understood as a simultaneous process of progress and slippage, where empowerment frameworks can aggravate divides between women." Recognizing these divides, and how the privilege of access to certain spaces can be used to further divide women, is a primary tool for highlighting the insidious ways in which the patriarchal system utilizes difference, be it cultural, social, political, or other to keep us divided and perpetuate its own survival. As Reinharz (1992: 248) argues, our job is opening up the space to make the invisible visible, to bring the margins in to the center, to transform the trivial to important and to put "the spotlight on women as competent actors, as subjects in their own right rather than objects for men." Opening up space for progress will also take time, and time is the third concept which we will move to examine now.

Time, Control, Context

We return here for a moment to Massey's concept of power geometry, to examine in more detail "what is it that determines our degrees of mobility, that influences the sense we have of space and place?" For Massey, time-space compression, as associated with the impacts of globalization, "refers to movement and communication across space, to the geographical stretching-out of social relations, and to our experience of all this" (Massey, 2013: 147). Here Massey wants us to recognize the differentiation in the ways individuals experience time-space compression based on their place within the complex social structures we discussed earlier. Each individual will have a different degree of movement and communication, but also a different degree of control and initiation over their ability to navigate this. As Katz (2001) argues, we need to be cognizant of the processes related to globalization and how these restructure the landscape of places, and gendered social relationships within those places.

As MacLeavy et al (2021) argue, we should be orienting ourselves utilizing a multilinear and multidimensional model of time. Rather than viewing time as linear, and the progress toward women's equality as one-directional, this instead allows us to recognize and highlight the differentiated experiences, and the existence of continuity and discontinuity in practices over time. We can look to history for examples of how women's experiences have been altered by global events, how progress has been made and then revoked. As Litoff and Smith (1994) explain, women's identities and political and geographic horizons were altered during World War II when women, many for the first time, were employed in traditionally male roles. Financial independence gave women more control, more choice, over how to spend their time. But following the end of the war and the return of the men much of this progress was lost. As Berry (2017) argues, "[w]hile devastating, war is also a period of rapid social change that can disrupt gender norms and create space for women's increased participation in public, political life" (see Berry, 2018; Hughes, 2009; Hughes and Tripp, 2015). These moments can be found throughout history. Moments where women have appeared to make progress, only for it to diminish over time.

Globally, 75 percent of unpaid work is done by women, who spend between three and six hours per day on it compared to men's average of 30 minutes to two hours (Criado Perez, 2019). Here is a clear example of how men and women experience time differently. An example of how the ways in which spaces and places are gendered, and that even with the variation between cultures and over time, how "[w]omen's experiences continue to display both 'endless variety' as well as 'monotonous similarity' (referencing Rubin, 1975, quoted in Jays 1988: 139) across space and through time" (Martin, 2004). Women's time is limited, it is limited by the expectations of the tasks we are expected to undertake, the societal pressures we are placed under to fulfill our gendered roles.

However, if we return to the idea of time as multilinear and multi-dimensional this opens up space for a more radical and interesting approach. As Bastian (2011: 164) argues, "dislocating space and disjointed time enable multiple histories, loyalties and modes of acting to exist simultaneously" and allows us to remove the constraints on feminist progress, action, and scholarship, currently confined to particular spaces and moments, which only limits its capacity to transform alongside other discourses, knowledges, and practices. Instead, if we open up our understanding of time, this allows us to "position feminist theory and politics not as a static or singular movement or project but as that which has the vitality to animate social change through open-ended invention and the desire to bring a different future into existence" (MacLeavy et al, 2021: 1573). This also enables us to recognize the culturally and historically specific forms which inequalities between the sexes take, and how the variation in how these inequalities are inflicted and shaped by their interaction with class and race (MacKinnon, 2017: 305). As Olufemi (2020: 21) powerfully argues, "[i]t is our job as feminists to rediscover the histories that have been purposefully withheld from us because it is the voices that speak to us from the past that help shape our vision for the future."

Bringing Place, Space, and Time Together

Throughout this chapter we have explored how complex gendered power relations intersect with the concepts of space, place, and time, and how these interactions either reduce or increase the barriers to women's agency. As we have demonstrated, women face a daily battle to navigate spaces that default male. Altering this reality requires changing the ways in which politics is both conceptualized and spatialized. Despite the progress that has been made, the artificial divides between the public and the private spheres are still enforced in many ways. It is also clear that simply adding more women to institutional structures and systems, designed for and by men, is not having the impact required to truly alter the inequalities between the genders. As Criado Perez (2019: 23) argues:

Whiteness and maleness are silent precisely because they do not need to be vocalised. Whiteness and maleness are implicit. They are unquestioned. They are the default. And this reality is inescapable for anyone whose identity does not go without saying, for anyone whose needs and perspective are routinely forgotten. For anyone who is used to jarring up against a world that has not been designed around them and their needs.

What is required is a new approach to how we understand the lived embodied experiences of women. We need to open up space for difficult conversation, to recognize that the path to progress is not the same for everyone. As Olufemi (2020: 71) argues: "If feminism means freedom, it means the right to self-determination and the right to be multi-dimensional, disorganised and even incoherent." We need to recognize the importance of solidarity, and solidarity across differences, for true progress to be made. We cannot rely on outdated and static approaches to changing the current systems and institutions. Instead we need to imagine alternatives, alternative spaces, alternative places, and alternative times.

References

Alcoff, L.M. 1996. Feminist theory and social science: New knowledges, new epistemologies. In *BodySpace: Destabilizing geographies of gender and sexuality*, edited by N. Duncan, pp. 13–27. London: Psychology Press.

Anderson, Kay. 2000. Thinking "post-nationally": Dialogue across multicultural, indigenous, and settler spaces. *Annals of the Association of American Geographers* 90: 381–391.

Bastian, M. 2011. The contradictory simultaneity of being with others: Exploring concepts of time and community in the work of Gloria Anzaldua. *Feminist Review* 97(1): 151–167.

Benhabib, Seyla. 1998. Models of public space: Hannah Arendt, the liberal tradition, and Jürgen Habermas. In *Feminism: The public and the private*, edited by Joan B. Landes. Oxford and New York: Oxford University Press.

Berry, M.E. 2015. When "bright futures" fade: Paradoxes of women's empowerment in Rwanda. *Signs: Journal of Women in Culture and Society* 41(1): 1–27.

Berry, M.E. 2017. Barriers to women's progress after atrocity: Evidence from Rwanda and Bosnia-Herzegovina. *Gender & Society* 31(6): 830–853.

Berry, M.E. 2018. *War, women, and power: From violence to mobilization in Rwanda and Bosnia-Herzegovina*. New York: Cambridge University Press. Brown, Wendy. 2000. Suffering rights as paradoxes. *Constellations* 7(2): 208–229.

Chouinard, V. 2001. Legal peripheries: Struggles over disabled Canadians' places in law, society and space. *Canadian Geographer* 45: 187–192.

Chouinard, V. 2004. Making feminist sense of the state and citizenship. In *Mapping women, making politics: Feminist perspectives on political geography*, edited by Lynn A. Staeheli, Eleonore Kofman, and Linda Peake. New York: Routledge.

Cohn, C. 1993. Wars, wimps, and women: Talking gender and thinking war. In *Gendering war talk*, edited by M. Cooke and A. Wollacott, pp. 227–246. Princeton: Princeton University Press.

Conway, J. 2008. Geographies of transnational feminisms: The politics of place and scale in the world march of women. *Social Politics* 15(2): 207–231.

Cope, M. 1996. Weaving the everyday: Identity, space, and power in Lawrence, Massachusetts, 1920–1939. *Urban Geography* 17: 179–204.

Cope, M. 2004. Placing gendered political acts. In *Mapping women, making politics*, pp. 74–89. New York: Routledge.

Criado Perez, C. 2019. *Invisible women: Data bias in a world designed for men*. New York: Abrams Press.

Davidoff, L. 1998. Regarding some "old husbands' tales": Public and private in feminist history. In *Feminism, the public and the private*, edited by Joan B. Landes. Oxford and New York: Oxford University Press.

Duncan, N. ed. 1996. *BodySpace: Destabilising geographies of gender and sexuality*. London: Routledge.

Enke, A. 2003. Smuggling sex through the gates: Race, sexuality, and the politics of space in second wave feminism. *American Quarterly* 55(4): 635–667.

Ferree, Myra Marx. 1992. The political context of rationality: Rational choice theory and resource mobilization. In *Frontiers in social movement theory*, edited by Aldon Morris and Carol McClurg Mueller, pp. 29–52. New Haven, CT: Yale University Press.

Fincher, R. 2004. From dualisms to multiplicities: Gendered political practices. In *Mapping women, making politics*, pp. 49–69. New York: Routledge.

Flanagan, M.A. 2018. *Constructing the patriarchal city: Gender and the built environments of London, Dublin, Toronto, and Chicago, 1870s into the 1940s*. Philadelphia: Temple University Press.

Flax, J. 1987. Postmodernism and gender relations in feminist theory. *Signs: Journal of Women in Culture and Society* 12(4): 621–643.

Folbre, N. 1994. *Who pays for the kids? Gender and the structures of constraint*. London: Routledge.

Giddens, A. 1990. *The consequences of modernity*. Cambridge: Polity.

Gilbert, M.R. 1998. "Race," space, and power: The survival strategies of working poor women. *Annals of the Association of American Geographers* 88(4): 595–562.

Hanmer, L. and Klugman, J. 2016. Exploring women's agency and empowerment in developing countries: Where do we stand?. *Feminist Economics* 22(1): 237–263.

Haraway, D. 1988. Situated knowledges: The science question in feminism and the privilege of partial perspective. *Feminist Studies* 14: 575–599.

Harding, S. 1986. *The science question in feminism*. Ithaca, NY: Cornell University Press.

hooks, bell. 1989. *Talking back: Thinking feminist, thinking black*. Boston: South End.

Hughes, Melanie. 2009. Armed conflict, international linkages, and women's parliamentary representation in developing nations. *Social Problems* 56(1): 174–204.

Hughes, Melanie and Tripp, A.M. 2015. Civil war and trajectories of change in women's political representation in Africa, 1985–2010. *Social Forces* 93(4): 1513–1540.

Hyndman, J. 2004. Mind the gap: Bridging feminist and political geography through geopolitics. *Political Geography* 23(3): 307–322.

Kabeer, Naila. 1999. Resources, agency, achievements: Reflections on the measurement of women's empowerment. *Development & Change* 30(3): 435–464.

Katz, C. 2001. On the grounds of globalization: A topography for feminist political engagement. *Signs: Journal of Women in Culture and Society* 26(4): 1213–1234.

Katz, C. and Monk, J. 1993. Making connections: Space, place and the life course. In *Full circles: Geographies of women over the life course*, edited by C. Katz and J. Monk, pp. 264–278. London: Routledge.

Keller, E.F. 1985. *Reflections on gender and science*. New Haven, CT: Yale University Press.

Kinser, A.E. 2004. Negotiating spaces for/through third-wave feminism. *NWSA Journal*: 124–153.

Kobayashi, A. 1997. The paradox of difference and diversity (or, why the thresholds keep moving). In *Thresholds in feminist geography, difference, methodology, representation*, edited by J.P. Jones, H. Nast, and S. Roberts. Lanham, MD: Rowman & Littlefield.

Lister, R. 1997. Citizenship: Towards a feminist synthesis. *Feminist Review* 57(1): 28–48.

Litoff, J.B. and Smith, D.C. 1994. Gender, war, and imagined geographies: United States women and the "far flung" fronts of World War II. In *Writing women and space: Colonial and postcolonial geographies*, edited by Alison Blunt and Gillian Rose. New York and London: Guilford.

Lorber, Judith. 1994. *Paradoxes of gender*. New Haven, CT: Yale University Press.

MacLeavy, J., Fannin, M. and Larner, W. 2021. Feminism and futurity: Geographies of resistance, resilience and reworking. *Progress in Human Geography* 45(6): 1558–1579.

MacKinnon, C.A. 2017. Butterfly politics. In *Butterfly politics*. Cambridge, MA: Harvard University Press.

Martin, P.M. 2004. Contextualizing feminist political theory. In *Mapping women, making politics*, pp. 20–34. New York: Routledge.

Massey, D. 1994. *Space, place and gender*. Cambridge: Polity Press.

Massey, D. 1995. Places and their pasts. *History Workshop Journal* 39: 182–192.

Massey, D. 2013. *Space, place and gender*. John Wiley & Sons. Meyers, D.T. 2002. *Gender in the mirror: Cultural imagery and women's agency*. Oxford University Press on Demand.

Narayan, U. 2018. Minds of their own: Choices, autonomy, cultural practices, and other women. In *A mind of one's own*, pp. 418–432. London: Routledge.

Nielsen, J.M. ed. 1990. *Feminist research methods: Exemplary readings in the social sciences*. Boulder, CO: Westview Press.

Olufemi, L. 2020. *Feminism, interrupted: Disrupting power*. London: Pluto Press.

Pateman, Carole. 1989. *The disorder of women, democracy, feminism and political theory*. Stanford: Stanford University Press.

Peterson, V.S. 1992. Transgressing boundaries: Theories of knowledge, gender and international relations. *Millennium* 21(2): 183–206.

Reinharz, S. 1992. *Feminist methods in social research*. New York: Oxford University Press.

Scott, J. 1986. Gender: A useful category of historical analysis. *American Historical Review* 91: 1053–1075.

Staeheli, L. 1996. Publicity, privacy, and women's political action. *Environment and Planning D: Society and Space* 14: 601–619.

Staeheli, L., Kofman, E. and Peake, L. 2004. *Mapping women, making politics: Feminist perspectives on political geography*. London: Routledge.

Tannen, D. 1990. *You just don't understand: Women and men in conversation*. New York: William Morrow.

Taylor, Verta. 1999. Gender and social movements: Gender processes in women's self-help movements. *Gender & Society* 13(1): 8–33.

Tickner, J.A. 1997. You just don't understand: Troubled engagements between feminists and IR theorists. *International Studies Quarterly* 41(4): 611–632.
Tickner, J.A. 2005. What is your research program? Some feminist answers to international relations methodological questions. *International Studies Quarterly* 49(1): 1–21. Tilly, L.A. 1981. Paths of proletarianization: Organization of production, sexual division of labor, and women's collective action. *Signs* 7(2): 400–417.
Wajcman, J. 1991. The built environment: Women's place, gendered space. In *Women, science, and technology: A reader in feminist science studies*, edited by M. Wyer, M. Barbercheck, D. Cookmeyer, H. Ozturk and M. Wayne. London: Routledge.
Watson, I. and Heath, M. 2004. Growing up the space: A conversation about the future of feminism. *Australian Feminist Law Journal* 20(1): 95–111.
Young, Iris Marion. 1990. *Justice and the politics of difference*. Princeton, NJ: Princeton University Press.
Young, Iris Marion. 1994. Gender as seriality: Thinking about women as a social collective. *Signs* 19(3): 713–738.

8 Exploring the Power of Silence, Voice and the In-between in a Troubled World

Jane L. Parpart

Introduction

Rethinking Silence, Voice and Agency in Contested Gendered Terrains (Parpart and Parashar, 2019) explored silence, voice and agency in a complicated world. More current work is raising new concerns about silence, voice and the in-between in an ever-changing global world. This approach contests the conceptual divide between silence and voice as categories and actions, and instead focuses on how silence, voice and the in-between have worked together (and apart) around the world. The chapter draws on an increasing number of books concerned with silence and voice, including a forthcoming volume edited by Aliya Khalid, Georgina Holmes and Jane L. Parpart (2024), exploring the 'in-between' and/or liminal spaces where silence and voice interact with one another (or not) to produce unique experiences for individuals, groups and societies.

The conceptual divides between silence and voice are too often simply seen as categories and actions. Yet new approaches have begun to shift attention to exploring how silence and voice can be understood as co-constituted embodied practices and political acts, often used simultaneously by marginalized communities and individuals to counter or challenge oppressive power structures shaping people's daily lived experiences. Silence and voice are thus increasingly regarded as critical for survival in our complicated changing world, one that explores the experiences of people, who may reject or embrace silences, and/or raise their voices in an ever-changing, complicated world (Rowe and Malhotra, 2013, 1–22; Murray and Durrheim, 2019, 1–20; Achino-Loeb, 2006a).

At the same time, in this liminal in-between space, we find ourselves disconnected from silence and voice as major categories of difference, and instead focus on the spaces of functionality that people and institutions widely utilize. This space is thus not simply a lived relationship between two concepts. Instead it encapsulates the experiences of people, who may reject or embrace silences, or raise their voices, as well as those whose voices are muffled or severely controlled. Liminal in-between spaces enable actors (people and institutions) to utilize silence, to speak out in their

DOI: 10.4324/9781003281382-12

everyday historic, social, cultural, economic and technological contexts and to retreat, when needed, in order to rethink and develop new approaches so that voice, silence and the in-between can be explored, discussed and utilized together and apart.

The articulation of 'liminal, in-between spaces' has helped women to move away from the hegemons of power, who claim a global understanding, in order to explore the ways people's lived experiences and actions have often inspired political and social activism in an increasingly complex and changing world. This shift requires an interrogation into the way control over speech has often limited women's ability to speak out in times when women were expected to be seen and not heard. The struggle for voice has inspired a commitment to speaking out and building feminist movements, both in the early struggles for women's liberation, and during later movements surfacing around the world. These debates have inspired global perspectives and expanded women's global reach, enabling rich and important debates about the need to rethink women's positions, to encourage debates and to fuel actions aimed at exploring the relevance (or not) of silence, voice and the in-between in a turbulent gendered world. For example, the current struggles in Iran, led by women accustomed to constrained lives, are inspiring public gatherings where many women are coming together in order to listen and to speak out in public. These gatherings and expressions of determination in public and private arenas are encouraging Iranian women to speak out, and to demand change that will lead to a more gender equitable society. This is evidence of many women's and men's struggles to enable women to speak out, even in situations where they are in considerable danger. Some Iranians have been leaving the country, but many are staying to take up places in these crucial struggles (Murray and Durrheim, 2019). In fact, these struggles are emerging in many parts of the world, and are a testimony to the commitment of women (and some men) who are demanding their rights to speak and to challenge gender inequality around the world. As Fivush and Pasupathi (2019: 126–127) point out, "it is not that silence is bad and voicing is good. Rather, both operate together in ways that are important for constructing what happened in the past, as well as what that means for our present and future selves."

Personal Reflections

My own experiences have played a key role helping me to understand how silence, voice and the in-between can influence individuals caught up in complicated, often dangerous situations. My upbringing as a Quaker led me to realize the power of silence in Quaker meetings and the importance of peace. These meetings reinforced my own awareness of silence as a means, not only to influence and learn from people attending Quaker meetings, but also as important mechanisms for dealing with both silence and voice in challenging and even dangerous times. Sitting in those meetings revealed the power of silence in a room full of silent people. Reflections during periods of silence became a central mechanism for thinking about my life in deeper ways, including acknowledging the importance of silence as well as voice in Quaker meetings. In my teens, I became more reluctant to attend Quaker meetings, but later in life I have realized that reflections and silences are just as important as speaking out in public. I have gradually developed an awareness of the power of silence as well as the importance of silence, voice and peace in a turbulent world. This consciousness continues to shape much of my thinking, writing and speaking, as well as my continuing concern with the complexities and dangers of many life experiences.

But while Quaker meetings have continued to influence my life, I also began to read and listen to the writings and speeches of the women's movement. I was drawn to crucial feminist writings such as Betty Friedan's *The Feminine Mystique* (1963) and Marilyn French's marvelous book, *The Women's Room* (1977). Both highlighted the importance of women's power and voice in a world that often assumed women should be seen but rarely heard. Both books deeply influenced my thinking. At that time I had two small children and was working on my master's degree at Boston University's African Studies program. Studying the lives of African families broadened my perspective about women and families and reminded me of the importance of learning about different societies around the world. Along with my studies, I was also drawn into the feminist movement, where I discovered other women willing to join discussion groups dealing with children, marriage, careers and other important life concerns. These meetings opened my own eyes to the importance of family life as well as the writings and actions both of feminist scholars, and people concerned with issues of race and class. Indeed, my involvement in the African Studies program at Boston University inspired me to focus on the importance of African Studies and the Black Lives Matter movement. These movements aroused my interest in issues of race, gender and class and the importance of thinking about how these factors have interacted in a world that has too often ignored such matters. This included two years of research into the conditions for black laborers working on the Zambian Copperbelt. Accompanied by my two daughters, these years were a key period of my life, helping me to see the importance of gender relations and cultural differences around the world, including in Zambia and Africa as a whole, and the need to understand gender relations from a global perspective. This research led to my first book, *Labor and Capital on the African Copperbelt* (1983), and inspired further work focusing on women, gender and labor in the global North and South. These concerns have continued to shape my life.

Rethinking Gender, Silence and Voice in a Changing World

I began to think about the historic struggles to protect and strengthen women's voices, especially the use of public voices in Europe and the Americas. The fight for women's right to vote was enormously important, with roots in the 1800s. For example, the Grimke sisters, Sarah Moore Grimke

(1792–1873) and Angelina Grimke (1805–1879), took up the challenge of women's rights to speak out in public. The sisters grew up in a slave-owning family in South Carolina, where they became deeply upset by the many injustices on their parents' slave plantation. In their twenties they moved to Philadelphia and joined its substantial Quaker community. They joined the abolitionist movement, spoke out strongly against slave labor that they had experienced on their family's plantation and elsewhere. The sisters became key actors in social reform movements, giving talks in Philadelphia as well as in other key cities, such as Boston, Massachusetts. While no doubt upsetting many people with their talks about the injustices on slave plantations, their speeches were welcomed by the more educated women in Philadelphia and the Boston area, who continued to discuss among themselves the possibilities for the future of women and girls and the importance of women gaining the right to vote (Birney, 1885; Lerner, 1967, 1971). The gradual pressures to assert women's rights, no matter their education or color, began to take shape. This was a long struggle, with white women in the United States finally gaining the right to vote in 1920. This vote was an important achievement, but it ignored the rights of black and brown women, who continued to struggle for their rights to vote and to full citizenship in America. While some managed to vote, most had to wait for all women to be able to vote, no matter what their color. This important struggle influenced women of color in the United States, who became key players in the fight for women's rights to vote, to speak out and to take up action to protect the rights of women of all races and cultures in the United States (Jones, 2020). Indeed, these struggles continue to this day.

From the 1970s, a focus on global development inspired my interest in economic opportunities around the world. This literature too often assumed that women were the same everywhere and that women's development was similar around the world. Many of the large international projects for women aimed to bring Northern assumptions about gender and development goals to women in the global South. These projects often simply added women to the more masculine assumptions embedded in development practices around the world. Indeed, some development projects based in Europe assumed that women and girls could be important development advocates. For example, I attended a meeting in London in 2011, supported by the British government and a number of key development agencies. The discussions focused on developing stronger gender and development programs and the possibilities for improving these programs around the world. I was particularly interested in a research project for girls who had been given some small calves, with the goal of raising them well and encouraging breeding that would lead to more calves and cattle. This 'girl effect' was celebrated as a big success by development agencies in the global North. While encouraging, this case reminded me that while development projects in the global South have often grown in strength, women in the South have too often been seen as dependent partners who helped Southern males gain social and economic significance, but did not play key roles in the projects (Parpart, 2015, 14–23). Indeed, the goals for women in development have remained largely focused on global issues that too often focus on women's struggles in the global North, with limited attention to the roles of global masculinity and gendered power relations in patriarchal contexts around the world (Desai and Potter, 2014).

Positionality: A Global Perspective

The move toward a broader, more inclusive, approach has inspired a global perspective that has been (and is) increasingly attentive to historical and cultural differences around the world. This approach reminds me that gender relations and practices cannot simply be read off liberal and neoliberal assumptions from the West. A broader understanding of cultural and historic differences among peoples around the world has highlighted the need to accept differences as well as similarities in our increasingly complicated world. The push for a more inclusive approach allows for more detail understanding of the differences in people's positions, reminding us that understanding cultural and historic differences requires insightful and thoughtful interpretations of historical as well as current contexts. This global approach is also embedded in economic, cultural and political institutions that encourage multiple ways of presenting, understanding and evolving new ways of interpreting 'proper' gendered behavior and assumptions (Coles et al., 2015).

Indeed, a global perspective highlights the way cultural, economic and political factors are shaping our increasingly interconnected world. This shift has opened discussions about the importance of exploring gender equality (and inequality) in particular life worlds. These discussions, and silences, reveal the complexity of global cultures, practices and actions, reminding us that different worldviews and experiences affect the way peoples and cultures understand themselves and their position(s) in an ever-changing world. For example, interpretations of indigenous cultures and moral traditions have figured prominently in human rights discourses in and about Africa. Bonny Ibhawoh, a Nigerian scholar based in Canada, has written extensively on human rights history on the African continent. He calls for a counter-hegemonic approach to human rights history that focuses on the struggles for rights inclusion in Africa and elsewhere. At the same time, he points out that the exclusion of LGBTQ minority rights has often resulted in severe discrimination. These exclusionary boundaries have been particularly present in Africa (Ibhawoh, 2018). Megan Mackenzie has analyzed the challenges and triumphs of female soldiers in Sierra Leone, reflecting the growing interest in women soldiers around the continent. She highlights female soldiers as a reflection of a growing trend (Mackenzie, 2012). At the same time, these limitations and potential dangers also continue to plague persons concerned with global inequality, around the world and within particular contexts (Rowe and Malhotra, 2013). Clearly a broad interest in gender and conflict is critically important for scholars, policy makers, soldiers and civilians around the world.

For example, Wendy Urban-Mead's excellent book, *The Gender of Piety* (2015), has brought the Pietist Movement in Zimbabwe into the discussion of religion in that country. Pietism was a religious movement that originated in Germany in the 17th century, entitled the Brethren in Christ Church (BICC). The church spread across much of the United States in the 19th century, and began to move into Africa. The BICC sent its first overseas missionaries to Southern Rhodesia in 1898. Situated in the southern region of Zimbabwe, dominated by the Matabele (originally from the Zulu people of South Africa), the missionaries soon discovered considerable differences between Matabele male and female church members. Men born into the church tended to focus their interest on the more male-dominated political and economic institutions in their earlier years, later shifting to greater involvement in the BICC. In contrast, women members generally regarded the church as liberating from an early stage, especially with its emphasis on education and monogamy. Thus the church was deeply important for women church members throughout their daily lives. However, many more senior men also came to play important active roles in the church as they matured. By 2013 the BICC had over 30,000 members in more than 300 churches in the Bulawayo area, demonstrating the importance of the BICC in the region. Indeed, the church continues to play a critical role in the region today.

Other studies reveal the power of silence, voice and the in-between around the world. For example, Keith Basso (1970), a brilliant anthropologist who lived with and studied the Apache peoples in the American southwest for many years, discovered a complicated series of expectations about the use of voice and silence. He realized that both often depended on people's relationships, as well as the relevance of various 'traditions' requiring silence, and/or voice, or a mixture of both. In 1970 Basso's article, "'To Give up on Words': Silence in Western Apache Culture," argued that silence among the Western Apache is a response to uncertainty and unpredictability in social relations. This approach enabled Basso to explore the way Apache people deliberately speak or remain silent. He concluded that silence in Western Apache culture has often been associated with social situations where relative strangers can begin to know each other better. Drawing on both Navajo and Apache practices, Basso discovered that courting between girls and boys generally goes slowly, and often utilizes both silence and voice, depending on circumstances. These practices can lead to engagements between couples. In his 1996 book, *Wisdom Sits in Places: Landscape and Language,* Basso continued to emphasize the importance of wisdom, manners and morals as integral practices in Western Apache culture.

Saba Mahmood's *Politics of Piety* (2005) has raised important questions about the silence/voice dichotomy associated with the liberal and neoliberal global North. This literature has celebrated speaking out against patriarchy, supporting feminist voices willing to challenge patriarchy in open debate and to voice discontent about masculine power. In contrast, Mahmood decided to study the Pietist Movement in Egypt. She discovered that the women involved in the Pietist Movement often chose submission to rules and self-discipline within largely patriarchal structures. At the same time, she began to see that women in the movement also sought, and often achieved, respect, theoretical knowledge and embodied power, through attention to religious practices, modesty and silences as well as voice in an essentially patriarchal institution. Her study requires new ways of thinking about gender, voice, silence and power. Voice comes into question as a dominant liberating force, demonstrating the need to draw on silence as well as voice in order to explore gendered relations and practices in a complicated world. Thus, Mahmood challenges the idea that voice is always a liberating force and silence equals weakness. Interestingly, Eviatar Zerubavel (2019, 67) reminds readers that listening to the sounds of silence is a crucial method for studying the unsaid. Indeed, he argues that people need the ability to 'see' the conventionally invisible and 'hear' the conventionally inaudible in a confusing world.

Aliya Khalid (2022) has highlighted Pakistani women's ability to use both silence and voice for achieving family education goals. These complicated goals often require intense effort in challenging circumstances, but they also reveal the ability of Pakistani women to wield power in an often sexist world. Khalid focuses on the experiences of mothers determined to support their daughters' education in often hostile environments. Many women have had to struggle to get opportunities for a good education, both for themselves and for their children. Mothers play a serious role in this effort. Drawing on both silence and voice (alone or together), Khalid points out the strategic use of silence as well as voice in unstable situations, and reminds readers that these strategies are profoundly important for women seeking voice in an unstable world, whether for themselves or for their children.

In Southern Africa, especially South Africa, resistance to human mobility is high. Cross-border women who sell sex for survival cannot be understood simply as migrants. In most cases the women, labeled as victims of trafficking, often reflected the insecurity and vulnerability encountered every day. But they also have to deal with legislation that is aimed at supervising and controlling sex workers on the streets or in brothels. This situation continues to undermine the potential for effective supervision of sex work and the possibilities that sex workers could live healthy lives and gradually integrate into South African society (Walker and Galvin, 2019). Many other cases are being discovered around the world. Sachseder (2022) has explored violence against women in Colombia, South America. Her study highlights the impact of violence against women and the terrible experiences so often endured by women in an unstable country. These are just a few examples of the enormous literature highlighting the difficulties faced by women in our complicated, ever-changing world.

Rethinking Silence, Voice and the In-between in a Postcolonial World

Silence is often seen as disempowerment, but, as we have seen, it can also be powerful. Silence can be a coping mechanism for enabling reflection, healing and rethinking one's position. At the same time, silence and voice can work together to strategize, organize resistance and encourage healing in complicated postcolonial contexts. As Glenn (2004, 52) acknowledges, "speech and silence depend upon one another: behind all speech is silence and silence surrounds all speech." This complexity has highlighted the importance of creating in-between spaces, where silence and voice can work together and/or apart as suits various contexts. These in-between spaces often provide safe spaces for reflection, healing and rethinking one's position. They enable silence and voice to work together, or apart, in order to strategize, organize resistance, and encourage healing in a complicated postcolonial world. They also provide ways to rethink the connections and differences between silence and voice, and the importance of developing new ways of bringing these practices together, and sometimes apart (Clair, 1998, 2013).

Rethinking silence, voice and the in-between is a complex and challenging process. I have highlighted the power of silence, both individually and collectively, recognizing that there are many aspects of silence that need to be explored (Parpart and Parashar, 2019). At the same time, I have come to realise that voice and silence can work together (and apart). They can be affected by in-between spaces that provide sites for reflection and thought about how to deal with current challenges and how to move forward. Collective silences can also be very powerful, especially when bringing large numbers of people together. For example, Patricia Collins has described the way African women have often used silence to consolidate internal resources and to strategize ways to deal with the confines of race, class and gender oppressions (Collins, 1991). Audrey Lorde (1984a, 1984b), a black lesbian poet, wrote brilliant essays as she struggled with cancer. She died in 1993, but her work continues to influence scholars, activists and supporters who have recognized that silence and voice can work together (and apart) to strategize, organize resistance and encourage healing in a complicated world.

While voice can be powerful, both individually and collectively, it is also important to recognize the power of collective silence. For example during the harsh days of the Argentine dictatorship, the Argentinian Madres of the Plaza de Mayo (mothers of the disappeared) came together in front of government buildings in the capital. They came together in silence, holding hands as they circled the center, thinking quietly of the horrors that have been placed on their children (and themselves). They wore diapers on their heads to remind the government of the terrible killings of their children, young men and women who were challenging the brutal behavior of government officials. The repeated meetings reinforced the mothers' grim determination to continue challenging the ruthless government and highlighted the terrible costs for the mothers coming together to reinforce the importance of women's collective empowerment in a dangerous situation (Cockburn, 2007, 51). The South African women's Black Sash movement has also celebrated gatherings where silence and vigils brought women together seeking solace and demanding a better world (Cockburn, 2007, 51).

The Women in Black movement has also had a long history of powerful public silences in many places around the world. I joined the movement in London's Trafalgar Square in 2006. It was an amazing experience. The power of silence spread through the crowd that had chosen to support the movement and to reinforce the importance of silence in a cruel world. I was soon swept up in the silence and the intense sense of community and power felt by the crowd. I learned a great deal just standing together, watching and feeling the power of collective support. Cynthia Cockburn wrote about her experience of silence in the Square. She discovered that

> [t]here is something calming about vigiling, holding yourself in silence and stillness as city workers and tourists mill around you, and the taxis and buses stream past. ... What restores me as I stand there once again is the presence of other women at my shoulders ... the carefully thought-out message we are trying to put across and feeling hundreds of similar events are occurring around the world.
> (Cockburn, 2007, 51)

Indeed, Cockburn has described other meetings of the Women in Black movement around the world (2007, 53).

Silence and voice are often intertwined as well. Anita Hill is a good example of the importance of using both words and silence in order to raise questions about patriarchal power. Hill, who is an established lawyer, attended the meeting for assessing Clarence Thomas' suitability as a future Supreme Court justice. She raised some questions about his behavior, pointing out that during her two years as his assistant she had been forced repeatedly to resist his sexual advances. Her description of this behavior and her discomfort with his sexual advances reveal the challenges often faced by women working in powerful institutions with powerful males often in charge. This case reminds us that women, and less powerful men, often choose both words and silences in order to deal with patriarchal power. Silence as well as voice can raise questions about both the power of silence and the potential of voice, how they can or cannot work together, and their centrality for dealing with complicated worlds.

Conclusion

This exploration of silence, voice and the in-between has concluded that gendered power is not linked solely to voice. Silence, as well as voice, can be powerful. Indeed, silence is more powerful, complex and communicative than we have assumed. Taking a global perspective, understanding silence, voice and the in-between requires considerable investigation. Voice as a form of power has always been regarded as the clearest form of communication, one where words can be said and shared with others. However, when silence also becomes a form of communication, it is no longer possible to assume that voice is power and silence is disempowerment. Yet when these different approaches to life utilize voice, silence and the in-between, a broader picture begins to emerge. Silence can begin to be understood as an essential element of communication and agency (Murray and Durrheim, 2019; Fivush and Pasupathi, 2019, 129). Silence can be a form of power, one that constrains tendencies to speak out in unstable situations, and often provides a basis for internal reflection and strategizing that might encourage new ways of thinking and acting. At the same time, voice also has power that can be exerted on many levels. 'Listening to the Sound of Silence' reminds us that interactions between silence, voice and various in-betweens raises questions about the possibilities of silence, voice and the in-between in a changing, evolving world (Zerubavel, 2019, 59). These interactions and possibilities set the stage for deeper explorations of silence, voice and the in-between as a reminder that the world we are living in provides many, and growing, alternatives in a changing world.

References

Achino-Loeb, M. L. 2006a. Silence as the Currency of Power. In M. L. Achino-Loeb (Ed.), *Silence: The Currency of Power*. New York: Berghahn Books, 1–22.

Basso, Keith. 1970. To Give up on Words: Silence in Western Apache Culture. *Southwestern Journal of Anthropology*, 26(3): 213–230.

Basso, Keith. 1996. *Wisdom Sits in Places: Landscape and Language*. New Mexico: University of Mexico Press.

Birney, Catherine H. 1885. *The Grimke Sisters: The First American Advocates of Abolition and Women's Rights*. Boston: Lee and Shepard Publishers.

Clair, Robin. 1998. *Organizing Silence: A World of Possibilities*. Albany, NY: University of New York Press.

Clair, Robin. 2013. Imposed Silence and the Story of the Warramunga Woman: Alternative Interpretations and Possibilities. In Sheena Malhotra and Aimee Carrillo Rowe (Eds.), *Silence, Feminism, Power: Reflections at the Edges of Power*. Northridge: California State University, 85–94.

Collins, Patricia. 1991. *Black Feminist Thought: Knowledge, Consciousness, and the Politics of Empowerment*. Toronto: HarperCollins.

Cockburn, Cynthia. 2007. *From Where We Stand: War, Women's Activism and Feminist Analysis*. London: Zed Books.

Coles, Anne, Leslie Gray, and Janet Momsen (Eds.). 2015. *The Routledge Handbook of Gender and Development*. London: Routledge.

Desai, Vandana and Robert Potter (Eds.). 2014. *The Companion to Development Studies*. Third Edition. London and New York: Routledge.

Fivush, Robyn and Monica Pasupathi. 2019. Silencing Self and Other through Autobiographical Narratives. In Amy Murray and Kevin Durrheim (Eds.), *Qualitative Studies of Silence: The Unsaid as Social Action*. Cambridge: Cambridge University Press, 126–146.

French, Marilyn. 1977. *The Women's Room: A Novel*. Berkeley: Jove Books.

Friedan, Betty. 1963. *The Feminine Mystique*. New York: W. W. Norton and Co.

Glenn, C. 2004. *Unspoken: A Rhetoric of Silence*. Carbondale, IL: SIU Press.

Ibhawoh, Bonny. 2018. *Human Rights in Africa*. Cambridge: Cambridge University Press.

Jones, Martha S. 2020. *Vanguard: How Black Women Broke Barriers, Won the Vote and Insisted on Equality for All*. New York: Basic Books.

Khalid, Aliya. 2022. The Negotiations of Pakistani Mothers' Structure: Towards a Research Practice of Hearing "Silences" as a Strategy. *Gender and Education*: 1–15.

Khalid, A., G. Holmes, and J. Parpart. 2024. *The Politics of Silence, Voice and the In-Between Exploring Gender, Race and Insecurity from the Margins*. London: Routledge.

Lerner, G. 1967. *The Grimke Sisters from South Carolina: Rebels Against Slavery*. Houghton Mifflin. Lerner, Gerder. 1971. *The Grimke Sisters from South Carolina: Pioneers for Women's Rights and Abolition*. New York: Schocken Books.

Lorde, Audrey. 1984a. *Sister Outsider: Essays and Speeches by Audrey Lorde*. Freedom, CA: The Crossing Press.

Lorde, Audrey. 1984b. The Master's Tools Will Never Dismantle the Master's House. In *Sister Outsider: Essays and Speeches by Audre Lorde*. Freedom, CA: The Crossing Press, 110–113.

Mackenzie, Megan. 2012. *Female Soldiers in Sierra Leone: Sex, Security, and Post-Conflict Development*. New York and London: New York University Press.

Mahmood, Saba. 2005. *The Politics of Piety*. Princeton: Princeton University Press.

Murray, Amy Jo and Kevin Durrheim. 2019. Introduction: A Turn to Silence. In Amy Murray and Kevin Durrheim (Eds.), *Qualitative Studies of Silence*. Cambridge: Cambridge University Press, 1–20.

Parpart, Jane L. 1983. *Labor and Capital on the African Copperbelt*. Philadelphia: Temple University Press.

Parpart, Jane L. 2015. Men, Masculinities, and Development. In Anne Coles, Leslie Gray, and Janet Momsen (Eds.), *The Routledge Handbook of Gender and Development*. London and New York: Routledge, 14–23.

Parpart, Jane L. and Swati Parashar (Eds.). 2019. *Rethinking Silence, Voice and Agency in Contested Gendered Terrains*. London and New York: Routledge.

Rowe, A. C. and S. Malhotra. 2013. Still the Silence: Feminist Reflections at the Edges of Sound. In *Silence, Feminism, Power: Reflections at the Edges of Sound*. London: Palgrave Macmillan, 1–22. Urban-Mead, Wendy. 2015. *The Gender of Piety: Family, Faith and Colonial Rule in Matebeleland, Zimbabwe*. Athens, OH: Ohio University Press.

Walker, Rebecca and Treasa Galvin. 2019. Labels, Victims, and Insecurity: An Exploration of the Lived Realities of Migrant Women Who Sell Sex in South Africa. In Navtej K. Purewal and Sophia Dingli (Eds.), *Gendering Security and Insecurity*. London: Routledge, 110–125.

Zerubavel, Eviatar. 2019. Listening to the Sound of Silence: Methodological Reflections on Studying the Unsaid. In Amy Murray and Kevin Durrheim (Eds.), *Qualitative Studies of Silence: The Unsaid as Social Action*. Cambridge: Cambridge University Press, 59–70.

9 Paradise Lost, Paradigm Found?
Revisiting Assumptions for a New Paradigm for Women in the World

Tiffani Betts Razavi

Introduction: Assumptions, Observations and Paradigm Shifts

Human beings operate within paradigms – frameworks or models built on basic assumptions, ways of thinking, and approaches that are generally accepted by communities or societies. In many ways, paradigms facilitate collaboration and collective endeavor in advancing knowledge and understanding across various spheres of human activity, including science, art and culture. But they can also become a constraint and limit progress by imposing barriers based on unquestioned assumptions.

Despite the sweep of developments across a century or more, including the spread of feminist ideals and improvements in equality in relation to a range of social, economic, political and legal indicators, women in the world continue to face barriers – deprivation not merely of rights but also of dignity, challenges not only to their spheres of influence but also to the valuing of their contribution to the creation of more peaceful and prosperous societies. If we accept that real peace cannot be attained without universal participation, then there is a need to look again at the assumptions of the prevailing paradigm of equality and social development.

Challenging paradigm assumptions involves confrontation with an anomaly – a question, a contrast, an experience, an ideal, a value, even a statistic – that deviates from expectation, and is a necessary condition for paradigm shift by which "new ways of perceiving the world come to be accepted" (Nielsen, 2019). The assumptions underlying dominant worldviews can be exposed by consciously extending empirical reach and widening perspective and, according to findings, adjusted or abandoned to create a new paradigm.

The idea that cumulative observation and experience can shape paradigms and prompt change is the starting point for the approach adopted in this chapter, which begins with an overview of the current status of women in the world and then reviews empirical evidence relating to three prevalent assumptions about progress toward equality – time, absorption and biological predisposition. Reflection on the anomalies encountered then spurs a discussion of the necessary features of a new paradigm for the advancement of women, in which human

DOI: 10.4324/9781003281382-13

development is approached as a complex, integrated organic system and based on a conception of human nobility.

Where are Women in the World? Glancing at the Figures

The movement of women into the world's public spaces represents the first of many assumptions that were historically challenged on the path to equality – the assumption that polling stations, classrooms and university lecture halls, board rooms, the corridors of power, and the chambers of governments were not for women – and the efforts of women's rights activists and feminists resulted in the increased participation of women in spheres from which they were once excluded. Quantitative data tracking gender equality indicate significant progress as "more girls are going to school, fewer girls are forced into early marriage, more women are serving in parliament and positions of leadership, and laws are being reformed to advance gender equality" – in 46 countries, women now hold more than 30 percent of seats in national parliaments, and in more than 100 countries action has been taken to track budget allocations for gender equality (United Nations, 2021).

However, the representation of women in national parliaments at 23.7 percent "is still far from parity" (United Nations, 2021). Furthermore, "women are missing from negotiating tables" (UN Secretary-General, 2019); "only two women in history ... have ever served as chief negotiators, and only one woman ... has ever signed a final peace accord as chief negotiator" (Council on Foreign Relations, 2020).

In 2021, the Global Gender Gap report projected that the overall global gender gap will close in 135.6 years (World Economic Forum, 2021), a significant pandemic-induced setback from the previous year in which the figure was 99.5 years (World Economic Forum, 2019). By region, reaching gender parity is predicted to take 52.1 years in Western Europe, 61.5 years in North America, 68.9 years in Latin America and the Caribbean, 121.5 years in Sub-Saharan Africa, 134.7 years in Eastern Europe and Central Asia, 142.4 years in the Middle East and North Africa, 165.1 years in East Asia and the Pacific, and 195.4 years in South Asia (World Economic Forum, 2021). Across the four dimensions studied, gaps between women and men in economic and political empowerment are the largest, the education gap is predicted to close within the next 14.2 years, and the health gap is almost closed already, though there is significant regional variation. However, for both education and health, the rate of change has slowed, and though equality seems within reach, may yet take considerable time.

According to eight indicators (mobility, workplace, pay, marriage, parenthood, entrepreneurship, assets and pension) measured by the World Bank, in 2021, only ten countries gave women and men equal legal rights, and a typical economy gave women three-quarters of the legal rights of men (World Bank, 2021). The United Kingdom scored 97.5, Australia 96.9, and the United States 91.3 for overall legal equality. Scores in the Middle East and North Africa were often below 50, and never over 90, a reminder that impressions of progress can easily fall prey to the bias of the global north, the postcolonial position and liberal/neoliberal assumptions about women and development (Parpart, 2019). Far from liberal feminist concerns for political power, the reality of many women in the world is that they cannot live or move safely, without fear of violence (particularly sexual violence), and they face harsh and dangerous repercussions for speaking up about inequality (Parpart, 2010; Criado Perez, 2019).

In conflict and post-conflict societies, where women are generally affected differently to men, gendered implications in policymaking have historically been ignored or overlooked. Women and children associated with violent extremist groups are "often invisible in the eyes of international policy and law" as "much of the information gathering and scholarship has lacked a gendered analysis," women associated with violent extremism face additional stigma, particular mental and physical health issues, as well as economic consequences, and there remains a "chasm between on-the-ground realities and global policies" (Anderlini and Holmes, 2019).

In other spheres, though the presence of women consistently increased in recent decades (prior to the COVID-19 pandemic), significant disparity remains at leadership levels, even in sectors dominated by women. For example, in healthcare, women comprise approximately 70 percent of global healthcare workers, as doctors, nurses, pharmacists and other personnel, but are consistently under-represented in leadership (IFC, 2019). No women were included in Italy's 20-member group of experts appointed the technical scientific committee to advise the government during the COVID-19 outbreak (BBC News, 2020) and only 34 percent of all authors (29 percent first author) who published papers related to COVID-19 were women (Pinho-Gomes et al., 2020).

Figures such as these provide a clear picture: two decades into the twenty-first century, there is progress toward equality. Women are healthier, safer, more educated and present in most spheres of human activity in many, but not all, parts of the world, but still without parity, particularly in leadership.

Is Time All We Need? The Pattern and the Pace of Change

Based on historical progress, a common assumption is that to reach equality all that is needed is more time; if we "stay the course," according to the Global Gender Gap report predictions, gender parity will be reached in 2156. However, staying the course "is only a good idea if you're sure you're on course" (Meadows, 2012), and complex systems such as the human world are generally not well served by undeviating directives. Stark data trend reversals during the COVID-19 pandemic alone (such as in the Global Gender Gap report) are sufficient to call into question the assumption that time is all we need.

Even prior to pandemic-related setbacks for women, cross-generational comparisons cast doubt on the "stay the course" assumption. The Boomer to Generation X transition is a case in point. The Boomer generation confronted sexism at the macro level across many fronts, making it possible for women to do things that in previous generations had been barred. In the process, however, the emphasis on creating *opportunity* (women "*can* have it all") seems to have turned to *expectation* (women "*should* have it all"), generating additional pressure for women in a still unequal society (Calhoun, 2021). A 2009 study of women in the United States found that although by many objective measures their lives had improved, subjective well-being declined, both in absolute terms and relative to men (Stevenson and Wolfers, 2009). Similarly, despite the improvement of key economic metrics, 2017 Gallup statistics indicated declining overall well-being, characterized mainly by deteriorating emotional and psychological factors, was disproportionately felt by women and other non-dominant groups (Witters, 2019). Though the overall trend halted in 2019, Gallup continues to report challenges for working women in the United States (Brenan, 2020), as well as for single mothers worldwide (Crabtree and Kluch, 2020).

It is a timeline of gaps and gains and more gaps. The Pew Research Center reports a sharp increase in the share of mothers in the workforce, from 47 percent in 1975 to 73 percent in 2000 (Geiger and Parker, 2018), but also that mothers are now spending more time on childcare than in the past – 14 hours per week in 2016, compared to 10 hours in 1965 (Geiger et al., 2019). Despite increasing levels of education and presence in the workforce, only 25 percent of Gen X women (born in 1980) can expect to earn more in their working lives than their fathers did, compared to 45 percent for women born in 1940 (Chetty et al., 2017).

Tracking the development of gender stereotypes raises similar questions about progress toward equality. Research shows that stereotypes are dynamic over time (e.g., Diekman and Eagly, 2000), learned by observation, and therefore subject to change according to conditions and exposure. If we are on course, then as the gender gap narrows, we would expect a shift across generations and convergence toward androgyny, but the evidence does not support this clear pattern (Eagly et al., 2020).

Draw-a-scientist studies, for example, show that there has been some change. In the original research (carried out from 1966 to 1977), only 0.6 per cent of children (all girls) drew female scientists (Chambers, 1983), while a more recent meta-analysis shows that the average percentage has increased to 28 (Miller et al., 2018). However, a significant gender difference persists; boys drew female scientists only 5 percent of the time, compared to 45 percent for girls. The results also indicate that as children get older, they increasingly associate science with men, and even girls become more likely to draw scientists as men: 70 percent of 6-year-old girls draw scientists as women, but the proportion flips around age 10 or 11 and by 16, the pattern is reversed and 75 percent of girls draw scientists as men. The findings from the draw-a-scientist study stem from children's experience – not from some abstract notion of gender equality gone wrong – and confirm that children do not yet have the data to report back a significantly altered perception of women in science.

Another meta-analysis of studies from 1940–2019 (Eagly et al., 2020) shows consensus across generations of the major dimensions of gender stereotypes (communion, competence, agency and intelligence), and no change from distinct social perceptions of women and men, except in relation to competence. Seventy years of increased female presence in the workforce have not yet stimulated a convergence of the social perceptions of the sexes, but rather have generated a more strongly stereotypical view of women as more communal, and men having greater agency. The authors suggest that these stereotypes are based on actual inequalities that persist across various economic sectors and spheres of social influence and prominence, and point out that the increase in the perceived competence of women does not (yet) correspond to equal social status.

Cross-generational views expressed in opinion polls further illustrate unexpected trends in the perception of male and female qualities over time. In 2013, the Pew Research Center reported the widespread perception that equality between women and men remains elusive, particularly in relation to the workplace. However, there is a gender gap in these perceptions. Women, especially the most educated women in this American sample, were more likely than men to report that society favors men over women. More significantly, the gender gap is not even across generations and runs counter to expectation for the "stay the course" model. The data show the widest male–female discrepancy is among Millennials (the youngest adult generation surveyed) with 75 percent of women saying more changes are needed to bring about workplace equality, compared to 57 percent of Millennial men (Pew Research Center, 2013). Other data sets indicate that perceived social pressures on men and women remain disparate and stereotyped; for example, younger men are far more likely to report increased expectation to behave according to male stereotypes in their attitudes toward women, family and work (Parker et al., 2017).

Findings such as these expose the unevenness of progress toward equality, and the effect of continued exposure to disparity for girls and boys, women and men, as generation succeeds generation, leading to trends that run counter to the assumption of gradual gain as a function of time.

Add Women and Mix? Structures, Shapes and Opportunities

Closely related to the assumption about time is the assumption that equality can be achieved through the absorption of an increasing number of women into existing systems and structures, sometimes dubbed "add women and mix." Notwithstanding the importance of parity, the data surveyed in the previous section suggest otherwise; despite the increased presence of women in most domains there remain "two levels of status, of expectation, of opportunity" (Golan, 2019). Androcentric societies persist, in which structures, norms and systems were created by men, according to their needs, interests and inclinations. Androcentrism is not rooted in a deliberate ideology, nor necessarily intended to preserve male power. "In many cases, these things aren't even seen or grasped as male-shaped. For centuries they have been internalized, even by women, as natural" (Golan, 2019), "the product of a way of thinking that has been around for millennia and is therefore a kind of not thinking" (Criado Perez, 2019), an absence of conscious thought perpetuated by accumulated reinforcing experience.

Although men and women are evenly represented in the population, historically, public spheres of human activity have been characterized by the presence of fewer women than men, and greater male visibility, giving the impression that men are the majority or dominant group in society (Bailey et al., 2019). Human societies therefore have neither the perspective nor the data relating to the female half of the population.

Because the lives of men have been taken to represent those of humans overall, the stories we tell ourselves about our past, present and future, our news, our language, our literature, our science, our city planning and transport systems, our economics, and so on, are all subject to a gender data gap (Criado Perez, 2019). Evidence (or rather the lack of it) abounds, and the sheer ubiquity is staggering. Many instances of the gender data gap, such as in films and books, are in plain sight. For example, women account for only around a third of speaking characters in films (Annenberg Inclusion Initiative, 2020). An analysis of children's books (see Ferguson, 2018) found that the ratio of male to female characters was about 3:2, that male characters are twice as likely to be in leading roles, and that they have many more speaking parts than female characters. As for the 60 percent of non-human characters (such as animals, plants and crayons), 73 percent were assigned the male gender pronoun. Textbooks around the world also continue to under-represent women and to reinforce traditional roles (Global Education Monitoring Report Team, 2016), with particular imbalance in the depiction of adult females in physics and mathematics books, and books targeted at older children (Wilbraham and Caldwell, 2018).

So, when women enter the proverbial room, even today, there, on the other side of the door, lurks the "default male" (Smith and Zárate, 1992; Criado Perez, 2019). In terms of the workplace, much of what passes for neutral practice and is considered the basis for advancement is actually part of a masculine culture of contest aimed at proving manhood on the job and promoting values that engage gender identities, so that "real men" are the ones most likely to thrive. Focusing on the exceptional women who succeed in these organizations as evidence of equality does not prompt a shift in organizational values, but further reinforces contest culture norms (Berdahl et al., 2018). Even the move to more flexible work conditions rooted in second wave feminism has led to a 24/7 work culture that is at odds with the integrated and community-based vision that was at its core (Stoller, 2020).

On the face of it, flexible work and other equal opportunities policies are intended to level the playing field. However, for women, the reality of androcentric cultures combined with the faulty logic of meritocracy (Markovits, 2019) based on "all things being equal" (Golan, 2019) is problematic. Structural challenges persist, even in equal opportunity-oriented organizations. For example, one study sought to identify the factors preventing women from advancing and found that both women and men attributed the problem to work/family balance. Participants were often unable to overcome this assumption, for example "to account for such anomalies as childless women, whose promotion record was no better than that of mothers. ... Childless women figured nowhere in people's remarks, perhaps because they contradict the work/family narrative." The authors conclude that the problem was not the work/family challenge per se, but rather "a general culture of overwork in which women were encouraged to take career-derailing accommodations to meet the demands of work and family" and in which all "felt pressured to go along with these demands for overwork because they wanted to stand out as stars amid their highly qualified colleagues" (Ely and Padavic, 2020).

Most responses to the unequal participation of women in workplaces – "fixing the women, valuing the feminine, and reducing bias" (Berdahl et al., 2018) – do not confront the basic problem that the conception and structuring of work remain androcentric. For example, "leaning in" which encourages the individual woman to summon the effort to conquer difficult circumstances and reach the desired goal not only fails to promote systemic change but makes people "more likely to believe that women are responsible for the problem – both for causing it, and for fixing it" (Fitzsimons et al., 2018). Rather, such measures tinker at the margins of a faulty system. There is ample evidence of both the failure of androcentric approaches to enhance equality, and the success of initiatives that include the experiences of women (e.g., Leder et al., 2019; Malley, 2019), indicative of a basic need to forego the assumption of absorption into hierarchy as an organizing principle and to redefine the nature, purpose and value of human activity in individual and societal terms (Razavi, 2021).

Back to Biology? Brains and Biases

The final assumption addressed here concerns biological predisposition – that inherited biological characteristics, particularly in relation to the brain and cognitive and emotional functioning, incline women and men to different tendencies, interests and competencies, preferences, strengths and weaknesses, and "naturally" define social roles, responsibilities and possibilities. The assumption of the biological innateness of differences provides justification for patterns of social, economic and political participation and organization.

In the past, "nature" factors have often been used to exclude women. For example, brain size observations were historically advanced as evidence for lower intelligence and cognitive ability, while documented differences in brain functioning were seen to underlie an undesirable effect of emotion on rational processes and both were used to limit women's access to leadership roles. However, more recently, the idea that the female brain is wired to be more caring provides a rationale for increasing the role of women in problem-solving and decision-making at all levels. Grappling with the relationship between sex differences in the brain and the goal of equality has sometimes generated an eagerness to deny the existence of differences in an effort to prove that men and women are the same, sometimes an enthusiasm to highlight differences and prove the worth of undervalued feminine qualities, and (perhaps most constructively) sometimes an emphasis on the interpretation, implication and application of findings rather than the differences per se.

The literature – whether academic, policy or popular – can be confusing. The range of biological sex differences (not to mention their implications) is wide, and despite a long history of scientific research, a steady stream of popular books, and frequent review in news media, lack of consensus about these differences remains. There is a perception that many feminists deny the existence of significant differences, in order to cling to a notion of equality based on sameness, which some argue has not helped advance the essence of the feminist agenda (e.g., Solá, 2018). Cahill (2016) comments that for a long period addressing sex differences in brain research became virtually taboo:

> Due to a deeply ingrained, implicit (but false) assumption that "equal" means "the same," most neuroscientists *knew*, and even feared that establishing that males and females are not the same in some aspect of brain function meant establishing that they were not equal. This assumption is false and deeply harmful, in particular to the health of women … but remains deeply impactful nonetheless.
>
> (Cahill, 2016, p. 12)

Recent decades have witnessed a shift. A few examples serve to illustrate the trend – in 2017, the *Journal of Neuroscience Research* dedicated an issue to the theme of sex/gender influences on nervous system function (Cahill, 2016). The same year, there was an issue of *Stanford Medicine* devoted to sex, gender and medicine, which featured cognitive differences between women and men (Goldman, 2017), and an article in *Psychology Today* urged readers to accept "The Truth about Sex Differences" (Schmitt, 2017). In 2019, *Frontiers in Neuroscience* published a study that confirmed that male–female differences exist in whole-brain images, as well as in specific regions of the brain, concluding that "structural differences might be related to gender differences in cognition, emotional control as well as neurological disorders" (Xin et al., 2019).

In parallel, however, there is another read of this research history. In contrast to Cahill, cognitive neuroscientist Rippon (2019) describes an environment in the latter part of the twentieth century in which researchers were effectively encouraged to identify stereotypical female/male characteristics which may not have even been measured in the scanner. If a difference was found, it was much more likely to be published than a finding of no difference, and it would also breathlessly be hailed as an "at last the truth" moment by an enthusiastic media. Finally the evidence that women are hard-wired to be rubbish at map reading and that men can't multi-task! So the advent of brain imaging at the end of the 20th century did not do much to advance our understanding of alleged links between sex and the brain.

(Rippon, 2019, p. xiii)

Having started out looking for sex differences herself, Rippon claims that controlling for brain size, other sex differences in brain structures disappear, and concludes that there are no significant differences based on sex alone. Joel and Vikhanski (2019) argue that the brain is like a mosaic made up of a multiplicity of characteristics, each of which can be seen as "male" and "female," but which do not cluster to form distinctly male and female brains. Though sex differences are found in many brain characteristics, Joel (2011) notes that these findings do not imply that the brain as a whole must be either male or female. In fact, there are relatively few features that are sexually dimorphic; most show overlapping distributions.

The apparently contradictory patterns described above stem from two overlapping assumptions about the human brain, both based on false dichotomies. One, as pointed out by Joel and others, is the assumption that brains are binary, springing from an impulse to map the genetic sex chromosome categories which give rise to distinct male and female body forms and reproductive functions on to all other human characteristics. Whether as researchers, practitioners, policy makers, teachers, parents or casual observers, this assumption has led us to look for, and expect to find, only two categories. In effect, we confuse the biological variable "sex" with the sociocultural notion of "gender" which delineates masculine and feminine roles, and in so doing significantly limit explanatory power (Oldehinkel, 2017). The idea of the brain as a mosaic (Joel, 2011; Joel and Vikhanski, 2019) helps us to avoid the dichotomy trap and develop a more refined picture. Rather than defaulting to binary classifications, by exploring instead distributions, and seeing women and men equally as potential "carriers" of characteristics and qualities, we stand to enrich our understanding of the human condition. We need a mosaic mindset to increasingly set the tone for the way we look for answers, and – perhaps more importantly – the way we ask questions about human development and experience.

The second biology-based assumption that limits progress is that "nature" and "nurture" are dichotomous. This assumption is readily overturned, as brain plasticity is well established; it is an organ shaped by environmental factors from before birth (e.g., Eliot, 2010; Rippon, 2019). Observations of sex differences, even in physical structures, then, are not attributable to being genetically male or female; variations are generated through exposure to different conditions (e.g., Zaidi, 2010). Given the gendered nature of human society, we would expect to find clustering of characteristics in males and females based on their differentiated patterns of experience. Moreover, that certain traits are found more in men than women and vice versa does not imply that these distributions are unchangeable over time. For example, studies consistently show that females adopt a certain approach to moral reasoning based on the salience of caring (research largely generated by Gilligan, 1982), but the idea that women are more caring *by nature* is not a viable inference to draw from consistent observations of caring behavior in women compared with men; rather, there is some combination of nature and nurture that explains these findings.

When the interactive relationship between the development of the brain and physical and social environments is sidelined and mosaics are reduced to binaries, we lose something critical in relation to understanding the human condition and the ways in which it can be improved. By assuming that equality is about difference or sameness, nature or nurture, we run the risk of falling prey not only to over-simplification but to perpetuating knowledge systems that fail to serve the full range of humanity's needs.

Outlining a New Paradigm

Revisiting these three basic assumptions about reaching equality has exposed numerous anomalies – across space and time, in principle and practice – which point to the need for a new paradigm to allow for further advancement and a deeper understanding of the end goal. Based on the observations described in this chapter, such a paradigm must be characterized by revised conceptions of individual identity and human nature as well as various system-level features to capture collective dynamics, as described below and illustrated in Figure 9.1.

Complexity and Organic Change

As discussed above, the paradigm that assumes a direct correlation between biological sex and emotional, cognitive and behavioral variables produces anomalies because there is empirical evidence of both biological similarities and differences between women and men (as could well be said of other human groups defined by physical characteristics, such as eye color), and also that these are neither fixed nor clear-cut categories. In a new paradigm, the binary assumption that focuses attention on elaborating a list of male and female traits is replaced with an acknowledgment of multiple dimensions of human characteristics – in the brain, in behavior and in social contexts – that interact as part of an integrated complex system and more adequately represents what it means to be human at this time.

The treatment of time from a developmental perspective is a relevant component of complexity because it accommodates non-linear progress. The persistence of inequality despite theoretical acceptance of equality as a human right and continued efforts to secure that right coherently and completely suggests that a framework that emphasizes presence versus absence or incremental quantitative change alone is inadequate. Like an individual human being developing into adulthood, humanity's collective self-awareness progressively but non-uniformly increases alongside its capacity to generate and absorb ever more textured explanations of itself and adopt corresponding modes of functioning. Reaching equality is therefore more effectively construed as part of a pattern of maturation of a complex system, a process of organic change.

Integration and Inclusivity

Similarly, complexity compels us to admit into the new paradigm the element of integration, and to view the system as a whole, rather than as a collection of separate issues or problems. However, in some measure, the response to the continued existence of barriers to equality seems to have become more fragmented rather than integrated, as feminism in its fourth wave (from around 2012; Brunell and Burkett, 2021) extends the emphasis on intersectionality which has been present since the 1980s (Chamberlain, 2017) and highlights the diversity of women's realities. The movement toward intersectionality might be seen to run the risk of dissipating the power of the underlying moral principle of equality, and some have questioned the extent to which the uptake of issues relating to women in the 2010s amounts to a new wave, or even feminism at all (e.g., Rivers, 2018).

Indeed, in the absence of a parallel emphasis on inclusivity, cohesion and a more fundamental unity of identity and purpose, there is a risk of fragmentation:

> Humanity is gripped by a crisis of identity, as various peoples and groups struggle to define themselves, their place in the world, and how they should act. Without a vision of shared identity and common purpose, they fall into competing ideologies and power struggles. Seemingly countless permutations of "us" and "them" define group identities ever more narrowly and in contrast to one another. Over time, this splintering into divergent interest groups has weakened the cohesion of society itself. Rival conceptions about the primacy of a particular people are peddled to the exclusion of the truth that humanity is on a common journey in which all are protagonists. Consider how radically different such a fragmented conception of human identity is from the one that follows from a recognition of the oneness of humanity.
> (Universal House of Justice, 2019, paragraph 7)

Though prevailing social norms urge us to view identity in competitive terms, the essence of feminism resists this fragmentation even as it raises consciousness of diversity and point us toward a new paradigm. Within a framework of standpoint epistemology, whether or not explicitly invoked, intersectionality reinforces the notion of the whole, encourages greater consciousness of complexity, and broadens participation in equality activism by removing the perceived barrier of competing identities. For example, describing the intersectional approach, a black feminist woman explains:

> I feel there's an understanding among people who identify that way [as black feminists], that we're all different, and we have multiple, shifting identities. The challenge that there has been with mainstream feminism and anti-racist movements in the past is that there has been a pressure to pick a side. It [the intersectional approach] holds the whole of who you are – your gender, ethnicity, sexuality, geographical location, ability status – everything is encapsulated.
> (Cochrane, 2013a, Chapter 6)

True intersectional awareness serves a means to elevate the discourse about women and equality, to consciously include the marginalized, and recognize how hierarchies of power are constructed and issues such as class, race, age, ability, and gender combine to affect efforts to reach equality (Cochrane, 2013b). Adichie (2015) comments on a frequently asked question in conversations about equality:

> "Why does it have to be you as a woman? Why not you as a human being?" This type of question is a way of silencing a person's specific experiences. Of course I am a human being, but there are particular things that happen to me in the world because I am a woman.
> (Adichie, 2015, np)

Participation in a common journey does not carry a moral requirement to forget particular aspects of identity, neither does defining ourselves in those terms imply that we are abandoning our human identity, nor that we are introducing divisiveness. Multiple identities generate anomalies in a paradigm that assumes separateness. In a new paradigm, therefore, orienting to the shared as the essential determinant of identity is important conceptually and practically, individually and collectively as the basis for a non-competitive, synergistic approach to diversity and an inclusive conception of humanity.

Human Nobility

With respect to inclusivity, there is value in explicit acknowledgment of the human spirit, a dimension of identity that is not often openly addressed in contemporary literature about equality (although there is historical precedent, e.g., Wollstonecraft, 1792; Grimké, 1838, 2015) but which can be seen as its essential and therefore fundamentally unifying feature. In every part of the world, beliefs in God, religion and the soul shape self-concepts, ethical frameworks and social structures, and motivate moral decisions and social activism. Indeed, a recent study reports that 88.7 percent of the global population identify as religious (Johnson and Crossing, 2020, p. 15: "the world was more religious in 2000 (87.0%) than in 1970 (80.8%), with that trend continuing in 2020 (88.7%) and 2030 (90.0%). This is not the case in every region, however, with Northern Europe and Western Europe experiencing a negative rate of change between 1970 and 2000, in the latter continuing to 2030"), which makes overlooking, underplaying or dismissing religion in relation to equality in favor of a secular default problematic. Dedication to the rigor of scholarship alone urges consideration of all possible explanations for phenomena, and in this case failure to include religion and a conception of spiritual equality in an emerging new paradigm would be remiss. Admitting religion as a demographic or sociological variable, for example through intersectionality as in many feminist approaches, is therefore significant.

However, as a feature of a new paradigm, there is another more fundamental way to include this dimension, which is to define human nature with reference to a spiritual quality, an inherent dignity or nobility not necessarily pinned to a particular religious belief, but usefully described from a faith perspective:

> In man there are two natures; his spiritual or higher nature and his material or lower nature. ... Signs of both these natures are to be found in men. In his material aspect he expresses untruth, cruelty and injustice; all these are the outcome of his lower nature. The attributes of his Divine nature are shown forth in love, mercy, kindness, truth and justice, one and all being expressions of his higher nature.
> ('Abdu'l-Bahá, 1911; translated from the Persian, in which the pronoun is ungendered)

A paradigm that embraces this dual material-spiritual conception of human nature, with its promise and its pitfalls, can accommodate non-linear progress and apparent anomalies in attitudes and behaviors or intentions and actions as part of a complex and multi-layered developmental process. Consciuos and consistent focus on human nobility offers a helpful baseline for addressing the structural problems stemming from the default male, the persistence of stereotypes and the cultural pressures of gender roles within a broad framework of "a spiritual maturation of the human sexless soul" (Conow, 1988, p. 50). Treating people and their environments with a vision of enhancing the higher nature cuts across subordinate descriptors and concentrates energy on the elevation of the human condition and, by extension, the common good.

Creativity and Coherence

The process of identifying the features of a framework within which past anomalies can be explained and women can more significantly advance brings us to an interesting and important conclusion about the notion of equality itself. The old paradigm falters because of the most fundamental of assumptions – that the meaning of equality as a finite end-goal is known. While there may be aspects that can be described in an aspirational sense, the reality is that the equality we seek to establish is a condition that humanity has yet to experience, and the inequality we strive to overcome is a barrier to an unknown peace. A new paradigm must cultivate invention and creativity – simultaneously convergent and divergent, embracing both the particular and the general, and drawing on both deduction and induction.

The paradigm begins to sound very much like the elusive future society it seeks to promote. Therein lies another key feature needed at this stage in human social evolution, a tenet to which feminists and pacifists alike adhere: the coherence of means and ends. To propel the advance of our highly complex system depends on processes that consistently defend and uphold the nobility of the human spirit, encompass the material and moral components of human development, the individual and the collective, the private and the public sphere, in a framework that shapes our attitudes and actions, approaches and structures.

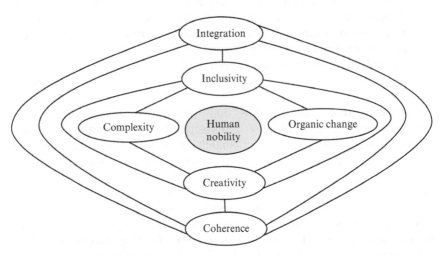

Figure 9.1 Features of a new paradigm
Source: Created by author

Now, New and Next

Paradigm shifts seem to imply a bold break with the past, a stark rejection of conceptions or approaches that are no longer fit for purpose, or that constrain development. However, paradigms are based on learned behaviors, and "although we are profoundly influenced psychologically and socially by the structures, it is ourselves who create and can change them" (Reardon, 1985). The protagonists of change are always people who have been raised in the old paradigm, and gradually, by choice, replace the old with the new. Change comes from those who know – and often have proven themselves – in the methods, tools and techniques of the old paradigm, but choose to put them to new uses.

We have arguably reached such a juncture in relation to women, equality and peace. There are gaps and inequities, and geographical unevenness, but women participate and hold leadership roles in androcentric systems. This presence, pressing toward parity, is proof of capacity and skill. There is no longer a performance-based case to exclude women from any sphere of human activity, nor to restrict their influence on the shaping of future structures and society. At the same time, through the involvement of women, we have realized the inadequacy of current systems to meet the needs of humanity defined in equal measure male and female. If we acknowledge the need for a new approach, a new paradigm, the first step, the "central transformational task" (Reardon, 1985), is to choose it. We choose to make the shift, individually and collectively. We make a conscious decision to change learned behaviors.

That decision sets us on a course. We do not have a precise pre-determined vision of our destination, but we have a purpose, and we have a path. Although a long-range goal can be too general to dictate strategy, over time a method may serve to give meaning to an aspiration (Ruddick, 1989). The features of a new paradigm described in the previous section provide some indication of such a method, that may eventually serve to create the states of equality and peace that lie beyond our current capacity to envisage. In keeping with the complexity of the system, for example, promoting growth and change implies multi-faceted simultaneous actions in relation to key components of the system, some of which have obvious immediate effects, and some of which set in motion or reinforce processes that ensure long-term viability. Although there are conceivably infinite particular forms that such actions could take, they are all expressions of a method coherent with the aim of creating structures of equality. Revisiting assumptions is a necessary part of that method, lending impetus to another press forward, another stage of growth and social progress, a "new" – or perhaps more aptly "next" – paradigm: the conscious and coherent pursuit of the equality of women and men in all its complexity, with the common purpose of building a world that upholds the nobility of the human spirit in equity and justice, compassion and kindness, prosperity and peace.

References

Abdu'l-Bahá (1911). *Paris Talks: AddressesGgiven by 'Abdu'l-Bahá in 1911*. Available at: www.bahai.org/library/authoritative-texts/abdul-baha/paris-talks/1#733601770.

Adichie, C.N. (2015). *We Should All be Feminists*. New York: Anchor Books.

Anderlini, S.N. and Holmes, M. (2019) *Invisible Women: International Civil Society Action Network Gendered Dimensions of Return, Rehabilitation and Reintegration from Violent Extremism*. United Nations Development Programme. Available at: https://icanpeacework.org/wp-content/uploads/2019/02/ICAN-UNDP-Rehabilitation-Reintegration-Invisible-Women-Report-2019.pdf [Accessed 24 May 2022].

Annenberg Inclusion Initiative (2020). *Inequality in 1,300 Popular Films*. Available at: http://assets.uscannenberg.org/docs/aii-inequality_1300_popular_films_09-08-2020.pdf.

Bailey, A.H., LaFrance, M. and Dovidio, J.F. (2019). Is Man the Measure of All Things? A Social Cognitive Account of Androcentrism. *Personality and Social Psychology Review*, 23(4): 307–331. doi:10.1177/1088868318782848.

BBC News (2020). Dateci Voce: Italian Women Demand Voice in Covid-19 Fight, May 8. Available at: www.bbc.com/news/world-europe-52588862.

Berdahl, J.L., Cooper, M., Glick, P., Livingston, R.W. and Williams, J.C. (2018). Work as a Masculinity Contest. *Journal of Social Issues*, 74(3): 422–448. doi:10.1111/josi.12289.

Brenan, M. (2020). Working Moms Get Little Reprieve From Household Demands. *Gallup.com*. Available at: https://news.gallup.com/poll/286739/working-moms-little-reprieve-household-demands.aspx [Accessed 9 June 2020].

Brunell, L. and Burkett, E. (2021). Feminism. *Encyclopedia Britannica*, March 24. Available at: www.britannica.com/topic/feminism.

Cahill, L. (2016). An Issue Whose Time Has Come. *Journal of Neuroscience Research*, 95(1–2): 12–13. doi:10.1002/jnr.23972.

Calhoun, A. (2021). *Why We Can't Sleep: Women's New Midlife Crisis*. New York: Grove Atlantic Press.

Chamberlain, P. (2017). *The Feminist Fourth Wave: Affective Temporality*. London: Palgrave Macmillan.

Chambers, D.W. (1983). Stereotypic Images of the Scientist: The Draw-a-Scientist Test. *Science Education*, 67(2): 255–265. doi:10.1002/sce.3730670213.

Chetty, R., Grusky, D., Hell, M., Hendren, N., Manduca, R., and Narang, J. (2017). The Fading American Dream: Trends in Absolute Income Mobility since 1940. *Science*, 356(6336): 398–406. doi:10.1126/science.aal4617.

Cochrane, K. (2013a). *All the Rebel Women: The Rise of the Fourth Wave of Feminism*. London: Guardian Books.

Cochrane, K. (2013b). The Fourth Wave of Feminism: Meet the Rebel Women. *The Guardian*. Available at: www.theguardian.com/world/2013/dec/10/fourth-wave-feminism-rebel-women.

Conow, B. (1988). The Active Force and That Which is its Recipient. *Dialogue Magazine*, 2(2–3): 46–50.

Council on Foreign Relations (2020). *Women's Participation in Peace Processes*. Council on Foreign Relations Interactives. Available at: www.cfr.org/interactive/womens-participation-in-peace-processes.

Crabtree, S. and Kluch, S. (2020). Single Moms Struggling Worldwide, Particularly in U.S. *Gallup.com*. Available at: https://news.gallup.com/poll/286268/single-moms-struggling-worldwide-particularly.aspx [Accessed 9 June 2020].

Criado Perez, C. (2019). *Invisible Women: Exposing Data Bias in a World Designed for Men*. S.L.: Vintage. Diekman, A.B. and Eagly, A.H. (2000). Stereotypes as Dynamic Constructs: Women and Men of the Past, Present, and Future. *Personality and Social Psychology Bulletin*, 26(10): 1171–1188. doi:10.1177/0146167200262001.

Eagly, A.H., Nater, C., Miller, D.I., Kaufmann, M., and Sczesny, S. (2020). Gender Stereotypes Have Changed: A Cross-Temporal Meta-Analysis of U.S. Public Opinion Polls from 1946 to 2018. *American Psychologist*, 75(3): 301–315. doi:10.1037/amp0000494.

Eliot, L. (2010). *Pink Brain, Blue Brain: How Small Differences Grow into Troublesome Gaps, and What We Can Do About It*. Oxford: Oneworld.

Ely, R.J. and Padavic, I. (2020). What's Really Holding Women Back? *Harvard Business Review*. Available at: https://hbr.org/2020/03/whats-really-holding-women-back.

Ferguson, D. (2018). Must Monsters Always be Male? Huge Gender Bias Revealed in Children's Books. *The Guardian*. Available at: www.theguardian.com/books/2018/jan/21/childrens-books-sexism-monster-in-your-kids-book-is-male.

Fitzsimons, G., Kay, A., and Kim, J.Y. (2018). "Lean In" Messages and the Illusion of Control. *Harvard Business Review*. Available at: https://hbr.org/2018/07/lean-in-messages-and-the-illusion-of-control.

Geiger, A.W. and Parker, K. (2018). For Women's History Month, a Look at Gender Gains – and Gaps – in the U.S. *Pew Research Center*. Available at: www.pewresearch.org/fact-tank/2018/03/15/for-womens-history-month-a-look-at-gender-gains-and-gaps-in-the-u-s/.

Geiger, A.W., Bialik, K., and Livingston, G. (2019). 6 Facts about U.S. Moms. *Pew Research Center*. Available at: www.pewresearch.org/fact-tank/2019/05/08/facts-about-u-s-mothers/.

Gilligan, C. (1982). *In a Different Voice: Psychological Theory and Women's Development*. Cambridge, MA and London: Harvard University Press.

Global Education Monitoring Report Team (2016). *Education for People and Planet: Creating Sustainable Futures for All*. Paris: Unesco.

Golan, G. (2019). Blocks to Equality, Lecture, Women in the World. Available at: https://youtu.be/3ls-fVr2uMM.

Goldman, B. (2017). How Men's and Women's Brains are Different. *Stanford Medicine*. Available at: https://stanmed.stanford.edu/2017spring/how-mens-and-womens-brains-are-different.html.

Grimké, S.M. (1838). *Letters on the Equality of the Sexes, and the Condition of Woman: Addressed to Mary S. Parker, President of the Boston Female Anti-Slavery Society*. I. Knapp.

Grimke, S.M. (2015). *Letters on the Equality of the Sexes, and the Condition of Woman. Addressed to Mary S. Parker, President of the Boston Female Anti-Slavery Society*. London: Andesite Press.

IFC (2019). Women's Leadership in Health. Available at: https://www.ifc.org/wps/wcm/connect/industry_ext_content/ifc_external_corporate_site/health/publications/womens+leadership+in+health.

Joel, D. (2011). Male or Female? Brains are Intersex. *Frontiers in Integrative Neuroscience*, 5(57). doi:10.3389/fnint.2011.00057..

Joel, D. and Vikhanski, L. (2019). *Gender Mosaic: Beyond the Myth of the Male and Female Brain*. New York: Little Brown Spark.

Johnson, T.M. and Crossing, P.F. (2020). The World by Religion. *Journal of Religion and Demography*, 7(1): 4–91. doi:10.1163/2589742x-12347101.

Leder, S., Shrestha, G., and Das, D. (2019). Transformative Engagements with Gender Relations in Agriculture and Water Governance. *New Angle: Nepal Journal of Social Science and Public Policy*, 5(1): 128–158. doi:10.53037/na.v5i1.50.

Malley, R. (2019). Why Research on Gender and Conflict Matters. Crisis Group. Available at: www.crisisgroup.org/global/why-research-gender-and-conflict-matters [Accessed 30 November 2020].

Markovits, D. (2019). *The Meritocracy Trap: How America's Foundational Myth Feeds Inequality, Dismantles the Middle Class, and Devours the Elite*. S.L.: Penguin Books.

Meadows, D. (2012). Dancing with Systems. The Academy for Systems Change. Available at: http://donellameadows.org/dancing-with-systems/ [Accessed 11 February 2021].

Miller, D.I., Nolla, K.M., Eagly, A.H., and Uttal, D.H. (2018). The Development of Children's Gender-Science Stereotypes: A Meta-Analysis of 5 Decades of U.S. Draw-A-Scientist Studies. *Child Development*, 89(6): 1943–1955. doi:10.1111/cdev.13039.

Nielsen, J.M. (2019). *Feminist Research Methods: Exemplary Readings in the Social Sciences*. New York: Taylor & Francis.

Oldehinkel, A.J. (2017). Editorial: Let's Talk about Sex – the Gender Binary Revisited. *Journal of Child Psychology and Psychiatry*, 58(8): 863–864. doi:10.1111/jcpp.12777.

Parker, K., Horowitz, J.M., and Stepler, R. (2017). Americans See Different Expectations for Men and Women. Pew Research Center's Social & Demographic Trends Project. Available at: www.pewsocialtrends.org/2017/12/05/americans-see-different-expectations-for-men-and-women/.

Parpart, J.L. (2010). Choosing Silence: Rethinking Voice, Agency and Women's Empowerment. In R. Ryan-Flood and R. Gill (eds.), *Secrecy and Silence in the Research Process: Feminist Reflections*. London: Routledge.

Parpart, J.L. (2019). Exploring the Power of Silence in a Troubled World: A Gendered Approach. Lecture, Women in the World, September. Available at: www.bahaichair.umd.edu/video; https://youtu.be/ZYtSaBah84s.

Pew Research Center (2013). On Pay Gap, Millennial Women Near Parity – For Now: Despite Gains, Many See Roadblocks Ahead. 11 December. Available at: www.pewsocialtrends.org/2013/12/11/chapter-2-equal-treatment-for-men-and-women/.

Pinho-Gomes, A.-C., Peters, S., Thompson, K., Hockham, C., Ripullone, K., Woodward, M., and Carcel, C. (2020). Where are the Women? Gender Inequalities in COVID-19 Research Authorship. *BMJ Global Health*, 5(7): e002922. doi:10.1136/bmjgh-2020-002922.

Razavi, T.B. (2021). A Bahá'í Perspective on the Meaning of Work and Values. In S. Shahvar (ed.), *The University of Haifa Lectures in Bahá'í Studies*. New York: Peter Lang.

Reardon, B. (1985). *Sexism and the War System*. New York: Teachers' College Press.

Rippon, G. (2019). *Gender and Our Brains: How New Neuroscience Explodes the Myths of the Male and Female Minds*. S.L.: Vintage.

Rivers, N. (2018). *Postfeminism(s) and the Arrival of the Fourth Wave: Turning Tides*. S.L.: Springer.

Ruddick, S. (1989). *Maternal Thinking: Toward a Politics of Peace*. Boston: Beacon Press.

Schmitt, D.P. (2017). The Truth About Sex Differences. *Psychology Today*. Available at: www.psychologytoday.com/us/articles/201711/the-truth-about-sex-differences.

Smith, E.R. and Zárate, M.A. (1992). Exemplar-Based Model of Social Judgment. *Psychological Review*, 99(1): 3–21. doi:10.1037/0033-295x.99.1.3.

Solá, A. (2018). Different is Fine: The Science of Sex Differences is Nothing for Feminists to be Afraid of. *Quartz*. Available at: https://qz.com/1218680/the-science-of-sex-differences-is-nothing-for-feminists-to-be-afraid-of/.

Stevenson, B. and Wolfers, J. (2009). The Paradox of Declining Female Happiness. *American Economic Journal: Economic Policy*, 1(2): 190–225. doi:10.1257/pol.1.2.190.

Stoller, S. (2020). How Did Flexible Work Turn from a Feminist Ideal to a Trap? *Aeon Essays*. Available at: https://aeon.co/essays/how-did-flexible-work-turn-from-a-feminist-ideal-to-a-trap.

United Nations (2021). United Nations: Gender Equality and Women's Empowerment. United Nations Sustainable Development. Available at: www.un.org/sustainabledevelopment/gender-equality/.

Universal House of Justice (2019). 18 January 2019 – Message on World Peace. Available at: www.bahai.org/library/authoritative-texts/the-universal-house-of-justice/messages/20190118_001/1#276724432 [Accessed 8 July 2021].

UN Secretary-General (2019). Women and Peace and Security: Report of the Secretary-General. Available at: www.securitycouncilreport.org/atf/cf/%7B65BFCF9B-6D27-4E9C-8CD3-CF6E4FF96FF9%7D/s_2019_800.pdf.

Wilbraham, S. and Caldwell, E. (2018). Children's Books are Adding to Science's Gender Problem. *The Conversation*. Available at: https://theconversation.com/childrens-books-are-adding-to-sciences-gender-problem-98522.

Witters, D. (2019). U.S. Wellbeing Declines Halted in 2019. *Gallup.com*. Available at: https://news.gallup.com/poll/266978/wellbeing-declines-halted-2019.aspx.

Wollstonecraft, M. (1792). *Vindication of the Rights of Woman*. S.L.: Verso.

World Bank (2021). *Women, Business and the Law 2021*. World Bank. Available at: https://wbl.worldbank.org/en/reports.

World Economic Forum (2019). *Global Gender Gap Report 2020*. World Economic Forum. Available at: www.weforum.org/reports/gender-gap-2020-report-100-years-pay-equality.

World Economic Forum (2021). *Global Gender Gap Report 2021*. World Economic Forum. Available at: www.weforum.org/reports/ab6795a1-960c-42b2-b3d5-587eccda6023.

Xin, J., Zhang, Y., Tang, Y., and Yang, Y. (2019). Brain Differences Between Men and Women: Evidence From Deep Learning. *Frontiers in Neuroscience*, 13. doi:10.3389/fnins.2019.00185.

Zaidi, Z.F. (2010). Gender Differences in Human Brain: A Review. *The Open Anatomy Journal*, 2: 37–55. doi:10.2174/1877609401002010037.

Conclusion
Women and the Potential for New Paradigms for Peace

Kate Seaman, Hoda Mahmoudi and Jane L. Parpart

We are now well into the third decade of the twenty-first century and women continue to face obstacles to their equal participation in all areas of daily life, political, social, and economic. These obstacles persist despite the growth in the education of girls, large-scale social movements, and three political waves pushing for women's rights. Without understanding the way patriarchal values define current dysfunctional systems there can be no change or challenge to that system. Throughout this volume the contributors have examined the ways in which current systems constrain women, and how the performance and presence of women is overlooked, leading to what Hoda Mahmoudi in the Introduction terms the 'voids of the never happened.'

Each of the chapters touches on key themes for understanding the varied experiences of women across the world, and how these experiences can be both hugely different and remarkably similar. These themes include the question of agency, the continuing impact of patriarchy on the organization of society, and the need to radically restructure society to counteract this. The chapters also touch on the broader systems of oppression that interact with patriarchy, and various ways to challenge these. The volume also emphasizes the importance of an intersectional approach to understanding the challenges women face today.

When compiling this volume we organized the chapters into three sections, placing chapters in conversation with each other based on their overlapping or connected themes. Each section includes chapters from different disciplines and approaches, and each brings a different perspective to the radical changes necessary within our social systems, at the individual, institutional, and societal levels. These changes are designed to end the current patriarchal paradigm, and to open up the possibility for us to imagine a new paradigm or paradigms, an imagining of a better world.

Part I focuses on the ideas of transformation, intervention, and disruption. Understanding the contribution of women to the creation of more peaceful and prosperous societies requires a deeper investigation of the different forms of violence women face in their daily lives, and the different understandings of what peace means to women whose daily experience varies depending on their age, class, race, location, and more. Together the three chapters examine

DOI: 10.4324/9781003281382-14

the intersecting challenges that women face on a daily basis, which vary depending on their positionality and identity. The chapters in this section also highlight how the lived identities of women can provide a means of solidarity and a foundation for challenging the status quo.

Within her chapter Brandy Thomas Wells argues that in order to construct a new paradigm for peace, we must challenge the patriarchy and how it works in tandem with other systems of oppression. In Wells' work we find links to Denise Segura's chapter as she identifies the ways in which Black women remain on the margins, or in the borderlands. Wells argues that race must be included as an analytic in peace studies, linking to Laura Sjoberg and her arguments about the coloniality of gender, notes that gender has been privileged more than race, class, or sexuality, and that these processes are actually intertwined in the continued oppression of women.

By examining the history of Black women's peace activism, through the current period, Wells highlights why we need to rethink the Women, Peace, and Security agenda, in ways which could lead to agency, inclusion, and justice. She argues that in the current formulation, where women are made visible in Women, Peace, and Security, they are essentialized, devoid of the realities of their lived experience. Instead Wells argues for an intersectional approach, that highlights the ways women experience life differently, and recognizes the range of intersecting social and political identities that women hold. This links directly to Denise Segura's contribution, where we find a focus on activism, and on reframing and contesting ideological and material forms of oppression.

Utilizing the concept of the 'borderlands' Segura identifies these as spaces with spatial, social, and spiritual features, and argues that we need to focus on these forces, the ways in which they frame social life, and how they pose barriers to social justice and wellbeing. Within the borderlands Segura identifies how identities shift and are negotiated in response to forces from above and below, linking to Sjoberg's chapter on how women's identities shift in response to external factors.

Within Segura's contribution we also find a connection to the chapters in Part III, including Jane L. Parpart's examination of voice and silence, as Segura notes that power within the borderlands is connected to the acquisition of knowledge, and also the acquisition of language that helps to unpack institutional settings and power arrangements. Continuing the thread running through the volume, Segura argues that women are constantly negotiating economic and political space in both psychic and geographic borderlands, and that the identity formation of women is linked to multiple sites and spaces. Connecting to Tiffani Betts Razavi's arguments about social change in her chapter in Part III, Segura argues for social change that heals not only the conditions under which we live, but also the mind and spirit of individuals. Segura's chapter focuses on the work of scholar activists, and how they can contribute to the empowerment of communities. Her focus is on how this empowerment occurs in alternative sites, spaces that emphasize community assets. Segura's arguments also link to Kate Seaman and Hoda Mahmoudi's chapter, also in Part III, and their focus on how women's roles are constructed, and how the concept of place can be understood as a position with social relationships which shifts over time.

As Laura Sjoberg argues in this volume, the progress toward gender inequality has been uneven, and women currently live in a world of both unprecedented gender equality, but continued gender oppression. Sjoberg argues that in the twenty-first century women are expected to both do more and be more than men, that old expectations of femininity have been added to new expectations about equality. Sjoberg also notes the essentializing of women in the process of gender equalizing, most notably the ways in which women are assumed to have gender, while men are assumed to occupy the standard space. Sjoberg asks us to focus on the politics of who we identify as having more or less gender equality, how we define gender equality, and how this interacts with other constructs such as class, race, sexual orientation, and more.

Part II delves deeper into the experiences of women in the workplace, and connects these experiences to wider questions of equality while providing insight into different women's experiences. The burden women carry is highlighted in the chapter by Lee, Lee, and Parpart, who focus on the impact of the COVID-19 pandemic on gender inequality in the workplace, and the ways in which the pandemic has exacerbated gender inequalities at home too, with women expected to perform the overwhelming share of unpaid care work at home.

Connecting to Parpart's chapter on silence, Lee et al. also highlight both the visibility and silence of women surrounding gender concerns. The chapter also argues that the social construction of gender is a dynamic practice of difference between women and men, and here the chapter connects to the contribution by Seaman and Mahmoudi, as they discuss the power processes and ongoing creation of gender inequalities in the workplace. Further, they also argue that these processes are used to silence competing interpretations, and that we need to be sensitive to the cultural context of gender imbalances.

Continuing the understanding of how agency can look different and have different meanings in different contexts, Chantal A. Krcmar's chapter explores the connection between the human security paradigm and the ways in which female construction workers in India conceptualize and experience their particular challenges. With a focus on local understandings and experiences, Krcmar highlights the interactions between the global and local, and how these women navigate their circumstances where the interaction between gender, agency, and human security is complex.

The contribution from Galia Golan provides insights from her life and experiences as a feminist activist scholar. Throughout, Golan highlights the ways that society is currently shaped by patriarchy, and underlines the importance of reorganizing society in ways which would benefit everyone. Golan has spent her life pushing for change, both within academia and outside, through her political activism and involvement in legal cases designed to change society. Golan has consistently challenged the status quo, but is also cognizant of the double burden which women now carry, again connecting back to Sjoberg's earlier chapter.

Part III takes a broader view of the ongoing challenges to gender equality, and each chapter utilizes a different conceptual approach to identify the limitations of the current paradigm, and the need for new approaches. As Kate Seaman and Hoda Mahmoudi argue, the current world is designed to limit women, their agency, and their potential. Utilizing the concepts of space, place, and time, they argue that we need to focus on how these intersect with complex power relations, by examining the webs of power that exist within social relationships, and how gender as a structure impacts on the entirety of human experience. The underlying argument put forth is the need for a new approach to understanding the lived embodied experiences of women, and how this understanding can help us to imagine alternatives to the way things are currently done, help us challenge boundaries, subvert expectations, and emphasize the potential that women hold. More attention needs to be paid to how different inequalities intersect and impact on the lives of women in different places and spaces.

The question of agency connects this contribution with that of Jane L. Parpart, which subverts the traditional understanding of voice, and the ability to use one's voice as a demonstration of agency. Instead Parpart argues that silence should also be associated with choice, power, and agency. She argues that silence and voice are co-constituted practices, and that both are political acts. The fundamental issue here is the question of control over speech, and how and when women have the option to choose to remain silent, or to use their voice to speak out to counter oppressive power structures. Silence for Parpart also represents a way for women to navigate oppressive structures, and can be a key part of the struggle for voice. Again this is a question of agency, and requires an examination of how current structures limit women's agency, connecting back to arguments outlined by Seaman and Mahmoudi. Parpart argues that we need to examine the in-between spaces, to avoid dichotomies, and to explore further to understand how women's experiences differ, and how these differences can open up new avenues for change.

These avenues for change are identified by Tiffani Betts Razavi, whose contribution challenges the current paradigm, and the way in which it constrains and limits progress, creating barriers for women based on unquestioned assumptions. Building up to her argument for a new paradigm, Razavi highlights the ways in which the current paradigm perpetuates existing stereotypes, connecting back to Sjoberg's arguments in relation to the image of the 'twenty-first century woman'. Razavi notes again the argument that time is all that is needed to reach equality, but pushes back against this by highlighting the setback to women's equality triggered by the COVID-19 pandemic, where the time needed to close the gender gap has grown from 99.5 years in 2019 to 135.6 years in 2021 (see p. 000).

In order to construct a new paradigm, Razavi argues that we need to approach human development as a complex, integrated organic system. That we need to acknowledge the uniqueness of human spirit, a call out to Denise Segura's chapter, to recognize the inherent dignity and nobility of each human being, and to reorient ourselves to the concept of the shared, rather than a focus on the different. As Sjoberg argues, in the next figuration of 'woman' we need to push harder to recognize the continued subordinations, augmented expectations, and double standards women face on a daily basis.

Throughout the volume the contributors have explored the realities and complexities of women's daily lives from a range of viewpoints and disciplinary groundings. The chapters in the volume all demonstrate the importance of engaging with women's lived experience, and the ways in which doing so can uncover the challenges women face, as well as the collective feminist action being taken to overcome these (Keller et al., 2018). These actions are aimed at challenging the systems of oppression that limit women's participation in various ways. These systems are 'messy' and complex (Nash, 2010) with many different systems intersecting to create multiple marginalisations for individual women, what Crenshaw (1990) terms 'structural intersectionality.'

Intersectionality provides an insight, or lens, into social stratifications (Yuval-Davis, 2011). It is an analytical tool that helps illuminate the hidden workings of power (Collins & Bilge, 2016). As Collins (2019) argues, intersectionality also offers a radical alternative to traditional scholarship, which is often viewed as removed from the social world. Instead, Collins argues, intersectionality offers an opportunity to "redefine social actions as a way of knowing that, because it valorizes experience" has the potential to strengthen intersectional theorizing. Because it allows for the conceptualization of 'ontological complexity' by recognizing that "analytical categories such as race, gender, and class, analytical categories like 'race', 'gender', 'class' and the hegemonic practices associated with them (racism, sexism, classism to which imperialism and homophobia certainly could be added) are mutually constitutive, not conceptually distinct" (Hancock, 2016, p. 71; see also Collins, 1990), intersectionality also plays a role in the emergence of new forms of feminist activism, particularly in relation to the representation of multiply marginalized women (Evans & Lépinard, 2019).

Going back to Crenshaw's (1990) 'structural intersectionality,' these new forms of activism are often found in the self-organization of women, seeking to represent themselves. This self-representation is often a response to the ways in which the needs of women who are multiply marginalized are often invisible or ignored in feminist discourses and other political platforms. Self-representation is then a key strategy in order to ensure access, representation, and social justice. The lack of representation raises important questions for the future of feminism, especially when "social movements often struggle to adopt inclusive intersectional politics and recognise difference and privilege" (Evans & Lépinard, 2019, p. 2).

Within feminism, this difficulty in recognizing difference and privilege can be illuminated through the concept of powerblindness, the failure to recognize one's own racial power and its connections to the systems and structures of racial power that are inherent in the societies we occupy, and within the institutions we work (Tomlinson, 2018). While, as feminists, we are more than aware of the ways in which institutions that influence our daily life are structured and dependent on dominance and subordination, and we are aware of the ways power is deployed to maintain these systems, we are often less willing to recognize our own power, the ways in which we deploy it, and how this is influenced by "deeply divided differences in social experiences, understandings, and aspirations" (Tomlinson, 2018).

In order to create a holistic approach to peace we must actively seek to remove the long history of oppression perpetuated by continuing patriarchal systems. But to do this, we must also recognize our own conflicts within this system, especially by recognizing the ways in which some women benefit, at the exclusion of others. This will require individual work, and one means of undertaking this work are the tools of 'rooting' and 'shifting.' As Lykke (2020) explains, "rooting" requires situating our own stakes along the lines of feminist epistemologies of situated knowledges, while "shifting" requires seriously trying to imagine what it takes to inhabit the situated perspective of interlocutors. Here the concept of a global duty of care can help, as this requires both a sensitivity to context, and a desire not to impose outside practices, but instead to support local practices (Miller, 2010). It also requires us to recognize the variations in context that produce both specific types of violence, and also the resistance to these violences, because as Emejulu and Sobande (2019) argue, "[i]t is in that space between the particularity of difference and the similarity of experience that a new world can be born."

As we noted above women's experiences can be both hugely different and remarkably similar, we need to work on recognizing the differences and building truly intersectional coalitions across these differences. Women are a key part of the creation of solutions to removing barriers to global peace. Women's full participation in constructing a different world in which they have full equality of education and opportunity and an equal voice in decision-making is required in order to create a new just, sustainable social order. However, it is imperative that this participation is full participation for all women, and not just some women, as without a truly inclusive approach, the challenges women face will not be resolved, and we run the risk of reinforcing and deepening the already existing divisions and inequalities.

References

Collins, P.H. 1990. *Black feminist thought: Knowledge, consciousness, and the politics of empowerment*. New York: Routledge.

Collins, P.H. 2019. *Intersectionality as critical social theory*. Durham, NC: Duke University Press.

Collins, P.H. & Bilge, S. 2016. *Intersectionality*. Cambridge: Polity Press.

Crenshaw, K. 1990. Mapping the margins: Intersectionality, identity politics, and violence against women of color. *Stanford Law Review* 43: 1241.

Emejulu, A. & Sobande, F. 2019. *To exist is to resist: Black feminism in Europe.* London: Pluto Press.
Evans, E., & Lépinard, É. 2019. *Intersectionality in feminist and queer movements: Confronting privileges.* Oxford: Taylor & Francis.
Hancock, Ange-Marie. 2016. *Intersectionality: An intellectual history.* Oxford: Oxford University Press.
Keller, J., Mendes, K., and Ringrose, J. 2018. Speaking "unspeakable things": Documenting digital feminist responses to rape culture. *Journal of Gender Studies* 27: 22–36.
Lykke, N. 2020. Transversal dialogues on intersectionality, socialist feminism and epistemologies of ignorance. *NORA-Nordic Journal of Feminist and Gender Research* 28(3): 197–210.
Miller, Sarah Clark. 2010. Cosmopolitan care. *Ethics and Social Welfare* 4(2): 145–157.
Nash, J.C. 2010. On difficulty: Intersectionality as feminist labor. *The Scholar and Feminist Online* 8(3): 1–10. http://sfonline.barnard.edu/polyphonic/nash_01.htm
Tomlinson, B. 2018. *Undermining intersectionality: The perils of powerblind feminism.* Philadelphia: Temple University Press.
Yuval-Davis, N. 2011. Beyond the recognition and re-distribution dichotomy: Intersectionality and stratification. In H. Lutz, M. T. Herrera Vivar, & L. Supik (eds.) *Framing intersectionality: Debates on a multifaceted concept in gender studies* (pp. 155–169). Aldershot: Ashgate.

Index

agency 98–9, 133–134, 136

borderlands 36–39; and the academy 40–42; *see also* liminal spaces

chaebols 74–76
complexity 168–170
Confucianism 75, 79
construction 96; and women 101–106
corporate social responsibility (CSR) 71, 77, 87; and gender 79; gender inequality 71; and masculinity 74–75; postcolonial thought 72
COVID-19 71; and gender inequality 2, 71, 82–87, 107–108, 161; impact on children 2, 108 Human Security 96, 98, 100, 107, 109

feminism 114–115, 118, 120–121, 126, 132–133, 144; and art 45–46; and Black women 3, 15–20, 170; and Latinas 41; within legal system 118–119, 135, 139; and military 18–9, 52, 74–75, 121–124; and place 136–140; within politics 18–24, 53, 58–59, 141, 149, 151–152, 154; and race 135, 141; and religion 171–172
feminist studies 15, 41, 43, 115–117

gender 2, 99, 124; asymmetries within 7, 124–126; and biological differences 57, 165–168; health disparities 2–3; and inequality 2–3, 97, 143, 160–165; and pay-gap 6, 80–82, 101, 143; and violence 2, 5–6, 52, 54, 57
Global South 73, 104, 151

human nobility 1, 170–71

intersectionality 16–17, 18, 54, 169–170, 182

liminal spaces 148–149

masculinity 58–59, 72–73, 133

oneness of humanity 8, 169
organic change 4, 8, 168

paradigms 4, 8, 159, 171–173, 178
patriarchy 4–6, 114–115, 134, 142
power geometry 133, 139, 142

silence 148–150, 153–157

war 121, 142
whiteness 138, 144

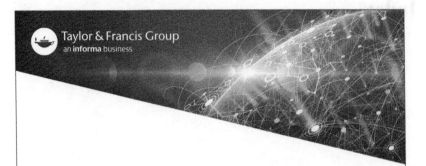